OXFORD CONSTITUTIONAL THEORY

Series Editors:

Martin Loughlin, John P. McCormick, and Neil Walker

The Global Model of Constitutional Rights

OXFORD CONSTITUTIONAL THEORY

Series Editors:
Martin Loughlin, John P. McCormick, and Neil Walker

One consequence of the increase in interest in constitutions and constitutional law in recent years is a growing innovative literature in constitutional theory. The aim of *Oxford Constitutional Theory* is to provide a showcase for the best of these theoretical reflections and a forum for further innovation in the field.

The new series will seek to establish itself as the primary point of reference for scholarly work in the subject by commissioning different types of study. The majority of the works published in the series will be monographs that advance new understandings of the subject. Well-conceived edited collections that bring a variety of perspectives and disciplinary approaches to bear on specific themes in constitutional thought will also be included. Further, in recognition of the fact that there is a great deal of pioneering literature originally written in languages other than English and with regard to non-anglophone constitutional traditions, the series will also seek to publish English translations of leading monographs in constitutional theory.

Blackburn
College

Library
01254 292120

Please return this book on or before the last date below

The Global Model
of Constitutional Rights

Kai Möller

OXFORD

UNIVERSITY PRESS

OXFORD

UNIVERSITY PRESS

Great Clarendon Street, Oxford, OX2 6DP,
United Kingdom

Oxford University Press is a department of the University of Oxford.
It furthers the University's objective of excellence in research, scholarship,
and education by publishing worldwide. Oxford is a registered trade mark of
Oxford University Press in the UK and in certain other countries

© K. Möller, 2012

The moral rights of the author have been asserted

First Edition published in 2012

Impression: 1

Crown copyright material is reproduced under Class Licence
Number C01P0000148 with the permission of OPSI
and the Queen's Printer for Scotland

British Library Cataloguing in Publication Data

Data available

ISBN 978-0-19-966460-3

Printed and bound in Great Britain by
CPI Group (UK) Ltd, Croydon, CR0 4YY

Links to third party websites are provided by Oxford in good faith and
for information only. Oxford disclaims any responsibility for the materials
contained in any third party website referenced in this work.

Acknowledgments

The idea to develop a substantive moral, reconstructive theory of constitutional rights first occurred to me in 2005 in Oxford, where I had just returned in order to write a second doctoral thesis. Much of the work was done at Lincoln College, Oxford, first as a postdoctoral fellow of the Thyssen Foundation between 2005 and 2007, and subsequently as a Junior Research Fellow in Law between 2007 and 2009. The book was completed at the LSE, where I have been teaching since 2009. I am grateful to Oxford University, Lincoln College, and the LSE for the outstanding research environments that they provided, which contributed greatly to making those years such a productive and intellectually exciting time.

The ideas proposed in this book are to a considerable extent the product of innumerable conversations with friends, colleagues and students in Oxford and London, but also in Berlin and elsewhere. My thanks for many inspiring and valuable observations, comments, criticisms, and discussions go to Virgílio Afonso da Silva, Robert Alexy, Trevor Allan, Nick Bamforth, Anne Barron, Jacco Bomhoff, Jo Braithwaite, Cathryn Costello, Timothy Endicott, Veronika Fikfak, Sandra Fredman, John Gardner, Simon Gardner, Conor Gearty, Carsten Gerner-Beuerle, Grant Huscroft, Mathias Hong, Aileen Kavanagh, David Kershaw, Tarunabh Khaitan, Maris Köpcke Tinturé, Stephen Kosmin, Liora Lazarus, Martin Loughlin, Maik Martin, Brad Miller, Yishai Mishor, Jo Murkens, Harry Papadopoulos, Tom Poole, Peter Ramsay, Mike Redmayne, Miriam Ronzoni, Prince Saprai, Christian Schemmel, Edmund-Philipp Schuster, Stavros Tsakyrakis, Alec Walen, Charlie Webb, Alison Young, Paul Yowell, and Katja Ziegler. I also thank my current and former students at LSE and Oxford, especially those of my various courses on jurisprudence and human and constitutional rights law and theory.

I owe special thanks to Alasdair Cochrane, Alon Harel, Jeff King, Dimitrios Kyritsis, George Letsas, Emmanuel Voyiakis, and Grégoire Webber, who, in addition to being valued conversation partners, have all read several chapters and provided helpful and much appreciated feedback.

Four scholars had a special impact on this book. Christopher McCrudden, as co-supervisor of the thesis out of which this book emerged, was continually impressive with his amazing breadth of knowledge and depth of understanding, which made the meetings with him exciting and inspiring highlights of those years; furthermore he became a mentor whose advice and support was invaluable. Nicos Stavropoulos, the other co-supervisor, constantly and mercilessly challenged the coherence of my views, which was enormously effective in helping me improve and refine my arguments; and his generosity with his time and ideas gave me a much better understanding of the philosophical complexities than I could otherwise have gained. Jeremy Waldron, the internal examiner of the dissertation, provided extremely valuable feedback on the work as a whole and raised a number of subtle and challenging questions with regard to several of its aspects in the viva and afterwards. Mattias Kumm, in addition to acting as external examiner, spent many unforgettable afternoons and increasingly late evenings in the summer of 2011 over intense discussions of the book with me. It truly has been a great fortune for me to have been able to work with and learn from these great scholars, to whom I am profoundly grateful.

Parts of this book were presented at the Colloquium on Global and Comparative Public Law at NYU, the LSE Forum in Legal and Political Theory, the Centre of the Study of Law in Society at Sheffield University, the Legal Philosophy Forum at UCL, and the Jurisprudence Discussion Group at Oxford. I am grateful to the conveners of those events for giving me the opportunities to test my ideas and to the participants for their engaging and helpful comments.

Further thanks go to the editors of the Oxford Constitutional Theory series for accepting the book into the series. I would also like to thank Natasha Flemming and Alex Flach at OUP for their kindness and professionalism, Catherine Cragg and Shanker Loganthan for efficiently taking the book through the production process, and Deborah Renshaw for her sharp-eyed copy-editing.

Very special thanks are due to Jeremy, for being there all along. I dedicate this book to my parents, with thanks and gratitude for the stability, love, encouragement, and support that they have provided from the very beginning.

★★★

Chapter 3 was previously published as 'Two Conceptions of Positive Liberty: Towards an Autonomy-based Conception of Constitutional Rights' in the *Oxford Journal of Legal Studies* and parts of Chapter 7 rely on a modified and extended version of the introductory sections of 'Proportionality: Challenging the Critics', published in the *International Journal of Constitutional Law*.

Kai Möller
AUGUST 2012

Contents

PART II: THE STRUCTURE OF JUSTIFICATION

Table of Cases

List of Abbreviations

BVerfG	Bundesverfassungsgericht (Federal Constitutional Court of Germany)
BVerfGE	Entscheidungen des Bundesverfassungsgerichts
ECHR	European Convention on Human Rights
ECtHR	European Court of Human Rights
EHRR	European Human Rights Reports
SA	South African Law Reports
SCR	Supreme Court Reports (Canada)
UKHL	United Kingdom House of Lords
U.S.	United States Supreme Court Reports
S.Ct.	Supreme Court Reporter (United States)
ZACC	South African Constitutional Court Cases

❧ 1 ❧

The Global Model of Constitutional Rights

I. THE PROJECT

Since the end of the Second World War and the subsequent success of constitutional judicial review, one particular model of constitutional rights has had remarkable success, first in Europe and now globally. In a nutshell, this *global model of constitutional rights* sees rights as protecting an extremely broad range of interests but at the same time limitable by recourse to a balancing or proportionality approach. Thus, it places itself in sharp contrast to the conceptions of rights proposed by most if not all moral and political philosophers who agree that rights protect only a limited set of especially important interests while enjoying a special, heightened, normative force. However, while the global model of constitutional rights does not seem to sit well with the philosophical conceptions of rights that have been proposed to date, it has itself still not been sufficiently theorized. The important and interrelated questions which it raises are the following. (1) Which *theory* or *conception of rights* explains best the global model of constitutional rights, including the questions of which values are protected by rights and what are their limits? (2) How does the judicial enforcement of *this particular conception* of constitutional rights relate to the value of *democracy*? (3) How does it relate to the value of the *separation of powers*, in particular to considerations of the *relative institutional competence* of courts on the one hand and the elected branches on the other? A comprehensive theory of constitutional rights must provide an *integrated* answer to these questions: the theory of rights which it proposes must also reflect attractive conceptions of democracy and the separation of powers. This book presents such a theory.

Its main features are the following. (1) The theory follows a *substantive moral approach* in that it is grounded in political morality; this can be contrasted with a formal theory such as Robert Alexy's influential theory of rights as principles or optimization requirements.[1] (2) It is *reconstructive*, i.e. it is a theory of the actual practice of constitutional rights law around the world. I will explain this in detail below. (3) It is *general* in that it does not focus on specific issues or rights but aims at identifying features of their moral structure which are shared by many or all constitutional rights.

II. THE GLOBAL MODEL AND THE DOMINANT NARRATIVE

This section will introduce the four central features of the global model of constitutional rights; and it will do so by contrasting them with what I shall call the *dominant narrative* of the philosophy of fundamental rights. The dominant narrative holds (1) that rights cover only a *limited domain* by protecting only certain *especially important* interests of individuals; (2) that rights impose exclusively or primarily *negative* obligations on the state; (3) that rights operate only *between a citizen and his government*, not between private citizens; and (4) that rights enjoy a *special normative force*, which means that they can be outweighed, if at all, only under *exceptional circumstances*. Of these features of the dominant narrative, the general acceptance of the second—rights as imposing negative obligations on the state—has already eroded considerably, mainly because of the growing recognition of social and economic rights.[2] The third—limitation to the relationship between citizen and government—while generally held to be true, does not normally attract much attention from rights theorists. The first and the fourth—special importance and special normative force— are still hardly controversial. However, under the global model of constitutional rights *all four* elements of this narrative have been given up—and often a long time ago. The doctrines and developments in constitutional rights law which have led to their erosion are rights inflation, positive obligations and socio-economic rights, horizontal effect, and balancing and proportionality. These doctrines and developments form the core of the global model of constitutional rights and provide the basic materials out of which the following chapters will reconstruct the theory of rights proposed here.

---

[1]   Alexy, *A Theory of Constitutional Rights* (Oxford University Press, 2002). My essay 'Balancing and the Structure of Constitutional Rights', (2007) 5 *International Journal of Constitutional Law* 453 criticizes Alexy's formal approach and recommends a substantive moral one; this book, by providing such a substantive moral theory of rights, can thus be read as offering a constructive response to what I regard as deficiencies in Alexy's methodology. For a generally positive review of Alexy's book see Kumm, 'Constitutional Rights as Principles: On the Structure and Domain of Constitutional Justice', (2004) 2 *International Journal of Constitutional Law* 574.

[2]   For a theoretical account of this development, see Fredman, *Human Rights Transformed: Positive Rights and Positive Duties* (Oxford University Press, 2008), ch. 1.

1. Rights inflation

Constitutional rights are no longer seen as only protecting certain particularly important interests. Especially in Europe a development has been observed which is sometimes pejoratively called 'rights inflation',[3] a name which I shall use in a neutral sense as referring to the increasing protection of relatively trivial interests as (prima facie) rights. The European Court of Human Rights (ECtHR) routinely reads such interests into the right to private life (Article 8 of the European Convention on Human Rights [ECHR]). For example, in the famous *Hatton* case, which concerned a policy scheme which permitted night flights at Heathrow airport, thus leading to noise pollution which disturbed the sleep of some of the residents living in the area, the Court discovered as part of Article 8 the right not to be 'directly and seriously affected by noise or other pollution',[4] dismissively dubbed 'the human right to sleep well' by George Letsas.[5] The broad understanding the Court takes towards the issue of private life becomes clear in one of its more recent attempts to circumscribe it:

> The Court recalls that the concept of 'private life' is a broad term not susceptible to exhaustive definition. It covers the physical and psychological integrity of a person. It can therefore embrace multiple aspects of the person's physical and social identity. Elements such as, for example, gender identification, name and sexual orientation and sexual life fall within the personal sphere protected by Art. 8. Beyond a person's name, his or her private and family life may include other means of personal identification and of linking to a family. Information about the person's health is an important element of private life. The Court furthermore considers that an individual's ethnic identity must be regarded as another such element. Article 8 protects in addition a right to personal development, and the right to establish and develop relationships with other human beings and the outside world. The concept of private life moreover includes elements relating to a person's right to their image.[6]

Thus, the Court has, for example, considered the storing of fingerprints and DNA samples by the state[7] and the publication of photographs of a

---

[3] Letsas, *A Theory of Interpretation of the European Convention on Human Rights* (Oxford University Press, 2007), 126.

[4] *Hatton v. United Kingdom* (2003) 37 EHRR 28, para. 96.

[5] Letsas, *A Theory of Interpretation of the European Convention on Human Rights* (Oxford University Press, 2007), 126.

[6] *S v. United Kingdom* (2009) 48 EHRR 50, para.66 (footnotes omitted).

[7] Ibid., para. 67.

person in her daily life by a magazine[8] as falling within the scope of 'private life'. With regard to sexual autonomy, the Court not only held that consensual homosexual sex was part of 'private life',[9] but came close to saying that homosexual sado-masochistic group sex orgies involving considerable violence were protected as well.[10] Article 8 also protects a right to access to the information relating to a person's birth and origin.[11]

While the ECtHR has not provided a comprehensive definition of the meaning of 'private life', it will still require that the interest in question be part of 'private life', whatever that term exactly means, and thus the Court will not necessarily accept *any* interest as falling within the scope of Article 8; in other words there is still a threshold which needs to be crossed for an interest to become a right. By way of contrast, the German Federal Constitutional Court has explicitly given up any threshold to distinguish a mere interest from a constitutional right. As early as 1957 it held that Article 2(1) of the Basic Law, which protects everyone's right to freely develop his personality, is to be interpreted as a right to freedom of action.[12] The Court provided various doctrinal reasons for this result, its main argument being that an earlier draft of Article 2(1) had read 'Everyone can do as he pleases' (*'Jeder kann tun und lassen was er will'*), and that this version had been dropped only for linguistic reasons.[13] The Court affirmed this ruling in various later decisions; most famously it declared that Article 2(1) of the Basic Law included the rights to feed pigeons in a park[14] and to go riding in the woods.[15]

It must be noted that the broad understanding of rights does not, of course, imply that the state is prohibited from interfering with the right in question. Rather, there is an important conceptual distinction between *an interference with* and *a violation of* a right: an interference will only amount to a violation if it cannot be justified at the justification stage. Thus, the broad understanding of rights at the prima facie stage must be seen in conjunction with the proportionality test which permits

---

[8]   *von Hannover v. Germany* (2005) 40 EHRR 1, para. 53.

[9]   *Dudgeon v. United Kingdom* (1982) 4 EHRR 149, paras. 40–41.

[10]   *Laskey, Jaggard and Brown v. United Kingdom* (1997) 24 EHRR 39, para. 36. The Court left open the question of whether the activities in question fell within the scope of Article 8 in their entirety, but proceeded on the assumption that they did.

[11]   *Odievre v. France* (2004) 38 EHRR 43, para. 29.

[12]   BVerfGE 6, 32 (*Elfes*).

[13]   Ibid., 36–7.

[14]   BVerfGE 54, 143 (*Pigeon-Feeding*).

[15]   BVerfGE 80, 137 (*Riding in the Woods*).

the limitation of prima facie rights when they are outweighed by a competing right or public interest. But it is notable that, contrary to the language used by philosophers, courts are very generous in labelling an interest a 'right', and therefore, again contrary to philosophical usage, they do not attach much weight to a right simply by virtue of its being a right. Furthermore, and again in contrast to some philosophical usage, what is referred to as the 'right' is only the prima facie right, not the definite right. So European lawyers routinely speak of human or constitutional rights to many things which people regularly do not have a definite right to.[16]

2. Positive obligations and socio-economic rights

Rights are no longer regarded as exclusively imposing negative obligations on the state. But while most theorists of rights only started to reconsider their views on this issue following the growing acceptance of socio-economic rights (particularly their inclusion in the South African Constitution), constitutional rights law abandoned the view that rights impose only negative obligations in the 1970s, when the doctrines of positive obligations or protective duties became established. The idea is that the state is under a duty to take steps to prevent harm to the interests protected by (otherwise negative) rights. Thus, the state must, as a matter of constitutional rights law, put in place a system which effectively protects the people from dangers emanating from other private persons, such as criminal activities which threaten, for example, life, physical integrity, or property; and it must also protect them from dangers which do not have a (direct) human cause, such as natural disasters.

In the jurisprudence of the ECtHR, the idea of positive obligations, first introduced in the *Belgian Linguistics* case of 1968,[17] is well-established. In the case of the right to life, it is even supported by the text of the Convention, which states in Article 2(1) that '[e]veryone's right to life shall be *protected* by law'. The *Osman* case provides a good

---

[16] This approach is sometimes criticized as 'guilty of "promoting unrealistic expectations"' (Webber, *The Negotiable Constitution: On the Limitation of Rights* [Cambridge University Press, 2009], 123), but whether it really is promoting such expectations depends on the way the word 'right' is used by the people. I am not sure that Europeans would be misled in the way Webber envisages; in any case the charge that they would is unsubstantiated. Furthermore, the linguistic meaning of the terms 'human right' or 'constitutional right' as used by the population is likely to change over time, following the developments in the courts.

[17] *Case Relating to Certain Aspects of the Laws on the Use of Languages In Education In Belgium* (1979–80) 1 EHRR 252, para. 3.

example of the Court's approach to this provision. A former teacher of Ahmet Osman, who was about 15 years old at the time, was obsessed with him and ultimately wounded the boy and killed his father. The family alleged that the police had not done enough to protect Osman and his father from the threat. The Court argued that Article 2(1) ECHR required not only that the state refrain from killing, but also that it 'put in place effective criminal law provisions to deter the commission of offences against the person backed up by law-enforcement machinery for the prevention, suppression and sanctioning of breaches of such provisions'[18] and that the provision may additionally 'imply in certain well-defined circumstances a *positive obligation* on the authorities to take preventive operational measures to protect an individual whose life is at risk from the criminal acts of another individual'.[19]

In the case of other rights there is no explicit textual basis supporting the acknowledgement of positive obligations, but the Court nevertheless consistently accepts their existence. Of the countless cases, the first *von Hannover* judgment provides a good example of the Court's approach. Princess Caroline of Monaco had unsuccessfully tried to stop the publication of certain pictures of her in German gossip magazines; she argued that the publication violated her right to private life under Article 8 of the Convention. The Court relied on its well-established case law to grant the existence of a positive obligation to protect privacy:

> The Court reiterates that although the object of Art. 8 is essentially that of protecting the individual against arbitrary interference by the public authorities, it does not merely compel the State to abstain from such interference: in addition to this primarily negative undertaking, there may be positive obligations inherent in an effective respect for private or family life. These obligations may involve the adoption of measures designed to secure respect for private life even in the sphere of the relations of individuals between themselves. That also applies to the protection of a person's picture against abuse by others.[20]

The legally difficult question in cases involving positive obligations is not the existence of positive obligations as such; this is well-established case law. Rather, it is the question of whether the state has done enough to comply with its obligation (in *Osman* it had, and in *von Hannover* it had

---

[18] *Osman v. United Kingdom* (2000) 29 EHRR 245, para. 115.

[19] Ibid. (emphasis added).

[20] *von Hannover v. Germany* (2005) 40 EHRR 1, para. 115.

not). But that is a separate question concerning the limits of the right, which does not affect the point to be made here, namely the move away from an understanding of rights as concerned exclusively with negative obligations.

The textual basis for the assumption that Convention rights generally impose positive obligations is weak. In particular, the limitation clauses, especially of Articles 8 to 11 (the rights to respect for private and family life, freedom of religion, freedom of expression, and freedom of association and assembly), regularly refer to 'restrictions', 'limitations', and 'interferences', which indicates a negative understanding of rights. In its more recent case law, the Court has tried to support its approach by reference to Article 1. For example, in a case involving the right to property (Article 1 of Protocol No. 1) the Court stated:

> The essential object of Article 1 of Protocol No. 1 is to protect a person against unjustified interference by the State with the peaceful enjoyment of his or her possessions. However, by virtue of Article 1 of the Convention, each Contracting Party 'shall secure to everyone within [its] jurisdiction the rights and freedoms defined in [the] Convention'. The discharge of this general duty may entail positive obligations inherent in ensuring the effective exercise of the rights guaranteed by the Convention. In the context of Article 1 of Protocol No. 1, those positive obligations may require the State to take the measures necessary to protect the right of property.[21]

But obviously, the reference to the word 'secure' in Article 1 ECHR does not even come close to a water-tight doctrinal argument for the general doctrine of positive obligations. The Court was certainly not forced to its conclusion by such textual subtleties; rather it must have found the idea of positive obligations attractive as a matter of the theory of rights underlying the Convention as a whole. But it has never spelt out what this theory is.

In German constitutional jurisprudence, the idea of *protective duties* (*Schutzpflichten*) was acknowledged for the first time in the first abortion decision of 1975, where the Federal Constitutional Court held that the state is under a duty to protect the fetus against the implementation of the woman's wish to have an abortion.[22] To establish the existence of the protective duty, the Court referred to the idea of an 'objective system

---

[21] *Broniowski v. Poland* (2005) 40 EHRR 495, para. 143.

[22] BVerfGE 39, 1 (*First Abortion Judgment*).

of values' set up by the Basic Law, which it had first established in the *Lüth* decision, discussed below, and to the principle of human dignity enshrined in Article 1 of the Basic Law.[23] In subsequent case law it dropped the reference to dignity and replaced the phrase 'objective system of values' with the less controversial 'objective dimension' of the basic rights. Today it is uncontroversial in Germany that the doctrine of protective duties is a *general* doctrine the application of which is not limited to certain rights; rather, the state is under a general obligation to take positive steps towards the protection of the rights of each person. In practice, however, most cases have been about life and physical integrity. In the *Schleyer* case of 1977, the Court held that the state was under a duty to take adequate steps to rescue Martin Schleyer, who had been kidnapped by the terrorist Red Army Faction (*Rote Armee Fraktion*). The following quotation shows nicely the Court's basic approach to the issue.

> Art. 2(2)(1) [the right to life] in conjunction with Art. 1(1)(2) Basic Law [the duty to protect and respect human dignity] obligate the state to protect every human life. This protective duty is comprehensive. It requires the state to protect and support each life; this implies mainly to protect it from illegal interferences by others. All state organs must, according to their special roles, orient their activities towards this task. As human life presents a supreme value, this protective duty must be taken particularly seriously.[24]

The Court also had to deal with cases relating to the risks or harm flowing from the use of nuclear energy,[25] aircraft noise,[26] and the storage of American chemical weapons.[27] It stuck to its earlier jurisprudence and affirmed the existence of protective duties in all cases.

The South African Constitution explicitly endorses positive duties by stating in its section 7(2): 'The state must respect, protect, promote and fulfil the rights in the Bill of Rights.' Here, 'respect' refers to negative duties, whereas 'protect' refers to positive duties. The South African Constitutional Court has affirmed the existence of positive duties in its case law:

> It follows that there is a duty imposed on the State and all of its organs not to perform any act that infringes these rights. In some circumstances there would also be a positive component which obliges the State and its organs

---

[23] Ibid., 41–2.   [24] BVerfGE 46, 160, 164 (*Schleyer*).   [25] BVerfGE 49, 89 (*Kalkar I*).
[26] BVerfGE 56, 54.   [27] BVerfGE 77, 170.

to provide appropriate protection to everyone through laws and struc-
tures designed to afford such protection.[28]

Furthermore, there is the aforementioned trend towards the acknowledgement of socio-economic rights, which obviously impose positive
duties on the state and thus conflict with the dominant narrative
according to which rights are concerned only with negative obligations.
Socio-economic rights are explicitly included in the South African Constitution, which contains in its sections 26, 27, and 29 rights to housing,
health care, food, water, social security, and education. Of course, it
would be naïve to think that the inclusion of such rights in a constitution
was a sufficient step to resolve poverty. As acknowledged by the South
African Constitutional Court in its first decision on socio-economic
rights, a major practical problem lies in the scarcity of resources,[29] and
this cannot be fixed by a constitutional provision. But the important
point for present purposes is that socio-economic rights are acknowledged at the constitutional level, however easily limitable those rights
may be.

While the South African Constitution is explicit about the inclusion of
socio-economic rights, as a matter of substance, similar rights have been
read into other constitutions. The ECtHR, while regularly stressing that
the ECHR 'does not, as such, guarantee socio-economic rights',[30] has
accepted some socio-economic entitlements mainly through the use of
its doctrine of positive obligations, discussed above, as flowing from
several Convention articles, including Articles 2 (life), 3 (prohibition of
inhuman or degrading treatment), 6 (fair trial), 8 (private and family life),
and 14 (non-discrimination).[31] The German Federal Constitutional Court
holds the view that a right to a social minimum follows from Articles 1(1)
and 20(1) of the Basic Law (the principle of human dignity in conjunction
with the principle of the welfare state).[32] Thus, in light of the relative
wealth of Germany compared to South Africa, the actual constitutional
entitlements of a poor person will be considerably higher in Germany

---

[28] *Carmichele v. Minister of Safety and Security*, 2001 (4) SA 938 (CC), para. 44. See also *Rail Commuters Action Group v. Metrorail*, 2005 (2) SA 359 (CC), paras. 70–71.

[29] *Soobramoney v. Minister of Health (KwaZulu-Natal)* (1997) ZACC 17, para. 11.

[30] See, for example, *Pançenko v. Latvia* (App No 40772/98), Decision of 28 October 1999, para. 2.

[31] For an overview, see Brems, 'Indirect Protection of Social Rights by the European Court of Human Rights', in Barak-Erez and Gross (eds.), *Exploring Social Rights* (Hart Publishing, 2007), ch. 7.

[32] Cf. most recently BVerfG, 1 BvL 1/09 of 9.2.2010 (*Hartz IV*), para. 133.

than in South Africa, in spite of the absence of an explicit commitment to socio-economic rights.

It is remarkable that while positive obligations were first acknowledged by courts in Europe on the basis of constitutional texts which at face value offered very little support for this view, the new South African Constitution, as the youngest constitution considered here, explicitly endorses both positive obligations and socio-economic rights. Both of these observations—the endorsement in absence of textual support and the subsequent explicit inclusion in the text of a new constitution—provide strong indicators that positive duties and socio-economic rights are indeed part of an emerging global consensus of thinking about constitutional rights which departs from the dominant narrative in important ways.

3. Horizontal effect

Constitutional rights are no longer seen as affecting only the relationship between the citizen and the state; rather, they apply in some way between private persons as well. For example, the constitutional right to privacy may protect a person not only against infringements of his privacy by the state, but also against such infringements by his neighbour, landlord, or employer. The doctrinal tool which achieves this is called the *horizontal effect* of rights, where 'horizontal' as opposed to 'vertical' indicates that rights operate between private persons. It is possible to see the horizontal effect of rights as a subset of positive obligations, discussed above: the state is under a positive obligation to ensure that private persons do not violate other private persons' rights. Alternatively, it can be seen as its own category which gives effect to constitutional rights between private persons.

The first court to acknowledge horizontal effect was the German Federal Constitutional Court in its famous *Lüth* decision of 1953.[33] Erich Lüth had called for a boycott of a new film by director Veit Harlan on the grounds of the latter's previous involvement with the Nazi regime. As this call for a boycott had the potential to result in substantial harm to the financial success of the movie, the producer and his distributing company obtained a court injunction against Lüth. When the

---

[33] BVerfGE 7, 198 (*Lüth*). English translation from the website of the University of Texas School of Law: http://www.utexas.edu/law/academics/centers/transnational/work_new/[copyright: Basil Markesinis].

matter came before the Federal Constitutional Court, it had to decide whether constitutional law, especially the right to freedom of opinion (Article 5[1] of the Basic Law) had any effect on the private law governing the relationship between Lüth and Harlan (and his distributing company). The Court first set out the traditional understanding of constitutional rights: 'There is no doubt that the main purpose of basic rights is to protect the individual's sphere of freedom against encroachment by public power: they are the citizen's bulwark against the state.'[34] But it then added one of the most famous paragraphs of its history:

> But far from being a value-free system the Constitution erects *an objective system of values* in its section on basic rights, and thus expresses and reinforces the validity of the basic rights. This system of values, centring on the freedom of the human being to develop in society, must apply as a constitutional axiom throughout the whole legal system: it must direct and inform legislation, administration, and judicial decision. It naturally influences private law as well; no rule of private law may conflict with it, and all such rules must be construed in accordance with its spirit.[35]

Applying this approach to the facts, it concluded that the lower court had failed to adequately take into account the right to freedom of opinion. The idea of an objective system (or order) of values subsequently became one of the cornerstones of German constitutional jurisprudence. It was heavily criticized by some academics in particular for its moralistic undertones; it was feared that the 'objective order of values' could easily lead to a 'tyranny of values' which would be relied upon to restrict individual freedom.[36] Presumably in response to these concerns, the Court later quietly replaced the term with the less controversial idea of an 'objective dimension' of the basic rights. But what exactly the objective system of values or the objective dimension of the basic rights mean remains something of a mystery to this day. In spite of this open question, the important lesson to be drawn is that the idea of constitutional rights affecting only the relationship between the citizen and the state was abandoned as early as 1953 in Germany. The Court affirmed the doctrine of the horizontal effect of rights in numerous later decisions, many but not all of which are about freedom of opinion; it is uncontroversial that the doctrine is not limited to certain rights but applies across

[34] Ibid., 204.

[35] Ibid., 205 (emphasis added; references omitted).

[36] Denninger, 'Freiheitsordnung—Wertordnung—Pflichtordnung', (1975) *Juristenzeitung* 545, 547.

the board. For example, the Court decided that a judgment of a lower court violated the claimant's personality right (Article 2[1] in conjunction with Article 1[1] of the Basic Law) by upholding a contractual agreement between the claimant's parents and their bank which led to the imposition of heavy debts on the claimant, who was a minor at the time;[37] and it declared a judgment which relied on aesthetic reasons to deny a Turkish tenant the right to install a dish antenna which would have enabled him to receive TV programmes from Turkey a violation of his right to freedom of information.[38]

In Canada, the question of whether constitutional rights operate between private persons was first considered by the Canadian Supreme Court in the *Dolphin Delivery* case in 1986, only four years after the Canadian Charter of Rights and Freedoms had come into force. Dolphin had obtained an injunction against a union, prohibiting secondary picketing; the union argued that this was unconstitutional in that it violated their right to freedom of expression. The important constitutional question was whether Charter rights applied between private litigants. While the Court in a first step denied the direct applicability of the Charter when the relevant law was, as in the case at hand, common law, it then continued by stating that even though the Charter was not directly applicable, the common law ought to be developed in a way consistent with Charter values, thus installing what is technically called weak indirect horizontal effect.[39]

South Africa is, to my knowledge, the only jurisdiction today which has explicitly endorsed horizontal effect in its constitution. Section 8(2) of the South African Constitution states in slightly awkward language: 'A provision of the Bill of Rights binds a natural or a juristic person if, and to the extent that, it is applicable, taking into account the nature of the right and the nature of any duty imposed by the right.' This explicit endorsement of horizontal effect in a young constitution strengthens further the view proposed here that horizontal effect is by now a well-established feature of the global model of constitutional rights.

There exist a number of complex and controversial issues about horizontal effect; in particular, first, the question of whether it is strong or weak, i.e. whether in a case where it is not possible to reinterpret the statute in question in line with the requirements of constitutional rights,

---

[37] BVerfGE 72, 155.   [38] BVerfGE 90, 27.

[39] *Retail, Wholesale & Dep't Store Union v. Dolphin Delivery Ltd.* (1986) 2 SCR 573, 605. The subsequent judgment in *Hill v. Church of Scientology of Toronto* (1995) 2 SCR 1170 confirmed this approach and fleshed it out further.

the statute is unconstitutional or not; and second, whether horizontal effect should be direct or indirect, i.e. whether constitutional rights 'directly' create rights between private persons or whether they do so only 'indirectly' via the (re-)interpretation of the existing private law.[40] The brief overview presented above cannot do justice to the complexities. But it does show that the practice of constitutional rights law no longer sees rights as exclusively concerned with the relationship between the individual and the state; rather, in some way, they have an impact on the relationship between private individuals as well.

4. Balancing and proportionality

Contrary to the dominant narrative, it is not the case that constitutional rights generally enjoy a special or heightened normative force in legal practice. While it is true that some rights, such as the right to freedom from torture and degrading or humiliating treatment or punishment in Article 3 ECHR, or the right to a fair trial in Article 6 ECHR, are absolute, most rights—including the rights to life, physical integrity, privacy, property, freedom of religion, expression, assembly, and association—can generally be limited in line with the proportionality test, at the core of which is a balancing exercise where the right is balanced against a competing right or public interest. Proportionality has become *the* central concept in contemporary constitutional rights law, and, in addition to the jurisdictions examined in this book, has been accepted by virtually every constitutional court in Central and Eastern Europe and is increasingly employed in Central and South American jurisdictions.[41] Different courts use different formulations of what is essentially the same test. The German Federal Constitutional Court follows a four-pronged test according to which the policy interfering with the right must be in pursuit of a legitimate goal; it must be a suitable means of furthering the achievement of the goal (suitability or rational connection); it must be necessary in that there must not be a less restrictive and equally effective alternative (necessity); and it must not impose a

---

[40] On these distinctions and other doctrinal problems involved in the doctrine of horizontal effect cf. Gardbaum, 'The "Horizontal Effect" of Constitutional Rights', (2003–4) 102 *Michigan Law Review* 387; Gardbaum, 'Where the (State) Action is', (2006) 4 *International Journal of Constitutional Law* 760; Kumm and Ferreres Comella, 'What is so Special about Constitutional Rights in Private Litigation? A Comparative Analysis of the Function of State Action Requirements and Indirect Effect', in Sajó and Uitz (eds.), *The Constitution in Private Relations* (Eleven, 2005).

[41] Stone Sweet and Mathews, 'Proportionality Balancing and Global Constitutionalism', (2008–9) 47 *Columbia Journal of Transnational Law* 72, 112.

disproportionate burden on the right-holder (balancing or proportion-ality in the strict sense). The ECtHR demands that the policy further a legitimate goal and a pressing social need and that it be proportionate to the achievement of the legitimate goal.[42] The Canadian Supreme Court adopted proportionality analysis, which has become known as the '*Oakes* test', in its most famous judgment to date:

> First, the measures adopted must be . . . rationally connected to the object-ive. Second, the means, even if rationally connected to the objective in this first sense, should impair 'as little as possible' the right or freedom in question . . . Third, there must be a proportionality between the effects of the measures which are responsible for limiting the *Charter* right or freedom, and the objective which has been identified as of 'sufficient importance'.[43]

Proportionality is also accepted in South Africa. It was first established in the *Makwanyane* case, which was decided under the Interim Constitu-tion, where the Court held:

> The limitation of constitutional rights for a purpose that is reasonable and necessary in a democratic society involves the weighing up of competing values, and ultimately an assessment based on proportionality . . . [T]here is no absolute standard which can be laid down for determining reason-ableness and necessity. Principles can be established, but the application of those principles to particular circumstances can only be done on a case by case basis. This is inherent in the requirement of proportionality, which calls for the balancing of different interests. In the balancing process, the relevant considerations will include the nature of the right that is limited, and its importance to an open and democratic society based on freedom and equality; the purpose for which the right is limited and the import-ance of that purpose to such a society; the extent of the limitation, its efficacy, and particularly where the limitation has to be necessary, whether the desired ends could reasonably be achieved through other means less damaging to the right in question.[44]

The Court later affirmed this approach in its interpretation of the final Constitution of 1996. Finally, the UK House of Lords (now Supreme Court) accepted as appropriate the test:

> whether: (i) the legislative objective is sufficiently important to justify limiting a fundamental right; (ii) the measures designed to meet the

---

[42] *Norris v. Ireland* (1991) 13 EHRR 186, para. 41.

[43] *R. v. Oakes* (1986) 1 SCR 103, para. 70 (emphasis in the original).

[44] *S. v. Makwanyane* (1995) 3 SA 391, para. 104.

legislative objective are rationally connected to it; and (iii) the means used to impair the right or freedom are no more than is necessary to accomplish the objective.[45]

In a later decision, it added the fourth stage (the balancing requirement): '[the judgment on proportionality] must always involve the striking of a fair balance between the rights of the individual and the interests of the community which is inherent in the whole of the Convention.'[46]

While these tests are all slightly different on the surface, they have in common a *balancing exercise* where the right is balanced against the competing right or public interest, which implies that in contrast to the dominant narrative, rights do not seem to enjoy any special or elevated status over public interests, but rather operate on the same plane as policy considerations. This has been captured in Robert Alexy's influential theory of rights as principles which have to be balanced against competing principles which include policy considerations;[47] remarkably, this theory is widely regarded as the best reconstruction of constitutional rights law available.[48]

III. TERMINOLOGICAL CLARIFICATIONS

1. *Global?*

The notion of 'the global' model of constitutional rights requires explanation. My claim is not that the model introduced in the previous section is global in the sense that it is accepted in every jurisdiction; rather its global character flows from the combination of two factors: first, that its appeal is not limited to certain countries or regions (e.g. Europe); and second, that it can claim greater appeal on a global scale than any rival model (such as, in particular, the US model of rights[49]). Indicators of its dominant global appeal are, first, the convergence in the doctrinal arsenal that is employed globally, in particular the ideas of horizontal effect, positive obligations, and balancing and proportionality, and, second, the historical links which provide explanations of how ideas and concepts travelled between jurisdictions. Some of the historical

---

[45] *R (Daly) v. Secretary of State for the Home Department* (2001) UKHL 26, para. 27.

[46] *Huang and others v. Secretary of State for the Home Department* (2007) UKHL 11, para. 19.

[47] Alexy, *A Theory of Constitutional Rights* (Oxford University Press, 2002), ch. 3.

[48] Kumm, 'Constitutional Rights as Principles: On the Structure and Domain of Constitutional Justice', (2004) 2 *International Journal of Constitutional Law* 574, 596.

[49] See s. IV on the question of whether the US follows a different model of rights.

roots of the global model lie in Europe. The doctrine of horizontal effect was first acknowledged by the German Federal Constitutional Court in 1953; the doctrine of positive obligations was first developed in the late 1960s by the ECtHR and from the mid-1970s by the German Court. The origin of the principle of proportionality—which is *the* core concept of constitutional rights law today—lies in German administrative law[50] and was imported into constitutional law by the Court as early as 1957 in its famous *Pharmacy Judgment (Apothekenurteil)*.[51] These doctrines, and inseparable from them, a certain model of rights, travelled from Germany and the European level to other European jurisdictions, such as in particular the ex-communist countries, and to other parts of the world, such as Canada and South Africa.[52] This explains why some authors loosely speak of the 'European' model of rights; but this has to be understood in the sense of 'originating from Europe' as opposed to 'being endorsed (only) in Europe'; because of its global appeal it is more precise to speak of the global model of constitutional rights.

2. Constitutional rights

This book mainly considers materials—mostly cases—from the ECtHR, Germany, the United Kingdom, South Africa and Canada. This selection may raise questions relating to its usage of the terms 'constitution' and 'constitutional'. I include the ECHR here in spite of the fact that it is technically not a constitution but an international treaty; however, the ECtHR performs a review function very similar to that of the highest domestic courts, the main difference arguably being a somewhat relaxed intensity of review. Furthermore, I will generally refer to 'constitutional' rights in this book, a term which has some advantages over its alternatives, 'human' or 'fundamental' rights, in that it makes clear that we are concerned with *legal* (often justiciable) rights of a certain *elevated status* over that of ordinary legislation. This includes the rights of the ECHR and also the rights protected under weak systems of judicial review such as the one in the United Kingdom. Furthermore, I will refer to the courts adjudicating upon constitutional rights (in the sense just explained) as

---

[50] Cf. Stone Sweet and Mathews, 'Proportionality Balancing and Global Constitutionalism', (2008–9) 47 *Columbia Journal of Transnational Law* 72, 97; Cohen-Eliya and Porat, 'American Balancing and German Proportionality: The Historical Origins', (2010) 8 *International Journal of Constitutional Law* 263, 271.

[51] BVerfGE 7, 377 (*Pharmacy Judgment*).

[52] Stone Sweet and Mathews, 'Proportionality Balancing and Global Constitutionalism', (2008–9) 47 *Columbia Journal of Transnational Law* 72, 112–31.

'constitutional' courts, independently of whether they are technically supreme courts, constitutional courts, or—as in the case of the ECtHR— international courts.

IV. THE US: AN OUTLIER?

This book excludes US jurisprudence from the set of materials which it seeks to reconstruct. The reason for this lies not in any claim to the effect that the US follows a model of rights which is different from that of the rest of the world; the book leaves this issue open. Rather it is that at this particular point of its history, US practice is *on the surface* different enough from the global model to justify leaving it aside, in order to avoid the long, complicated and controversial argument which would inevitably be needed to justify its inclusion and which would only distract from the book's main claims.

US constitutional rights law can be regarded as differing from that of the rest of the world in several respects. Most obviously, it is different with regard to the outcomes that it produces: many substantive views of the US Supreme Court about what rights do or do not require are not shared by other courts, for example on issues relating to abortion, hate or other offensive speech, or gun control, to name a few. But more important in the present context is that it seems, at least on the surface, that the US follows a structurally different understanding of rights which seems much closer to the dominant narrative. First, there is no rights inflation in the US Supreme Court, or at least not to the same extent as in Europe: the Court will only accept a liberty interest as a right if it can be shown to be 'deeply rooted in this Nation's history and tradition';[53] its reason for this caution is that '[b]y extending constitutional protection to an asserted right or liberty interest, we, to a great extent, place the matter outside the arena of public debate and legislative action. We must therefore "exercise the utmost care whenever we are asked to break new ground in this field"'.[54] Second, there is no general acknowledgement of horizontal effect; rather, constitutional rights will only apply when there is 'state action'.[55] Third, there is no endorsement of positive duties and

---

[53] See, for example,*Washington v. Glucksberg* (1997) 521 U.S. 702, 720.

[54] Ibid.

[55] For an overview, see Barendt, 'The United States and Canada: State Action, Constitutional Rights and Private Actors', in Oliver and Fedtke (eds.), *Human Rights and the Private Sphere* (Routledge-Cavendish, 2007), 399.

certainly none of socio-economic rights. The *DeShaney* case illustrates this approach: the petitioner was a child who was subjected to a series of beatings by his father until he eventually suffered permanent, serious brain damage. He and his mother argued that the state had violated his constitutional rights by failing to protect him from his father. The Supreme Court, however, held that the Fourteenth Amendment, which states that 'no State shall...deprive any person of life, liberty, or property, without due process of law', was not violated. It relied on textual and historical reasons to support this conclusion, arguing that the clause was phrased as a limitation on the state's power to act, not as a guarantee of certain minimal levels of safety and security, and that its history showed its purpose to be the prevention of government abusing its power or employing it as an instrument of oppression. 'Its purpose was to protect the people from the State, not to ensure that the State protected them from each other. The Framers were content to leave the extent of governmental obligation in the latter area to the democratic political process.'[56] This understanding of constitutional rights thus places the US Supreme Court in diametrical contrast to the ECtHR, which would have applied its general doctrine of positive obligations and held that the right to life and the right to private life (into which the Court reads a right to physical integrity) place obligations on the state to protect people's lives and physical integrity from violations by third parties. Finally, US constitutional law has not subscribed to the proportionality test to determine the permissible limitations of rights, but uses a variety of standards, including the strict scrutiny test which demands that a law interfering with a fundamental right must serve a compelling government interest and be narrowly tailored to the achievement of that interest. According to common wisdom, this requirement is harder to fulfil than proportionality; as the saying goes, strict scrutiny is '"strict" in theory and fatal in fact'.[57]

It must be noted that all the above observations on the current state of US law are controversial; and it would seem possible to construct an argument to the effect that upon closer inspection the US model of rights is not far removed from the global model. With regard to rights inflation, it is arguable that the rational basis test which the US Supreme

---

[56] *DeShaney v. Winnebago County Department of Social Services* (1989) 489 U.S. 189, 196.

[57] This famous phrase was coined by Gunther, 'The Supreme Court, 1971 Term—Foreword: In Search of Evolving Doctrine on a Changing Court: A Model for a Newer Equal Protection', (1972) 86 *Harvard Law Review* 1, 8.

Court applies to interests not deemed fundamental does in substance award those interests a protection similar to the protection offered to trivial interests under, for example, the German or European approaches, albeit without labelling those interests as 'rights'. With regard to horizontal effect, the simple reference to the 'state action' doctrine raises the question of what counts as state action: under the broadest possible understanding, the creation of any (private law) statute or common law doctrine amounts to state action, from which it follows that there is indeed state action in *every* legal dispute; and furthermore, court decisions adjudicating claims between private individuals can always be constructed as involving state action.[58] At times the Supreme Court has come close to taking this view,[59] which, taken seriously, would in substance lead to a broad acknowledgement of horizontal effect via the state action doctrine. Thus, referral to the requirement of 'state action' does not resolve the problem of whether and to what extent constitutional rights have an impact on the legal relationship between private parties. With regard to the absence of positive obligations, the *DeShaney* judgment has been sharply criticized as relying on a mistaken interpretation of the US constitution.[60] And finally, with regard to balancing and proportionality, even within the US Supreme Court, Justice Breyer has shown sympathies for the European approaches on balancing and proportionality and would prefer to see those approaches used more widely within the interpretation of the US Bill of Rights.[61] Furthermore, it is arguable that the current tiered scrutiny (strict and intermediate scrutiny; rational basis review) amounts in substance to something similar to proportionality analysis.

Thus, it is certainly a possibility that upon deeper analysis it turns out that US practice, too, is best explained by the global model and the reconstructive theory developed in this book. Furthermore, it remains of course true that US constitutional rights law is a part of a Western liberal tradition of rights discourse and that for this reason examples and cases drawn from it will be useful for the analysis of specific issues even if its

---

[58] Kumm and Ferreres Comella, 'What is so Special about Constitutional Rights in Private Litigation? A Comparative Analysis of the Function of State Action Requirements and Indirect Effect', in Sajó and Uitz (eds.), *The Constitution in Private Relations* (Eleven, 2005).

[59] *Shelley v. Kramer* (1948) 334 U.S. 1.

[60] Strauss, 'Due Process, Government Inaction, and Private Wrongs', (1989) *Supreme Court Review* 53.

[61] *District of Columbia v. Heller* (2008) 128 S.Ct. 2783, 2852 (Breyer J, dissenting). For an insightful discussion, cf. Cohen-Eliya and Porat, 'The Hidden Foreign Law Debate in *Heller*: The Proportionality Approach in American Constitutional Law', (2009) 46 *San Diego Law Review* 367.

doctrinal structure arguably differs from the global model. Therefore this book will occasionally rely on US cases to illustrate a point. But for the reasons given, a comprehensive analysis of how US law relates to the global model is beyond the scope of this book.

It is an interesting point to note that many of the leading philosophers of rights—Ronald Dworkin, Robert Nozick, James Griffin and others—are Americans; their theories may be influenced by or, as in Dworkin's case, reconstructions of the US practice which, as explained, at least on the surface seems to be much closer to the dominant narrative. If so, then this makes even clearer the need for a theory of rights which is developed against the backdrop of the global model of constitutional rights.

V. THE RECONSTRUCTIVE APPROACH

The theory proposed in this book is *reconstructive*, which means that it is a theory of the practice of constitutional rights law around the world ('the practice') and especially those features of the practice which I summarized under the label of 'the global model of constitutional rights'. This can be contrasted with what we might call a *'philosophical'* theory of constitutional rights which is insensitive to the practice. A philosophical theory will aim at providing the morally best account of constitutional rights while ignoring the question of the extent to which this account fits the practice. When the practice departs from the philosophical theory then this is for the philosophical theory a reason for regret only insofar as the practice is deficient; but it does not affect the validity of the philosophical theory. The reconstructive theory, by way of contrast, aims at providing a theory which, like the philosophical theory, is morally coherent, but unlike it, need not be the morally best ('the one right') theory, where 'morally best' is understood as morally best independently of the practice. Of the several morally coherent theories, the reconstructive theory will pick the one which fits the practice better than any other coherent theory. Thus, the reconstructive theory is sensitive to both moral value and the practice it seeks to reconstruct; it is, in Ronald Dworkin's terminology, an *interpretive* theory.[62]

There are two reasons why this book chooses the reconstructive approach. First, the practice of constitutional rights adjudication around the world provides scholars with a wealth of case law and doctrines produced by judges who often deal with questions of constitutional

---

[62] On interpretivism see Dworkin, *Law's Empire* (Hart Publishing, 1986), ch. 2.

rights on a daily basis and accumulate a practical expertise in this area which philosophers cannot hope to match. It would simply be imprudent to ignore this wealth of materials and experience when developing a theory of rights. Second, the extraordinary amount of political power exercised by constitutional courts raises particularly urgent questions of legitimacy and requires an assessment of the moral justifiability of the practice; and for this the reconstructive account can be used.

The reconstructive theory can be employed for two further purposes. First, it can be used to assess specific aspects of the practice; where the practice departs from the reconstructive theory, this particular aspect of the practice is, all things being equal, a mistake which should be corrected. For example, if the reconstructive account holds that the practice is best reconstructed as excluding moralism, then we can conclude that those cases in which moralism nevertheless features are, all things being equal, mistakes and should have been decided differently. Second, one can assess the reconstructive account in light of a philosophical account and use the philosophical account to criticize the reconstructive one and recommend reform. However, for any philosophical theory to convincingly claim the need for reform of the practice, it must first provide the best possible understanding of the practice; otherwise the philosophical account risks fighting against a distorted account of the practice or a straw man.

There are two kinds of reconstructive theories. The first can be called *moral reconstruction*; this is the kind of theory which I have outlined above and which will be proposed in this book. It aims at finding moral value in a practice: something which makes it worth continuing with that practice. It is of course possible that there is no such moral value, in which case this would have to be acknowledged by adopting the perspective of what Dworkin calls the internal sceptic;[63] the consequence is that the practice ought to be discontinued. The second kind of reconstruction is morally neutral; we might call it *zeitgeist reconstruction*. Rather than aiming at identifying moral merit it aims at reconstructing the practice in a way which shows the *zeitgeist* predominant in shaping the practice. *Zeitgeist* reconstruction is a valid scholarly enterprise and can be important for, in particular, historical and sociological purposes. Two examples will show the difference between the two kinds of reconstruction. We might be interested in a *zeitgeist* reconstruction of Nazi law. So we would look at the practice of Nazi law and try to identify

---

[63] Ibid., 78–9.

important themes in it; and we would find one important theme which is the idea of the racial superiority of Aryans over Jews. So we might say that one aspect of our *zeitgeist* reconstruction of Nazi law is this presumed superiority. By way of contrast, if we had engaged in a *moral* reconstruction of Nazi law, we could not have held that the idea of a superiority of Aryans over Jews was a valid reconstruction: it lacks moral value; or in other words, it is not a principle but a falsity. So a moral reconstruction of Nazi law would look very different from a *zeitgeist* reconstruction. The second example is closer to contemporary constitutional rights law. Suppose that a look at the practice shows that sometimes the practice rejects moralism and sometimes it approves of moralism. For example, moralism towards homosexuals is no longer regarded as acceptable today by the courts, whereas 50 years ago it clearly was; but recently the German Federal Constitutional Court regarded moralism towards people engaging in incest as acceptable.[64] Someone engaging in moral reconstruction must give a morally coherent account of the legitimacy of moralism which also fits the practice. She could not just argue that the correct moral reconstruction held that moralism was acceptable when directed against whoever is the unpopular group of the day: that blatantly lacks moral coherence because the mere fact that a group is unpopular does not justify limiting this group's freedom. But it might be a very good *zeitgeist* reconstruction: it might be the case that the *zeitgeist* in Western societies is such that it is regarded as permissible to engage in moralism towards a group only if that group is really unpopular. So, again, two persons engaging in reconstructive enterprises might come up with very different reconstructive accounts depending on what the goal of their reconstruction is. Since the aim of this book is to assess the moral legitimacy of the practice it seeks to reconstruct, it must engage in a moral reconstruction.

VI. A SUMMARY

The book will rely on the four features of the global model of constitutional rights presented in section II in order to develop its theory of rights: first, rights inflation and the broad understanding of (prima facie) rights, including a right to privacy which protects almost all, at least all non-trivial, interests; second, the existence of positive obligations and the

---

[64] BVerfGE 120, 224, 248 (referring to a 'sense of wrongness *[Unrechtsbewusstsein]* anchored in society' as reinforcing the reasons supporting the prohibition).

growing acceptance of socio-economic rights; third, the acknowledgement of horizontal effect; and fourth, the use of the doctrines of balancing and proportionality. My claim is that on the basis of this set of
materials it is possible to construct a theory of constitutional rights
which fits these materials and is morally coherent. To this end, the
structure of this book will reflect the unanimous practice of courts in
distinguishing between the prima facie stage of rights and the justification stage.

In Chapters 2–4, the book develops a theory of the scope of prima
facie rights which makes sense of the broad understanding of rights,
horizontal effect, positive obligations, and socio-economic rights.
Chapter 2 ('Negative and Positive Freedom') argues that the value
protected by constitutional rights must be positive freedom, or *personal
autonomy*: in particular the doctrines of positive obligations and horizontal effect and the increasing acceptance of socio-economic rights indicate
that the point of rights is to *enable* people to live their lives autonomously, as opposed to *disabling* or limiting the government in certain
ways.

Chapter 3 ('Two Conceptions of Autonomy') discusses two competing conceptions of personal autonomy which I term the *excluded reasons
conception* and the *protected interests conception*. The excluded reasons
conception—related in particular to Dworkinian theories of rights—
holds that in order to respect a person's autonomy, the state must not
rely on certain (excluded) reasons in its treatment of him, in particular
moralistic or paternalistic reasons or reasons based on the idea that some
people are worth less than others. The chapter argues that while this is a
coherent and intuitively appealing conception of autonomy, it cannot
explain the broad scope of (prima facie) rights accepted today. The
second and preferable conception of autonomy—the protected interests
conception—focuses directly on the actions and personal resources
which are important for the purpose of leading an autonomous life.
For example, it recognizes the importance for autonomous persons of
being able to choose one's intimate partners, utter one's political views,
and control what happens to one's body, and takes the importance of
these interests as the reason for protecting them. It is then possible to
assess the weight of a specific autonomy interest with reference to its
importance *from the perspective of the self-conception of the agent*. This
approach is related but preferable to similar concepts used by courts
and philosophers, such as the idea of developing one's personality,
which is widely used in European human rights law, James Griffin's

idea of living one's conception of a worthwhile life, or the idea of self-realization. The chapter demonstrates that the protected interests conception is successful and superior to the excluded reasons conception in explaining the broad scope of rights under the global model.

Chapter 4 ('The Right to Autonomy') proposes a comprehensive conception of (prima facie) rights. It demonstrates that it is coherent to accept rights to whatever is in the interest of the autonomy of a person, including socio-economic rights (which protect the preconditions of autonomy) and rights to engage in trivial activities (such as pursuing one's hobbies) and even immoral and harmful activities (such as murder). It thus concludes that the almost unanimously held view that there is a *threshold* which separates interests from rights should be given up. The point and purpose of constitutional rights under the global model is thus not to single out certain especially important interests for heightened protection but rather to ensure that *all* autonomy interests of a person are *adequately protected* at all times. The broad understanding of prima facie rights is simply a tool which ensures that all autonomy interests survive the prima facie stage in order to assess the adequacy of their protection at the justification stage, using, in particular, the proportionality test.

In the subsequent three chapters, Chapters 5–7, the book develops a theory of the justification stage, focussing on the core doctrinal tools used at that stage, namely balancing and the principle of proportionality. Chapter 5 ('Towards a Theory of Balancing and Proportionality: The Point and Purpose of Judicial Review') starts from the premise that in order to develop a substantive moral theory of balancing and proportionality, we first need an account of the point and purpose of judicial review under the global model. This account must integrate the reconstructive theory of rights as it has emerged in the previous chapters with attractive accounts of the values of democracy and the separation of powers. Having established in Chapter 4 that constitutional rights comprehensively protect a person's autonomy, this chapter goes one step further and argues that not only rights but also (almost all) policies are oriented towards autonomy. It follows that constitutional rights and policy-making are concerned with the same subject-matter, namely *the specification of the spheres of autonomy of equal citizens*. This raises a problem for the legitimacy of judicial review because it seems to imply that there is no room left for democratic decision-making. Relying on a reinterpretation of Mattias Kumm's work, the chapter proposes a solution to this problem by arguing that for a policy to be constitutionally legitimate and democratic properly understood, it must represent a *reasonable* specification of the spheres of autonomy of equal citizens, as opposed to *the one correct* specification. The chapter further integrates this result with the value of the separation of powers by arguing that even if one accepted the controversial proposition that considerations relating to institutional competence are the key to a proper appreciation of that value, no objection to judicial review would arise because it is plausible to assume that courts will be capable of assessing constitutional legitimacy in the specific sense just described.

The following two chapters build on these conclusions to develop an account of balancing and proportionality. Chapter 6 ('Balancing') presents the operative heart of the doctrine proposed in this book: a theory of personal autonomy under conditions of *conflict*. When there is such conflict between the autonomy interests of one person with the autonomy interests of another person, constitutional law recommends that the competing autonomy interests are to be 'balanced'. The chapter first clarifies the various possible meanings of this idea by presenting four concepts of balancing: balancing as autonomy maximization, interest balancing, formal balancing, and balancing as reasoning. It argues, negatively, that equating, without further argument, balancing with consequentialist reasoning or mechanical ways of quantification would be misguided; at the most general level, the doctrine of balancing, properly understood, simply refers to the need to resolve a conflict of autonomy interests in line with sound moral arguments (balancing as reasoning). Positively, the chapter proposes a set of moral principles to adequately deal with such conflicts, illustrating this with analyses of a broad range of important constitutional rights cases relating to issues including abortion, hate speech, religious drug use, euthanasia, and many others. Thus, it explores the considerable complexity that hides under the convenient doctrinal label of 'balancing' and develops a workable theory of how this balancing ought to be conducted in the resolution of actual cases.

The final chapter ('Proportionality') integrates the results of the previous chapters into a comprehensive theory of proportionality. It argues that the principle of proportionality is a tool for the structured resolution of conflicts of autonomy interests. Each of the four stages of the proportionality test (legitimate goal; suitability or rational connection; necessity; balancing or proportionality in the strict sense) has its own role to play in this regard. The purpose of the legitimate goal stage is to exclude goals which, while sometimes autonomy-related, must not be accorded any weight: in particular moralistic or impermissibly paternalistic goals. The point of the suitability stage is to establish the extent to which there is a genuine conflict between the two autonomy interests at stake. The necessity stage deals with alternative policies which are less restrictive of the right. At the balancing stage the conflict is ultimately resolved, using the framework developed in Chapter 6. In assessing the balance, courts grant the original decision-maker what in Europe is called a 'margin of appreciation'; other courts do the same under different terminologies. This margin of appreciation incorporates the reasonableness requirement proposed in Chapter 5 into constitutional rights law: a policy will be regarded as constitutionally legitimate if it falls within the margin of appreciation of the elected branches, i.e. if it resolves a conflict of autonomy interests in a way which is reasonable (as opposed to correct). Thus, the principle of proportionality, properly applied, guides judges through the reasoning process as to whether a policy is constitutionally legitimate.

PART I

THE SCOPE OF RIGHTS

$\mathcal{\infty}$ 2 $\mathcal{\infty}$

Negative and Positive Freedom

The starting point of the reconstructive enterprise undertaken by this book is to ask whether it is possible to identify in the practice of constitutional rights law a value or a set of values protected by (prima facie) rights. The main candidates which come to mind are liberty, or freedom (I will use the two synonymously[1]), in their positive and negative dimensions. Isaiah Berlin introduced the distinction between negative and positive liberty in his famous essay *Two concepts of liberty*,[2] and his account is helpful for present purposes. *Negative* freedom, for Berlin, is about the question 'What is the area within which the subject—a person or group of persons—is or should be left to do or be what he is able to do or be, without interference by other persons?'[3] In short, negative freedom is 'freedom *from*'; it is about the absence of constraints, or, as it is sometimes put, 'the right to be left alone'.[4] Its focus is not on the liberty-holder but on the potential violator: he has to stand back and let the liberty-holder enjoy his liberty, and the less he interferes, the greater is the liberty-holder's liberty. *Positive* freedom, by way of contrast, is concerned with the question 'What, or who, is the source of control or interference that can determine someone to do, or be, this rather than that?'[5] Thus, positive freedom is about *control*, it is 'freedom *to*'; in contrast to negative freedom, the focus here is on the individual person rather than the potential violator. For the purposes of this book, I will

---

[1] This reflects common usage in English; also, most languages only have one word for both terms (*Freiheit*; *liberté*). Note that Dworkin ascribes distinct meanings to them: *Is Democracy Possible Here?* (Princeton University Press, 2006), 67. For his understanding of liberty, see *Sovereign Virtue* (Harvard University Press, 2000), ch. 3.

[2] Berlin, 'Two Concepts of Liberty', in Berlin, *Liberty* (Oxford University Press, 2002).

[3] Ibid., 169.

[4] Roberts, 'Privacy, Autonomy and Criminal Justice Rights: Philosophical Preliminaries', in Alldridge and Brants (eds.), *Personal Autonomy, the Private Sphere and the Criminal Law* (Hart Publishing, 2001), 59.

[5] Berlin, 'Two Concepts of Liberty' in Berlin, *Liberty* (Oxford University Press, 2002), 169.

regard positive freedom as synonymous with *autonomy*, in particular *personal autonomy*:[6] it is about the control an individual has over her own life.

It is well known that Berlin was sceptical about positive freedom and much preferred negative freedom. Whatever the merits of his work in this respect, in recent decades philosophers have by and large disagreed with him and turned towards positive freedom or autonomy. The best-known and most influential example is Joseph Raz who argues in *The Morality of Freedom* that '[n]egative freedom, freedom from coercive interferences, is valuable in as much as it serves positive freedom and autonomy'.[7] The argument of this chapter will be that a similar shift has occurred in constitutional rights law: the global model of constitutional rights is best explained not by the once uncontroversial idea that the point of constitutional rights is to protect the people from their governments, but rather by reference to the value of positive freedom. Having made its case in favour of positive freedom or autonomy, the chapter considers two further values often invoked in constitutional rights discourse, namely human dignity and equality. It concludes that while they may have a role to play in a theory of constitutional rights, under the reconstructive, 'bottom-up' methodology employed here it is preferable to begin with personal autonomy.

I. NEGATIVE FREEDOM

1. *Freedom from the state: limited government*

An understanding of constitutional rights as being about freedom from the state, or limited government, sits relatively well with civil and political rights in their vertical dimension. It is common rhetoric among constitutional rights lawyers to speak of civil and political rights as preserving 'a zone of non-interference from the state'—a formulation which indicates that we are concerned with freedom from the state. If, for example, individuals have a right to design their sex lives according to their preferences, speak their minds freely, or worship whichever god they prefer, then this means that the government is limited in that it must not decide for them what kind of sex lives to lead, or what speech to speak, or which god to pray to. However, even with regard to these

---

[6] Chapter 5 will introduce a second kind of autonomy, namely political autonomy.

[7] Raz, *The Morality of Freedom* (Clarendon Press, 1986), 410.

rights, one can doubt whether regarding the limitation of the state as their moral point does full justice to them. Take the right to demonstrate: if I want to hold a demonstration in central London, it is not a sufficient protection of my right to demonstrate if the government just stands back according to the principle that its power is limited by my right. Rather, it may, for example, have to get involved in the planning of the route, make arrangements for the traffic, and provide security measures in order to protect me from counter-demonstrations. Thus, the right to demonstrate is a bundle of different things: first, the government must not prohibit or otherwise make impossible my demonstration; in that sense my right can arguably be regarded as being about negative liberty. Second, the government must employ *positive* measures to enable me to exercise my right; and this part of the bundle cannot be explained in terms of limited government.

I do not want to push this point further because there is enough other evidence to discredit the idea that constitutional rights are about limited government. Most importantly, it fails to explain positive obligations and socio-economic rights. As the name makes clear, 'positive' obligations require the state to become active and protect the interests protected by rights against violations especially by third parties. Socio-economic rights, too, require the state to provide certain goods and thus expand rather than limit the state.

The matter is more complicated with regard to horizontal effect. On one interpretation, horizontal effect is simply a subcategory of positive obligations; it thus requires the state to become active and prevent the violation of the rights of one private party by another; it follows that horizontal effect, too, expands rather than limits the state. However, one might try to pull horizontal effect under the umbrella of limited government by arguing that the point of horizontal effect is to limit the state by stopping it from 'outsourcing' rights violations to private parties.[8] There is, however, not much evidence that this view underlies the global model. In the German context, the existence of horizontal effect has famously been justified with regard to an 'objective order of values' established by the Basic Law, which must influence the interpretation of all private law.[9] This phrase is notoriously mysterious, and I cannot offer

---

[8] This approach finds resonance in the case law of the US Supreme Court, according to which there is state action when the state 'has provided such significant encouragement, either overt or covert, that the choice must in law be deemed to be that of the state'. *Blum v. Yaretsky* (1982) 457 U.S. 991, 1004.

[9] BVerfGE 7, 198, 204 (*Lüth*).

a complete investigation into its meaning here. However, the wording indicates that something bigger is at stake than just the desire to limit government; the 'objective order of values' seems to stipulate positive requirements rather than negative ones. In Canada, the Supreme Court demands that the common law be developed in light of the values of the constitution.[10] Thus, even the courts, when developing the common law, are bound by constitutional rights in some way, and it seems absurd to assume that the courts developed this doctrine in order to prevent themselves (in a Ulysses-like fashion) from creating common law rules which were designed to encourage private persons to violate the rights of others. Thus, an approach that sees the point of constitutional rights in limiting government does not sit well with the existence of horizontal effect. It can therefore be concluded that while an understanding of constitutional rights as being about limited government can possibly make sense of civil and political rights in their vertical dimension, it fails to explain horizontal effect, positive obligations and socio-economic rights. Thus, it is an unsuitable candidate for a comprehensive theory of constitutional rights.

2. *Freedom from everyone?*

Before rashly excluding negative freedom from the list of candidate values, another understanding of negative freedom must briefly be examined. As laid out above, one problem with the 'negative freedom as limited government' approach is that it cannot explain horizontal effect. To cure this defect, maybe it is sufficient to understand the point of freedom not as limiting *government*, but as limiting *everyone*? Under this interpretation, constitutional rights would still preserve a zone of 'freedom from', but the agents from whom they protect the right-holder would not only be the government but also private actors. The right to freedom of speech, for example, would mean that a person has the right to speak his mind, and that both the state and all other persons are limited in that they must not interfere with his speech.

While this model may explain horizontal effect, it would obviously still be unable to account for positive rights. However, it fails also for another reason, namely its lack of moral appeal compared to an autonomy-based approach. The problem is what exactly the value protected by 'freedom from everyone' is supposed to be. In the case of negative

---

[10]   *Retail, Wholesale & Dep't Store Union v. Dolphin Delivery Ltd.* (1986) 2 SCR 573, 605.

freedom as limited government, the value at stake must flow from the idea that government is the greatest threat to freedom and that its power should therefore be limited. But in the case of freedom from everyone, this idea does not work. I cannot think of a value served by an understanding of negative liberty as freedom from everyone except for *personal autonomy*. If private persons ought to be prevented from violating individuals' speech, religious practice, privacy, etc., then the most plausible justification of this lies not in *limiting* everyone, but rather in *enabling* everyone to take control of his life: to autonomously engage in speech, religion, or private activities. Therefore, the real value at stake is not negative liberty but personal autonomy, to which we must now turn.

II. POSITIVE FREEDOM OR PERSONAL AUTONOMY

1. *Civil and political rights in their vertical dimension*

While, as pointed out in the previous section, it is largely possible to regard civil and political rights in their negative dimension, such as the rights to freedom of expression, freedom of religion, and the right to privacy, as being about negative liberty, as a matter of ordinary language it is also possible to conceptualize them as autonomy-protecting: they can be regarded as enabling individuals to make choices in these areas. Much here is simply a matter of rhetoric: either one speaks about the right *to* sexual autonomy—thus indicating that it falls into the 'freedom to' category, or one speaks of the right to freedom *from* state interference in matters of sexuality, stressing the negative character of the right. Since the question of whether these rights are about negative or positive liberty cannot be decided by rhetoric or definition, we have to ask which approach sits better with the core features of the practice.

Autonomy can easily accommodate those rights which are about *actions*: a central element of autonomy is about making choices about one's life and acting upon them.[11] Among civil and political rights, there are, however, some rights which are not about actions but protect what we might call the right-holder's *personal resources*, such as his physical integrity, property, reputation, or personal data. So the question is whether these rights can be explained in terms of personal autonomy. A first idea would be to regard personal resources as a *precondition* of autonomy: unless we are, for example, physically alive, we cannot

---

[11] Cf. Raz, *The Morality of Freedom* (Clarendon Press, 1986), 369: 'The ruling idea behind the ideal of personal autonomy is that people should make their own lives.'

pursue any autonomous projects; and if we are alive but our physical integrity has been interfered with—for example, because we have been beaten up—then this will at least in some cases be a hindrance to the autonomous pursuit of our projects. The same reasoning could be applied to property: one might say that unless one has at least some property, one cannot really live an autonomous life—at least not a *meaningfully* autonomous life: maybe one can survive on state benefits, but a truly autonomous life requires the availability of more options than just that.

However, this explanation of the rights to physical integrity and property is deficient because it cannot convincingly explain some of our intuitions about what constitutes an interference with those rights. Take the case of being beaten up: we regard this as an interference with the right to physical integrity not because it limits the victim's ability to pursue his projects—for example, because he will have to go and see a doctor to fix him, and that costs him time which he could otherwise have used for better purposes. Rather, we are confident to conclude that an interference has occurred without engaging in such considerations. Similarly, even a minor interference with the property of a very rich person will be regarded as an interference with that person's property right, independently of whether it affects the person's ability to pursue her projects.

The correct approach is that personal resources are not preconditions but *elements* of autonomy. Personal autonomy, properly understood, is not only about actions. Rather, to use Berlin's language, it is ultimately about *control*, namely, generally speaking, control over one's life. That naturally includes at least some (maybe all) actions because it is through actions that a person controls in which direction to move her life. It must, however, go further than that and also include control over one's personal resources. Thus, an autonomous person does not only control her actions, but also what happens to her body or her property, and violations of a person's property or physical integrity are also violations of that person's autonomy.

Which domains are protected in this way will be a matter of moral debate. The right to physical integrity is uncontroversial[12] and the right to property is widely accepted.[13] The German Federal Constitutional

---

[12]   Art. 2 ECHR; Art. 2(2) of the German Basic Law; s. 7 of the Canadian Charter of Rights and Freedoms; ss. 11 and 12(2) of the South African Constitution.

[13]   Art.1 of Protocol No. 1 ECHR; Art. 14 of the German Basic Law; s. 25 of the South African Constitution.

Court and the ECtHR go further and accept, for example, a right to control one's public image, which means a right to decide which information about oneself may be released to the public, in particular by the media.[14] The question of the exact determination of what ought to be considered as part of a person's resources need not be resolved here; my point is only to show that an autonomy-based approach does not have to limit itself to the protection of actions but can, indeed should, include personal resources as well.

2. Horizontal effect

An autonomy-based understanding of constitutional rights sits well with horizontal effect: if what matters is personal autonomy, then our primary concern is not the identity of the potential violator (the state or a private actor?); rather, the focus is on the right-holder and the degree of control she has over her life. Private and state actors may have different ways of interfering with autonomy (an employer dismisses an employee because of something he said, or adds clauses to the employment contract prohibiting certain speech, whereas the state prohibits certain speech under threat of official punishment), but the effect is the same: it limits the degree to which an individual is in control of his life.

This argument may seem too simple, and there are two possible objections with which I will deal in turn. The first is that the doctrines regarding horizontal effect proposed by the German Federal Constitutional Court and the Canadian Supreme Court are not, at least not on the surface, about personal autonomy. Rather, the arguments rely on the idea that the respective constitutions set up a system of *values* which has an impact on private law. This raises the question of what the value-based approach means and whether it can be reconciled with an understanding which places personal autonomy at the heart of constitutional rights. In response to this concern, what courts must mean when they talk about the 'values' underlying constitutional rights is, precisely, personal autonomy. The term 'value' does not hold any explanatory force; it is a truism that constitutional rights must be interpreted in light of their underlying values. So the question is *which* value(s) constitutional rights protect. It must be a value that leads to an endorsement of

---

[14] Cf. BVerfGE 34, 269 (*Princess Soraya*) (concerning the publication of an interview with a celebrity which had never taken place); *von Hannover v. Germany* (2005) 40 EHRR 1 (concerning the publication of unauthorized pictures from a celebrity's private life).

horizontal effect. If the courts thought that the point of constitutional rights was limited government, then there would simply not be any reason for them to ever think about horizontal effect: there is no reason to bind a private person in certain ways if what one wants to achieve is limited government.[15] In such a case, even under a constitution such as the South African one, which explicitly makes constitutional rights applicable between private parties, 'taking into account the nature of the right and the nature of any duty imposed by the right',[16] the courts would have to reject horizontal effect: taking into account the nature of the right as being about the limitation of government, it would follow that there is no need for horizontal effect. Conversely, if courts regarded the protection of personal autonomy as the point of constitutional rights, then even in a case where the constitution has a clause which establishes that it only applies to the state,[17] it would be clear that the state must be under a duty to protect personal autonomy, and that includes producing laws that protect individuals from violations of their autonomy by third parties. Thus, when courts speak about the values underlying constitutional rights and rely on those values to defend horizontal effect, this makes sense only if they mean the value of personal autonomy.

The second possible objection is that my account misses something which almost all scholars take to be one of the crucial issues in any discussion of horizontal effect, namely the conceptual distinctions between various forms of direct and indirect horizontal effect, and the relevance of these distinctions for a comprehensive grasp of horizontal effect. Given that these distinctions do not feature in my account, it may be suspected that my account is simplistic and misses something import-ant. Conventional arguments about horizontal effect usually take the following form. First, it is established that according to the respective constitution, rights bind only state organs, and not explicitly private persons. Then it is discussed what this implies for horizontal effect. There are a number of approaches to this issue: at the poles, verticalists say that from the fact that only state organs are bound it follows that constitutional rights apply only where there is state action, and that therefore they are irrelevant in disputes between private parties.[18] Hor-izontalists point out that all law, including private law, is produced by

---

[15] With the exception of the issue of the 'outsourcing' of rights, discussed above.

[16] S. 8(2) of the South African Constitution.

[17] Art. 1(3) of the German Basic Law; s. 32 of the Canadian Charter of Rights and Freedoms.

[18] This is the prevailing view in the US.

state organs and must therefore comply with constitutional rights.[19] An intermediate position ('indirect horizontal effect') accepts the verticalists' argument but claims that this leaves open the possibility that while there is no direct applicability, the 'values' implicit in constitutional rights demand that private law be interpreted in their spirit.[20] It is remarkable, though, that the debate between direct and indirect horizontalists gets off the ground only on the assumption that constitutional rights are about autonomy. If they were about limited government, then there would be no point in discussing *any* impact of constitutional rights— direct or indirect—on the relationship between private persons. So both indirect and direct horizontalists must already assume that the point of constitutional rights is to protect personal autonomy. Thus, the debate between the two is best understood as being about constitutional *interpretation*: it tries to reconcile the fact that constitutional rights are about autonomy with a constitution whose text and history—following what I called the 'dominant narrative'—suggest that constitutional rights are not applicable between private persons. So it is an argument about whether the 'spirit' of constitutional rights or a more narrowly textual or historical reading of the respective constitution should prevail. What the debate is *not* about is any *substantive* disagreement about the values protected by constitutional rights.[21]

3. Positive obligations

Regarding constitutional rights as autonomy-protecting immediately makes plausible the existence of positive obligations on the state to protect persons from the illegal acts of other private persons or other threats to the interests protected by the right because, as argued above, under an autonomy-based framework the main consideration is the

---

[19] Chemerinsky, 'Rethinking State Action', (1985) 80 *Northwestern University Law Review* 503, 524–5; Butler, 'Constitutional Rights in Private Litigation: A Critique and Comparative Analysis', (1993) 22 *Anglo-American Law Review* 1, 18–22.

[20] Hunt, 'The "Horizontal Effect" of the Human Rights Act', (1998) *Public Law* 423, 434–5.

[21] A parallel point has been argued convincingly by Kumm and Ferreres Comella. They demonstrate that the choice between direct and indirect horizontal effect has no consequences for the outcomes of cases: in Germany, not a single case would have been decided differently had the Federal Constitutional Court chosen direct horizontal rather than indirect horizontal effect; and in Canada, the seemingly weaker form of horizontal effect endorsed by the Canadian Supreme Court in common law cases can best be explained by considerations relating to inter-institutional dialogue rather than substantive differences about the scope of constitutional rights. See Kumm and Ferreres Comella, 'What is so Special about Constitutional Rights in Private Litigation? A Comparative Analysis of the Function of State Action Requirements and Indirect Effect', in Sajó and Uitz (eds.), *The Constitution in Private Relations* (Eleven, 2005).

extent to which an agent has control over his life, and not the identity of the violator of his right. For example, it is not of primary importance for the autonomy of an agent whether he is killed by the police or by a criminal; what matters instead is the fact that his life has been taken away from him. This point is reinforced by the jurisprudence of the ECtHR which consistently holds that the standards of review in cases involving negative and positive obligations are 'similar'.[22]

4. Socio-economic rights

Furthermore, it must be examined whether an autonomy-based approach to constitutional rights makes sense of socio-economic rights such as those of the South African Constitution, which includes rights to a healthy environment (section 24), access to housing (section 26), healthcare, food, water, and social security (section 27), and basic and further education (section 29). The answer is straightforward: not only are socio-economic rights *compatible* with an autonomy-based under-standing of rights; they are indeed *required* by it because they protect the *preconditions of autonomy*. In simple terms, setting up a framework which results in the people having many options but no food and water would fail to enable them to live an autonomous life. Similar, if less dramatic, considerations apply in the case of the rights to housing, healthcare and social security. In the case of the right to education, at least a basic education including the ability to read and write must be regarded as a precondition of autonomy because illiteracy has a disabling effect in that it forecloses so many options that the remaining ones are not sufficient to enable a person to live a meaningfully autonomous life. A right to further education goes beyond this, but even here it is generally true that the more education a person has enjoyed, the more options are available to him; in that sense higher education increases one's autonomy by being a precondition for having more options.

5. Procedural rights

The claim that constitutional rights are best explained as autonomy-based may seem problematic with regard to procedural rights such as the right to a hearing or the right to a fair trial: those rights are not, or at least not primarily, concerned with the achievement of certain substantive

---

[22] See, for example, *von Hannover v. Germany* (2005) 40 EHRR 1, para. 57.

outcomes (such as an adequate protection of autonomy), but rather with the proper procedures to be used in reaching those outcomes; thus it seems that their justification must rely at least partly on an independent value. While this book will mainly focus on substantive rights, it is important to address this point, not in order to develop a comprehensive conception of procedural rights but to assess whether the existence of procedural rights poses a problem for an autonomy-based approach and, if not, to locate the place of procedure within an autonomy-based framework.

The most fruitful way of analysing the issue is to focus on the relationship between substantive outcomes and procedures. Roughly speaking, procedural rights become applicable when a public authority makes determinations about someone's legal rights. It will become clear in the course of this book that legal rights, just as constitutional rights, are concerned with personal autonomy;[23] and therefore it can be said that procedural rights have a role to play only in relation to autonomy: they complement the substantive protection of personal autonomy. For example, in the case of court proceedings between two private persons about a contractual obligation of one person to pay the other a certain amount of money, a judgment denying or awarding one of them a certain sum relates to property which, as has been argued above, is a part of autonomy; and it is this relevance to autonomy which triggers the applicability of procedural rights such as the right to an independent and impartial tribunal. Similarly, in criminal trials, the accused person's liberty—another element of his autonomy—is at stake, and this triggers the applicability of procedural rights, including those specifically pertaining to criminal trials, such as the presumption of innocence and the privilege against self-incrimination. To give a final example, when a public authority makes a determination of someone's legal rights, for example by prohibiting his demonstration or awarding him a benefit such as a place at a university, certain welfare benefits, or the permission to run his business in a certain way, then this specifies the person's sphere of autonomy; if the act in question did not have relevance for his autonomy, then the applicability of his procedural rights—for example his right to a hearing—would not be triggered. Thus, procedural rights can only be understood in relation to personal autonomy as a complement to its substantive protection. This leaves their precise content and

---

[23] See Chapter 5, section IV.4.a, where I argue that policy-making is aimed at securing the conditions of personal autonomy.

justification open but shows that they can, indeed should, be integrated into an autonomy-based framework.

6. A combination of positive and negative freedom?

So far, this chapter has operated on the assumption that constitutional rights are based on *either* negative *or* positive freedom, and it has demonstrated that an understanding of rights as protecting personal autonomy can explain many features of the global model. However, it is conceivable that not all constitutional rights are based on the same value; in particular, the possibility seems to remain that civil and political rights in their vertical dimension are about limited government, as they have long been regarded. Someone might therefore argue that vertical civil and political rights are about limited government, whilst civil and political rights in their horizontal dimension, positive duties, and socio-economic rights are about personal autonomy. However, this view must presuppose that vertical and horizontal rights are two more or less *separate* sets of rights, and this distorts the way constitutional lawyers think about them. First, they do not normally speak of horizontal *rights* but of the horizontal *effect* of constitutional rights, which indicates that they conceive of vertical and horizontal rights not as two separate sets of rights but rather view each single right as having a vertical and a horizontal dimension which flow from one and the same core value. For example, take section 8 of the South African Constitution: the heading of the section is 'Application'; subsection 1 sets out that the rights bind the government; and subsection 2 stipulates their horizontal effect. Second, this view is also supported by the constitutional doctrines on horizontal effect which were first developed by the German Federal Constitutional Court and later by the Canadian Supreme Court. As I pointed out above, the German Court argued that the *values* enshrined in the Basic Law must guide the interpretation of all law, and concluded from this that horizontal effect must be endorsed. This shows that the Court conceived of horizontal effect as something which was simply a different expression of the very same value which underlies negative rights. The same argument applies in the Canadian case: when the Canadian Supreme Court argued that the common law must be interpreted in light of the values of the Charter, it must have had in mind that the values of the Charter are autonomy values, and not limitation of government values. Thus, the arguments which both the German and the Canadian courts have used to support the recognition of horizontal effect make sense only on the assumption that constitutional rights are about personal autonomy and not about a combination of autonomy and limited government.

III. EQUALITY AND HUMAN DIGNITY

There are two other candidate values which I have not addressed so far, namely human dignity and equality. Human dignity is an extraordinarily popular concept in constitutional rights law and is often described as the basis of human or constitutional rights.[24] There is certainly great intuitive appeal in the idea of human and constitutional rights as flowing from human dignity, and therefore it would be foolish to dismiss this value lightly. However, human dignity does not recommend itself as the starting point of a *reconstructive* theory for the following reason. It seems plausible to assume that any attractive conception of human dignity must award a prominent place to personal freedom: a life in dignity will normally require personal freedom. If this is true, then it might be the case that the practice of constitutional rights law is best explained in terms of personal freedom, which can in turn be explained as part of an even more abstract and complex value of human dignity. But then the starting point of a reconstructive, 'bottom-up' analysis must be personal freedom and not dignity. This leaves open or even supports the possibility of regarding human dignity as the foundational value of constitutional theory or indeed political morality without, however, making it the first port of call for a reconstructive theory.

Equality could feature in one of two ways in a comprehensive theory of constitutional rights. First, one could consider it as the one fundamental value of constitutional rights law, similar to the way in which many regard dignity as fundamental. This is the approach favoured by Ronald Dworkin who sees the more specific rights such as freedom of speech as flowing from the axiomatic right to equality of concern and respect.[25] My response to this approach is similar in structure to the one presented

---

[24] For a comprehensive analysis of the use of the concept of human dignity in human rights law see McCrudden, 'Human Dignity and Judicial Interpretation of Human Rights', (2008) 19 *European Journal of International Law* 655.

[25] Dworkin, *Sovereign Virtue* (Harvard University Press, 2000), 1: 'Equal concern is the sovereign virtue of political community—without it government is only tyranny.' For his right to equal concern and respect, see, for example, *Taking Rights Seriously* (Duckworth, 1977), ch. 11. In his book, *Is Democracy Possible Here?* (Princeton University Press, 2006), 10, Dworkin now relies on what he calls 'the two principles of human dignity' as the basis of rights.

against the suitability of human dignity. Dworkin may be right in his appraisal of equality. Again, however, this does not imply that equality ought to be the starting point of a *reconstructive* analysis. For example (and, I believe, roughly faithful to Dworkin's intentions), it could be argued that treating people as equals requires respecting their autonomous choices about what the good life requires, rather than imposing on them the majority's choices. But then there is nothing wrong with starting with an account of the proper meaning of autonomy and bringing in the idea of equality at a later stage of the analysis.

Second, there is the possibility that equality features in a theory of constitutional rights not as the sole fundamental value but as one which *complements* autonomy. In light of the fact that constitutions generally include equality or non-discrimination provisions, one might argue that some constitutional rights are autonomy-protecting and others (in particular the rights to equality and non-discrimination) are equality-protecting. Thus, the two values of autonomy and equality would stand next to each other as the two fundamental values of constitutional rights law. The picture has intuitive appeal and corresponds to how many think about the point and purpose of constitutional rights ('Constitutional rights protect our freedom and equality.'). Its problem is, however, that, as it stands, it leaves the relationship between the two values unresolved. Two possibilities present themselves. The first is to regard autonomy and equality as two separate values setting up distinct moral standards. This approach, however, does not sit well with the practice of constitutional rights law: many rights issues can be approached from an autonomy perspective or an equality perspective, and often the same considerations apply, independently of the doctrinal starting point. For example, a case involving the dismissal of soldiers from the army because of their homosexuality can be constructed as being about an interference with their right to private life (this is the approach that the ECtHR chose in *Smith and Grady v. United Kingdom*[26]), or alternatively as being about discrimination on the ground of sexual orientation; and in both cases the proportionality assessment the outcome of which determines whether the interference with the right to private life or the unequal treatment are justified proceeds in the same way. The second and more promising possibility is to regard autonomy and equality as in some way related to each other. But then, given that a

---

[26] *Smith and Grady v. United Kingdom* (2000) 29 EHRR 493.

reconstructive theory must start *somewhere*, it makes sense to consider first the value which offers the better fit and bring in the other at a later stage. This is precisely the approach chosen by this book, which starts with an analysis of autonomy and leaves the role of equality open until Chapter 5.[27]

[27] In that chapter (Chapter 5, section IV.4.a) the value of equality will be introduced and its proper role in constitutional rights law, including the role of a *right* to equality, will be assessed. It will be concluded that its point is to guide the resolution of clashes between different people's autonomy interests: such conflicts must be resolved in line with each person's status as an equal. Furthermore, it will be argued that a separate *right* to equality, while not incoherent, is unnecessary in that the protection offered by the right to equality does not add anything to an autonomy-based understanding of constitutional rights.

⚬ 3 ⚬

Two Conceptions of Autonomy

I. INTRODUCTION

This chapter builds on the conclusion of Chapter 2, which argued that constitutional rights are best explained as protecting personal autonomy, and takes the inquiry one step further by asking a follow-up question: which *conception* of autonomy is at work in the jurisprudence of the courts? My starting point, in good Berlinian tradition, is the notion of *control*.[1] The ECHR as interpreted by the ECtHR, for example, gives a person some control over her physical integrity, liberty, expression, religious and moral beliefs, private and family life, property, personal data, and more. Other constitutions have similarly expansive lists, with slight variations.[2] The most recently drafted major constitutional rights document, the Charter of Fundamental Rights of the European Union, affirms this broad understanding of rights; interestingly, it is widely regarded as providing an accurate account of the current state of affairs in European-style constitutional rights law.[3] The question for an autonomy-based theory of all these rights is what holds them together: we need to know how to distinguish those exercises of autonomy which ought to be protected by constitutional rights from those which ought not.

To simplify the task, I will restrict myself to negative vertical rights in this chapter, and only deal with horizontal effect, positive obligations and socio-economic rights in the next chapter. I shall present two competing conceptions of personal autonomy, which I shall refer to

---

[1] Cf. Berlin, 'Two Concepts of Liberty', in Berlin, *Liberty* (Oxford University Press, 2002), 169.

[2] Notably (and intentionally) absent from the Canadian Charter of Rights and Freedoms is the right to property.

[3] Cf. Craig and de Búrca, *EU Law* (5th edn, Oxford University Press, 2011), 395: '[O]verall the Charter could perhaps best be described as a creative distillation of the rights contained in the various European and international agreements and national constitutions on which the ECJ had for some years already drawn.'

as the excluded reasons conception and the protected interests conception.[4] The excluded reasons conception represents a popular understanding of autonomy and is related in particular to Dworkinian theories of rights; in the legal domain a similar understanding of constitutional rights has recently been advocated by George Letsas.[5] The following section will first develop a coherent account of this conception and then examine whether it can sufficiently explain the practice of constitutional rights law. The conclusion will be that it cannot. In response to its main defects, the third section will develop the protected interests conception as an alternative model which provides a fuller account of the breadth of the practice.

II. THE EXCLUDED REASONS CONCEPTION OF AUTONOMY

The key feature of the excluded reasons conception of autonomy is that it is *relational*. It focuses on the relationship between the state and the citizen, and it shapes this relationship by making it impermissible for the state to rely on certain reasons in the treatment of the citizen. One is autonomous if one's treatment by the state is not governed by impermissible reasons.

1. The exclusion of moralism and paternalism

The first of two sets of excluded reasons that will be discussed in this section regards the exclusion of paternalistic and moralistic reasons as the key to autonomy. Personal autonomy, on this understanding, means freedom to conduct one's life without paternalistic or moralistic interference by the state. For example, it would be a violation of autonomy if

---

[4] This distinction is similar to the distinction between immunities theories and reason-blocking theories of rights (Letsas, 'Two Concepts of the Margin of Appreciation', [2006] 26 *Oxford Journal of Legal Studies* 705, 717; referring to a dispute between Richard Pildes and Jeremy Waldron: Pildes, 'Why Rights Are Not Trumps: Social Meanings, Expressive Harms, and Constitutionalism', [1998] 17 *Journal of Legal Studies* 725; Waldron, 'Pildes on Dworkin's Theory of Rights', [2000] 29 *Journal of Legal Studies* 301; Pildes, 'Dworkin's Two Conceptions of Rights', [2000] 29 *Journal of Legal Studies* 309). My choice of the term 'excluded reasons conception' is inspired by Mattias Kumm's discussion of excluded reasons in 'Political Liberalism and the Structure of Rights: On the Place and Limits of the Proportionality Requirement', in Pavlakos (ed.), *Law, Rights and Discourse: The Legal Philosophy of Robert Alexy* (Hart Publishing, 2007), 131, 142. I also find the term 'immunities conception' misleading because it suggests an absolute or near-absolute protection of the 'immunized' object which is neither reflected in the actual practice of constitutional courts nor in the conception which I propose in this book; therefore, I choose the weaker formulation of a 'protected interests conception', which indicates the non-absolute character of the respective interests.

[5] Letsas, *A Theory of Interpretation of the European Convention on Human Rights* (Oxford University Press, 2007), chs. 5, 6.

the government outlawed certain sexual practices on the grounds that they are, or are considered to be, immoral. Similarly, the prohibition of certain religions on the grounds that they are wrong or misguided or an insult to God would be a violation of autonomy. The underlying idea of this understanding of autonomy is the liberal claim that every person has the right to develop and act upon his or her own conception of the good life, rather than having to conform to the government's conception.[6] The excluded reasons conception imports this liberal political view into the concept of autonomy and thus claims that any imposition of views about the good life on the individual person is a violation of her autonomy, i.e. her right to decide for herself what the good life requires.

2. *From excluded reasons to the content of autonomy*

The ultimate purpose of this section is to explore the degree to which the exclusion of moralism and paternalism can explain the practice. To do that, I must flesh out the excluded reasons conception further and identify a list of actions and personal resources protected by autonomy. This task is, however, more difficult than it seems at first glance. The problem is that a governmental act does not have a label attached to it, indicating for which reasons it interferes with a person's liberty. Two possible tests suggest themselves: a subjective and an objective one. The *subjective test* refers to the *subjective motivation* of the legislators producing the legislation, as a matter of psychological historical fact. If the legislators voted for the legislation for moralistic or paternalistic reasons, then the legislation violates autonomy. There are many problems with this approach; in particular, it is not clear why, as a matter of substance, we should really be all that concerned with the subjective states of minds of legislators: there is an argument to be made that what legislators think when they cast a ballot is irrelevant and compatibility with rights should be seen as an objective matter. However, I shall leave this issue aside here because the subjective test has one obvious flaw: it requires us to identify the motivations of legislators, and that is often an impossible task. It is true that in some cases legislators or governments may actually tell courts that they enacted a piece of legislation for moralistic or paternalistic reasons; however, most cases are not as obvious and

---

[6] Cf. Rawls, *Collected Papers* (Harvard University Press, 1999), 365 ('...the capacity to decide upon, to revise, and rationally to pursue a conception of the good').

clear-cut. Therefore, irrespective of whether it would be desirable to have a subjective test, it will not work in practice.

The *objective test* leaves aside the legislators' motivation and seeks to determine *objectively* the moralistic or paternalistic *nature* of the legislation. One way to do so is to focus on the regulated activity and find some feature in it which makes it objectively the case that prohibiting or otherwise limiting it would be moralistic or paternalistic. For example, it seems that a prohibition of sodomy is a classic example of a moralistic piece of legislation, just as seat-belt laws are a classic example of paternalism.[7] But what is the test employed here?

It is helpful in this context to consider Joel Feinberg's discussion of paternalism. Feinberg compares the autonomy of persons with the sovereignty of nation states. He argues that just as it is unjustified for one nation state to interfere with the sovereignty of another nation state on the grounds that the latter is governing itself badly (imagine Germany somehow imposing an NHS reform on Britain on the grounds that Britain has proved itself incapable of doing so in a satisfactory way), it is equally unjustified for a government to interfere with the autonomy of an individual person simply on the grounds that that person makes bad choices for himself. In this sense, persons are sovereign.[8] In order to distinguish actions which fall within the sphere of personal autonomy from those outside it, Feinberg distinguishes between decisions which are *self-regarding*—'that is which primarily and directly affect only the interests of the decision-maker'—and those which are *other-regarding*—'that is which directly and in the first instance affect the interests or sensibilities of other persons'.[9] Feinberg thinks that the existence of a 'twilight area of cases that are difficult to classify' is no reason for concern but just a normal feature of many workable distinctions—'including that between night and day'.

Feinberg's approach is objective because it avoids the necessity of identifying subjective states of minds, and instead focuses on some objective feature of the regulated activity (its character as self- or other-regarding). His

---

[7] I do not mean to suggest that seat-belt regulations would necessarily be violations of autonomy under the excluded reasons approach. There are various ways to include subtle distinctions and allow some forms of paternalism while rejecting others (see for example Dworkin, *Sovereign Virtue* [Harvard University Press, 2000], 268–9; Kleinig, *Paternalism* [Manchester University Press, 1983], 67–70). Those distinctions are not the topic of this section; the example merely serves to demonstrate a general problem with the excluded reasons conception.

[8] Feinberg, *Harm to Self* (Oxford University Press, 1986), 47–51.

[9] Ibid., 56–7.

approach fails, however, because it implies a false simplicity: individual behaviour is not inherently self-regarding or other-regarding. Rather, it affects the agent and his environment in multiple ways, and some of these ways may give rise to legitimate public interests to interfere with the activity, while others do not. Take again the case of sodomy. It may seem that it is a clear example of an activity which is 'self-regarding', at least if carried out with consent and in the privacy of one's home, and regulation of which would therefore be moralistic. However, imagine the government prohibits or regulates sodomy not on the grounds of its supposed immorality, but rather in an effort to reduce the spreading of HIV. In this light, sodomy suddenly seems like an 'other-regarding' activity. The fact that a government may regard homosexual activity as immoral may or may not be a sufficient reason to justify its prohibition, and on quite a different plane, the fact that it may contribute to the spreading of HIV may or may not justify its restriction. Or consider the seat-belt example: while it seems plausible to assume that seat-belt laws are paternalistic because they protect some drivers against their will, possibly their point is not paternalism but reducing the amount of resources to be spent on treating injured drivers, or—as was once argued by the German Federal Constitutional Court[10]— decreasing the likelihood of injuries, thereby making it more probable that in an accident, an uninjured person could help and save an injured one. The general point is that whether or not an activity is protected by autonomy under the excluded reasons conception cannot be decided in isolation from the possible reasons in favour of its restriction. There is no way to determine the nature of an activity as self- or other-regarding, or in fact any other feature inherent to the activity, which would show that its prohibition would be moralistic or paternalistic.

Since focussing on the nature of the activity does not work, we have to concentrate on the reasons for its restriction instead. Here is a sound way of conducting an objective test to exclude moralism and paternalism: in a *first* step, one regards *all* behaviour as prima facie protected because we cannot exclude in advance the possibility that a limitation will be based on moralistic or paternalistic reasons. In a *second* step, all the possible justifications for the limitation are collected and examined: the impermissible ones (paternalistic and moralistic reasons) are excluded, and all the remaining ones are examined as to whether they justify the interference. Thus, in the case of a prohibition of sodomy, one would have to

---

[10] BVerfG, (1987) *Neue Juristische Wochenschrift* 180.

collect possible reasons for the restriction of this behaviour (its supposed immorality, the risk of HIV transmission, etc.), then discount the excluded ones (immorality) and finally ask whether the remaining ones (HIV) justify a prohibition. If the remaining ones indeed justify the prohibition, then the law does not violate autonomy because it can be justified without recourse to paternalistic and moralistic motives. If they do not, then the law violates autonomy because it cannot be justified except by recourse to considerations which ought to be excluded.

This leads to a further practical difficulty. The excluded reasons theorist wants to identify paternalistic and moralistic laws. To do so, it is not sufficient to exclude paternalistic and moralistic reasons; rather, he must also judge whether the *remaining* reasons are sufficiently strong to justify the interference. Two routes to achieve this suggest themselves. According to the first, government always prevails if it can point to *any* non-paternalistic and non-moralistic reason in favour of the restriction. For example, in the sodomy case, the government wins if it points to the risk of spreading HIV. The problem with this approach is that its test is *too loose* to provide any meaningful protection of autonomy because government will almost always be able to come up with *some* reason, however weak, which argues in favour of the restriction. On the second route, government must present reasons *of sufficient strength* to substantively justify the prohibition. Thus, it is not enough to simply point to any reason in favour of the restriction, but rather, the reasons have to be so strong that they provide a substantive justification of the interference. So in the example, one would have to examine whether fighting the spreading of HIV provides a substantive justification for the prohibition of sodomy.

The problem with this route is that it is no longer in line with the general strategy of the excluded reasons conception of autonomy: this conception wants to exclude paternalistic and moralistic reasons *and stop there*. It does *not* want to identify and assess the strength of all the *other* possible reasons arguing in favour or against the restriction because this would mean, among other things, assessing whether the legislature has given proper weight to the individual interests at stake; and that is beyond what the excluded reasons theorist with his focus on the exclusion of moralism and paternalism wants to engage in. Another way of making the same point is this: the excluded reasons theorist wants to say that autonomy is about the exclusion of moralism and paternalism. Under the approach discussed here, this is no longer true, however: a violation of autonomy can occur because of moralism, paternalism, *or* the failure to take the autonomy interests of the affected person sufficiently into account. Note that this conclusion is not just an unfortunate coincidence which can be avoided by refining the theory. Rather, it is a necessary feature of *any* coherent objective approach: the objective approach, qua being objective, must assess whether there is a substantive—objective!—justification for a limitation of individual liberty, and that implies that it must assess *all* the possible reasons for and against it.

Since the subjective approach is impossible to carry out from a practical point of view and the objective approach, properly understood, must extend the excluded reasons approach beyond excluded reasons, it seems that we are stuck. What is true is that, as has been demonstrated, there is no clear-cut way to identify moralistic or paternalistic legislation. In spite of this, however, we often feel confident to say that a specific piece of legislation is moralistic or paternalistic: take the case of anti-sodomy laws or seatbelt regulations. How do we arrive at such conclusions? I think that the solution lies in common sense: we have faith in our intuition that barring extraordinary circumstances, moralistic or paternalistic reasons must feature in the justification of such laws.

A look at Ronald Dworkin's early theory of rights helps develop this intuition into a workable test. In *Taking Rights Seriously*, Dworkin defended a conception of rights which is based on the distinction between personal and external preferences. Personal preferences state a preference about the assignment of one set of goods or opportunities to the agent himself, whereas external preferences are about the assignment of one set of goods or opportunities to others.[11] For Dworkin, utilitarianism properly understood prohibited counting the external preferences of voters or legislators. How was this to be achieved? Since Dworkin saw that it was not possible to look into every single legislator's or voter's head to identify the preferences he had based his vote on, rights come in as 'a response to the philosophical defects of a ultilitarianism that counts external preferences and the practical impossibility of a utilitarianism that does not':[12] according to Dworkin, rights exist in those areas where there is an *antecedent likelihood* that the majority would act upon external preferences.[13] I am not interested here in the viability of Dworkin's early theory of rights as such, parts of which he has modified since *Taking Rights Seriously*.[14] It is, however, illuminating

[11] Dworkin, *Taking Rights Seriously* (Duckworth, 1977), 275.

[12] Ibid., 277.   [13] Ibid.

[14] See in particular Dworkin, *Is Democracy Possible Here? Principles for a New Political Debate* (Princeton University Press, 2006), ch 2. For a comprehensive analysis of Dworkin's theory of rights, including

to examine how his theory deals with the difficulty of identifying impermissible justifications for interferences with liberty: rather than claiming that one could somehow establish the existence of these improper justifications (external preferences in Dworkin's case; paternalistic or moralistic justifications here) as a matter of historical fact—for example by looking into the legislators' heads—Dworkin works around this problem by acknowledging rights in areas where experience teaches that such justifications will often prevail.

So under this approach the test for whether a law is moralistic or paternalistic would be whether the law interferes with individual freedom in an area where experience teaches that legislation will often rely on moralistic or paternalistic justifications. This is in principle a coherent understanding of both autonomy and rights. It is, however, important to see that it is based on a *presumption*: while it may be true that laws interfering with sexual autonomy, political speech, or religious beliefs will often be based on moralistic or paternalistic grounds, this is not necessarily so in each and every case. To filter out those cases where the interference is not based on such beliefs, the test must be supplemented with a second stage where it is examined whether there is a non-moralistic and non-paternalistic justification for the law in question which is so strong that it overcomes the initial presumption. Take the popular example of falsely shouting 'fire' in a crowded theatre. There is a presumption that a law regulating the content of speech violates autonomy because experience teaches that the justification of such regulation will often rely on impermissible grounds. However, this presumption can be rebutted if, as in this case, there is a clear and strong case to be made for the regulation which does not rely on such impermissible arguments.

So this version of the excluded reasons approach operates on the basis of two presumptions: *first*, the presumption that in certain areas, experience teaches that an interference with liberty will be based on moralistic or paternalistic grounds, and will therefore be impermissible, and *second*, the presumption that if there are non-moralistic and non-paternalistic reasons *of great strength* in favour of the restriction, the initial presumption is rebutted. The advantage of this test over the objective test discussed above is that it is better tailored to the excluded reasons theorist's main concern, namely the exclusion of impermissible reasons.

its development in Dworkin's writings, cf. Yowell, 'A Critical Examination of Dworkin's Theory of Rights', (2007) 52 *American Journal of Jurisprudence* 93.

While it still needs to consider all the reasons for and against a particular piece of legislation at the second stage, it will only get to that second stage if the legislation falls within an area where experience teaches that moralism and paternalism often prevail; and as will be shown below, those areas can be relatively narrowly circumscribed. I will therefore proceed by accepting that for the excluded reasons approach, autonomy protects activities and personal resources which are subject to an antecedent likelihood of moralistic or paternalistic interference.

3. The exclusion of paternalism and moralism, and the practice

To what extent can the excluded reasons conception explain the prima facie rights acknowledged by the practice of constitutional rights law? It clearly has the ability to explain some of the more traditional rights. The reason why the rights to *freedom of religion* and *freedom of conscience* are acknowledged might be the antecedent likelihood that governments will impose the majority's religious and moral beliefs on the minority unless they are prevented from doing this.[15] The right to *freedom of expression* can at least partly be linked to the prohibition of paternalism and moralism: we must not outlaw certain speech on the ground that the ideas proposed are immoral or harmful to the speaker or those freely subscribing to them. A similar idea applies to the related right to *freedom of association*. Furthermore, some aspects of the *right to privacy* can be explained in terms of the excluded reasons conception, in particular the already mentioned *right to sexual autonomy*: homosexual behaviour and other sexual practices have often been outlawed on the perceived grounds of their immorality, and the right to privacy protects against governmental reliance on this motive. A part of the debate concerning the *right to commit suicide* centres on the individual person's right to decide for himself about the value of his remaining life and to prevent government from passing judgment in this matter. The *right to abortion* has been defended as being about governmental neutrality with regard to the question of the moral status of the fetus, arguing that outlawing abortion would amount to moralistic legislation.[16]

---

[15] Letsas, 'Two Concepts of the Margin of Appreciation', (2006) 26 *Oxford Journal of Legal Studies* 705, 719.

[16] This point is reflected in the much-derided passage of the US Supreme Court in *Casey*: 'At the heart of liberty is the right to define one's own concept of existence, of meaning, of the universe, and of the mystery of human life. Beliefs about these matters could not define the attributes of personhood were they formed under compulsion of the State.' *Planned Parenthood of Southeastern Pennsylvania v. Casey* (1992) 505 U.S. 833, 851.

The examples show that the excluded reasons conception has the capacity to provide justifications for some important and widely acknowledged constitutional rights. There is, however, a number of constitutional rights which are not easily explained by the excluded reasons conception as developed thus far. Notably missing are rights of equal importance to the ones mentioned above, namely the *rights to life, physical integrity, liberty* and *freedom from torture*, which are standard ingredients of constitutions. It is important to be clear about why exactly they are missing. The reason is not that life and physical integrity are of minor importance for individuals—they clearly aren't. However, the excluded reasons conception as developed so far protects individuals only in areas with an antecedent likelihood of moralistic or paternalistic interference. This could in principle justify a protection of physical integrity as well: think of societies where there exists a practice requiring male, or worse, female circumcision. In such a community it would make sense to acknowledge a right to physical integrity to prevent the majority from imposing its views of the good life as requiring this particular form of mutilation on those who disagree. The example shows that for the excluded reasons conception, the question of which rights are acknowledged will depend on the kinds of disagreement which exist in the respective community about what constitutes the good life. The reason that in today's Western communities we would not need a right to life or physical integrity under the excluded reasons conception as developed so far is simply that, fortunately, there is little antecedent likelihood (to use Dworkin's terminology) that the majority would kill or injure disagreeing members of the community for moralistic or paternalistic reasons.[17]

4. Equal worth of persons: the exclusion of unequal-worth-based reasons

The excluded reasons conception ultimately rests on an ideal of *respect for persons*. It would, for this conception, not respect a person if a conception of the good were imposed on him—hence the exclusion of paternalistic

---

[17] Hart ('Between Utility and Rights', in Hart, *Essays in Jurisprudence and Philosophy* [Clarendon Press, 1983], 198, 213) criticized Dworkin's early theory of rights by pointing to the fact that for Dworkin, in a society without relevant prejudices (which lead to policies which rights could trump), rights would 'wither away'; cf. also Yowell, 'A Critical Examination of Dworkin's Theory of Rights', (2007) 52 *American Journal of Jurisprudence* 93, 114. This shows an interesting feature of excluded reasons conceptions in general, namely that they only kick in in a society where the impermissible reasons are prevalent or popular; in societies without such tendencies, excluded reasons models are pointless because the reasons they want to exclude play no role anyway.

and moralistic reasons. If this is true, then there may be other excluded reasons flowing from the idea of respect. One group of excluded reasons may be that government must not base its policies on the idea that some persons are of *less importance* than others: that would deny their equal value and therefore fail to respect them properly. Imagine the government responds to an enemy country's declaration of war by requiring only members of a certain race or religion to defend the country, while the members of the other race or religion can stay at home, and it justifies this by pointing to its view that the people staying at home are worth more than those having to go to war. Such a policy does not rest on moralistic or paternalistic reasons; however, it rests on similarly illegitimate grounds: the government's decision fails to show proper respect towards the affected persons.[18]

How do we get from the exclusion of these unequal-worth-based reasons to the content of autonomy? Just as in the case of moralistic and paternalistic reasons, it will be impossible to look into the legislators' heads to identify the psychological motives on which they based their decisions. Rather, whether or not a policy relies on unequal-worth-based reasons must be determined objectively. Again, the only coherent way to do so seems to be to identify areas where there exists an antecedent likelihood of government treating one group less favourably than another, based on the idea of unequal worth. The areas of life, physical integrity and liberty may suggest themselves because arguably killing, torturing, injuring, and locking up people have often been a means of denying persons their equal worth.

5. The exclusion of unequal-worth-based reasons, and the practice

How far does the amended version of the excluded reasons conception carry us? We must be careful here: there is a risk that we redefine anything which unjustifiably affects a person's interests adversely into a

---

[18] Another way of making the same point is to regard both the exclusion of moralistic and paternalistic reasons and unequal-worth-based reasons as flowing from a requirement of equal concern and respect; see Letsas, 'Two Concepts of the Margin of Appreciation', (2006) 26 *Oxford Journal of Legal Studies* 705, 719. The problem with that approach is that it is not evident why the prohibition of moralism and paternalism should follow from a commitment to equality rather than autonomy (see Hart, 'Between Utility and Rights', in Hart, *Essays in Jurisprudence and Philosophy* [Clarendon Press, 1983], 198, 217–21; Dworkin, 'Rights as Trumps', in Waldron [ed.], *Theories of Rights* [Oxford University Press, 1984], 153, 161; see also Raz, *The Morality of Freedom* [Clarendon Press, 1986], ch. 9 [on equality]). I find it more plausible to classify the exclusion of moralism and paternalism as autonomy-protecting and the exclusion of unequal-worth-based reasons as equality-protecting. However, this classification does not affect the substance of the argument.

manifestation of the risk of that person being treated as worth less, and therefore acknowledge rights in every area where there exists a risk of making wrong decisions adversely affecting someone. Taken to extremes, we can reinterpret a law which for less than convincing reasons regulates the size or thickness of paper to be sold in stationers as a manifestation of the risk that their owners will be treated as being worth less than other persons. Many unsatisfactory laws involve a failure to take the *legitimate autonomy interests* of the affected persons adequately into account. But this is not something against which the excluded reasons conception wants to protect individuals, because if it did, it would collapse into its rival, the protected interests conception. To be sure, there may be appeal in the argument that to respect the equal worth of each citizen, the state must adequately respect his autonomy interests. All I am claiming is that we can neglect this particular interpretation of the equal importance principle here because that interpretation would lead to the conception of autonomy which I will discuss under the heading of the protected interests conception in the next section. Therefore, under the excluded reasons conception, the simple failure to adequately respect the autonomy interests of an individual does not in itself constitute a denial of his equal worth; rather, there must be a further criterion or filter, relating, for example, to the gravity of the failure or to whether the policy can be regarded as carried out in good faith. Which criterion should be adopted by the excluded reasons theorist is not my concern here because I do not believe that *any* plausible filter could lead to the catalogue of rights which the practice acknowledges.

In *Taking Rights Seriously*, Dworkin explicitly rejects a *right to property* on the ground that he 'cannot think of any argument that a political decision to limit such a right . . . is antecedently likely to give effect to external preferences'[19]. Dworkin is right: it is hard to see property owners as a group which is likely to suffer from being treated as worth less than persons not owning property. However, the German Basic Law, the ECHR, the EU Charter, and the South African Constitution protect a right to property,[20] and this indicates that they follow a conception of autonomy which is different from the excluded reasons approach.

The *right to freedom of profession* is another instance of a right which the excluded reasons conception cannot explain. While it is not as widely recognized as some more traditional rights, it is included in the German

---

[19] Dworkin, *Taking Rights Seriously* (Duckworth, 1977), 278.

[20] As mentioned above, it is notably absent in the Canadian Charter; this is an indicator of the controversial nature of the right to property.

Basic Law, the South African Constitution, and the EU Charter; and it seems unlikely that governments will make laws interfering with profession for paternalistic, moralistic, or unequal-worth-based reasons.

The *right to private and family life* goes beyond protecting activities likely to be moralistically regulated or prohibited; for example, it covers the right of access to information regarding the identity of one's natural parents,[21] and it seems absurd to speculate that governments or majorities will treat persons who do not know the identities of their parents as worth less than other persons, and will therefore deny them knowledge of their descent. The right to privacy also offers protection from media intrusion into one's private life;[22] and again, it is implausible and at best mere speculation to assume that persons who are the object of media interest are likely to be treated as worth less than other people.

The increasingly recognized *right to data protection* cannot be explained under the excluded reasons conception either because when governments collect data they often do so indiscriminately and do not restrict themselves to unpopular groups or persons. There are, however, areas where the data collected can arguably be used to identify and target unpopular groups: for example, in *Z v. Finland*,[23] the applicant complained that personal data relating to her HIV infection had not been adequately protected by the state, resulting in it becoming available to the public. One could certainly construct an argument to the effect that releasing data about a person's HIV infection was the manifestation of the likelihood that HIV carriers will be treated as worth less by the state than HIV negative persons, and that this was the reason for protecting this particular data. This is however not the line of argument which the ECtHR pursued. The Court did not at all refer to the role of the state in all this but focussed mainly on the interests of the claimant: it pointed to the effect of the disclosure of the data on her private and family life and her social and employment situation, and raised the concern that the risk of such data being published might discourage persons from seeking diagnosis or treatment and thus also undermine preventive efforts by the community.[24] The focus of this line of reasoning on the *interests* of the *claimant* in a case which could easily be constructed as being about *importance-based reasons* employed by the *government* is yet another

---

[21] Cf. *Odievre v. France* (2004) 38 EHRR 43, para. 29; *Gaskin v. United Kingdom* (1990) 12 EHRR 36, para. 37.

[22] *von Hannover v. Germany* (2005) 40 EHRR 1, para. 53.

[23] *Z v. Finland* (1998) 25 EHRR 371.

[24] Ibid., paras. 95, 96.

indicator of the deficiency of the excluded reasons approach in explaining the practice.

6. Conclusion

An assessment of the strength of the excluded reasons conception in explaining the practice provides us with a mixed picture. On the one hand, it can accommodate aspects of the more traditional negative rights such as the right to freedom of speech and assembly, freedom of religion, certain aspects of the right to privacy; and if amended it can additionally accommodate aspects of the rights to life, physical integrity, and liberty. This indicates that there is some appeal in the excluded reasons conception, and that it would be a mistake to reject it altogether. On the other hand, it has problems with the right to property and other, more recently acknowledged rights, such as aspects of the right to privacy, the right to data protection, and freedom of profession.

The main problem with the excluded reasons conception lies in what I described as its main feature: its relational character. For the excluded reasons conception, a particular action or resource will only form part of the content of personal autonomy if it is likely that the state will fail to show proper respect for the agent by interfering with the action or resource in question; and it turns out that such a likelihood does not seem to exist in some of the areas which are protected by constitutional rights today. In the following section, I will develop a model of personal autonomy which sets relational features aside and thus avoids the central weakness of the excluded reasons conception.

III. THE PROTECTED INTERESTS
CONCEPTION OF AUTONOMY

1. General

While the excluded reasons conception is concerned with the reasons on which the state may rely in treating its citizens, the protected interests conception takes a different, arguably more straightforward approach: it focuses directly on the actions and personal resources which are important for the purpose of leading an autonomous life. For example, the protected interests conception recognizes the importance for autonomous persons of being able to choose one's intimate partners, utter one's political views, and control what happens to one's body, and takes the importance of these interests as the reason for protecting them. Or put negatively: we think that, all things being equal, a person who does *not* have control over what happens to her body, or whom she chooses as an intimate partner, or which profession to take up, is less autonomous than she should be: something is lost if these particular instances of control are not available to her. So under this understanding, to be autonomous, a person must have some control over a number of (partly) independent domains of her life. This is reflected in the ways in which most of us think about giving our own lives meaning and direction: we are always working on several fronts and projects simultaneously. A typical person spends much of her time and energy trying to create or maintain a stable relationship with a partner of her choice, raising children, having close relationships with other family members, making progress in her professional life, having a decent social life with close friends, rewarding hobbies and activities, and so on. At the same time, she is making efforts to achieve some long-term security, maybe acquire property, improve or maintain her health and looks, work on her character, her relationship with her God, etc. And each of these projects will require ongoing efforts in a number of sub-projects. In addition, when circumstances change or the person's ideal changes of how to live *a* life or *her* particular life well, her projects need to be adapted.[25] She will at least partly judge the success of her life by her success in the projects she has come to pursue. It follows that because of the impact of the success in her individual projects on the success of her life as a whole, she has specific autonomy interests with regard to each of these projects.

The crucial question in this context is on which scale to determine the importance of different autonomy interests. We can imagine the widest possible understanding of autonomy and regard all actions and personal resources as protected. Then, autonomy would indiscriminately protect, for example, feeding the birds, giving a political speech, choosing a career, choosing an intimate partner, and watching TV. Intuitively, it seems that feeding the birds and choosing one's intimate partner are of different weight or importance for the autonomy of persons. How can the protected interests conception account for this? I suggest as the point of reference for assessing the weights of autonomy interests the importance of the act or resource in question *from the point of view of the self-conception of the agent*. For example, being able to choose an intimate partner is more important than being able to feed the birds, to the extent

---

[25] Cf. Dworkin, *Is Democracy Possible Here? Principles for a New Political Debate* (Princeton University Press, 2006), 18 with a similar point.

that choosing one's partner is a more important manifestation of the self-conception of the agent than feeding the birds. A person's self-conception is shaped by the answers to the two questions *'Who am I, and who would I like to be?'*[26]

> How one understands oneself depends not only on how one describes oneself but also on the ideals toward which one strives. One's identity is determined simultaneously by how one sees oneself and how one would like to see oneself, by what one finds oneself to be and the ideals with reference to which one fashions oneself and one's life. This existential self-understanding is evaluative in its core and, like all evaluations, is Janus faced. Two components are interwoven in it: the descriptive component of the ontogenesis of the ego and the normative component of the ego-ideal.[27]

There are several substantively similar concepts used in the literature and the jurisprudence of courts, and it may be useful to contrast them with the self-conception approach. Both the German Federal Constitutional Court and the ECtHR regularly rely on the notion of *developing one's personality*.[28] While in substance this may amount to much the same as the self-conception approach, it is unfortunate in that, first, it is too narrow: autonomy is not only about one's personality but also gives an agent control over, for example, his body: autonomy is about *persons* and not limited to the persons' *personalities*. It is also too narrow in that it seems to dictate the purpose for which autonomy ought to be used, namely to develop one's personality. At the same time, the end goal of all this remains mysterious: it is not clear to what end a person ought to develop his personality.

Another concept frequently employed by courts is that of *personal identity*. Identity comes close to self-conception, but it is narrower in that, again, just like self-development, it seems to be mainly concerned with a person's personality, which is too restrictive. Furthermore, it is also narrower in that at least in everyday usage it seems to be about *very important* elements of a person's self-conception, such as gender, sexual orientation, or religion, and as will become clear, this limits the usefulness of the concept too much in the context of constitutional rights.

---

[26] Habermas, *Justification and Application* (MIT Press, 1994), 4 (emphasis added). In the German original, Habermas speaks of a person's '*Selbstverständnis*' which is translated as 'self-understanding' in the English version; however, I prefer to speak of a person's 'self-conception' because 'self-understanding' underemphasizes the dimension of the ego-ideal.

[27] Ibid., 4–5.

[28] Cf. the quotations below.

In philosophy, the notion of *living one's conception of the good life* is a popular way to express largely the same idea as the self-conception approach.[29] One of my reasons for hesitating to subscribe to it is the controversial philosophical baggage that comes with it and that is not necessary for my argument here, in particular the twin concept of the 'right' which complements the 'good'. James Griffin uses a related term, namely *to live one's conception of a worthwhile life*.[30] While this avoids the philosophical baggage, it is otherwise subject to the same concerns: first, the expression contains confrontational and atomistic connotations ('my' versus 'your' conception of 'the' good/'a' worthwhile life), which is unfortunate because what is good or worthwhile for a person may depend on the individual person's life story rather than a given way (or set of ways) for everyone to live his or her life best. The self-conception approach, by way of contrast, captures better what's important about autonomy. One's self-conception involves an element of *where one is coming from and where one wants to go*, as well as of one's view of *oneself within one's social environment*; thus, the self-conception view places the agent in a historical and social continuum, which captures better, I think, the ways in which we reflect about our own lives. Second, the notion of living one's conception of the good life seems to suggest either the necessity of having a worked-out conception to be able to claim the right, or the assumption that every person has in fact one such, fully developed, conception; neither of which should be required: developing a conception of the good by means of trial and error, or struggling to find a coherent theme to one's different intuitions about the good life, are just as important and must be protected just as much as living one's fully developed conception. Finally, the notion of living one's conception of the good life does not give us any indications about the relative weights of autonomy interests: for example, it does not tell us the standard by which we are to judge whether feeding the birds is less important for autonomy than choosing a partner. Nor does it tell us anything about the *limits* of a person's right to live his conception of the good. The self-conception approach, by focussing on autonomy *interests* (the weights of which are assessed on a scale according to their importance for the agent's self-conception), acknowledges the possibility of conflicts between the agent's autonomy interests and the interests of the public or other persons, and thus does not create the false impression

---

[29] Rawls, *Collected Papers* (Harvard University Press, 1999), 365.

[30] Griffin, *On Human Rights* (Oxford University Press, 2008), 47.

that a special value, going beyond the weight of the respective autonomy interests, attaches to the ideal of 'living one's conception of the good'.

While the concepts discussed above are very similar to the self-conception approach and are sometimes used interchangeably, the self-conception approach must be distinguished from three related but different ideas. First, it is different from *self-realization* and *self-fulfilment*. As Joseph Raz has pointed out, autonomy and self-realization are not identical.[31] A person may autonomously decide to give up his career and dedicate his life to some good cause, purely out of a sense of moral obligation and not because he expects to achieve self-realization in the pursuit of that cause. While such a decision is not one which furthers self-realization, it is clearly very central from the point of view of autonomy—it is a manifestation of the self-conception of a person with certain moral views and the willingness to act upon them even at the cost of self-realization.

Second, the self-conception approach is different from one focussing exclusively on what people *want* for themselves, and it is equally different from one focussing on a person's *preferences*, narrowly understood. A person may really want or have a preference for steaks all the time, but it does not follow that being a steak-eater is an important element of his self-conception as a person (although it could possibly be). Another person may want to watch TV all day, but it does not follow that she regards watching TV as important for her self-conception, either. An activity is important for the self-conception of an agent only if it affects or reflects something which the agent considers to be giving meaning and value to his or her life, and not everything a person happens to want or has a preference for necessarily qualifies for that.

Third, the self-conception approach does not judge the value of the self-conceptions people hold; in that sense it can be described as *neutral* and can be contrasted with some (not all) versions of *perfectionist* understandings of autonomy.[32] It does not regard some exercises of autonomy as more important than others on the ground that they are, or are

---

[31] Raz, *The Morality of Freedom* (Clarendon Press, 1986), 375–6.

[32] While I do subscribe to a neutral understanding of autonomy here, I do not (yet) take sides in the debate between perfectionism and antiperfectionism. Perfectionists believe that state action (and inaction) should be judged by its contribution to individual well-being. A perfectionist will endorse the protected interests conception as developed here if he believes that by not judging people's self-conceptions, we contribute most to their well-being; a claim that certainly has some plausibility. I shall, however, reject perfectionism's main premise, namely its focus on well-being rather than autonomy, in Chapter 7.

considered to be by people other than the agent, more valuable. For example, if religion X has an important role in the self-conception of a person, then the self-conception approach respects this and does not accord this feature little weight on the ground that arguably, religion X should not have that importance, but rather religion Y should, or no religion should play any role at all. By taking the self-conceptions of individual persons as its reference point, the protected interests conception adopts an 'internal' perspective about what adds value to one's life, as opposed to an 'external' perspective of what a person's self-conception *ought* to consist of or how important this or that feature of it *ought* to be; something I regard as indispensable to an attractive account of freedom. Therefore, under this conception, an autonomy 'interest' is not necessarily connected to a person's 'well-being'.[33] Rather, what I have in mind when speaking of autonomy interests could also be called an 'instance' of a person's autonomy; something that falls into the sphere which he is prima facie entitled to control.

One last general remark about the protected interests conception: as argued above, when we ask what importance some action or resource has, we have to look at the agent's self-conception. It follows that the same action or resource can be of different value for different persons. Therefore it is misguided to assume that an interest theory of human rights must necessarily be based on the assumption that there is a list of interests universally shared by all individuals.[34] There may be one list of interests common to one species of animals: maybe dogs have the same interests universally. But for humans, if we take the idea of autonomy seriously, our autonomy interests will at least partly depend on our self-conceptions. This will affect both the question of what qualifies as a relevant autonomy interest (feeding the birds?; sexual autonomy?) and the weight of a specific autonomy interest. If it is true that an Englishman attaches special value to the privacy of his home, then it makes sense to regard an invasion into the home of an Englishman as worse from the point of view of the agent's self-conception and autonomy than one into the home of, say, a Spaniard. Therefore, on the basis of the protected interests theory, a balancing exercise between privacy and (for example) public security may lead to different results, depending on whether we are in England or Spain.

---

[33] In contrast to Raz's understanding; see *The Morality of Freedom* (Clarendon Press, 1986), ch. 12, esp. 295.

[34] Letsas, 'Two Concepts of the Margin of Appreciation', (2006) 26 *Oxford Journal of Legal Studies* 705, 717.

2. *The protected interests conception and the practice*

When examining the extent to which the protected interests conception of autonomy explains the practice of constitutional rights law, the central question must be whether the actions and resources protected by the practice reflect what most people consider as important for their autonomy. So if we discover that the practice protects all or most of what people regard as important for their autonomy, we can confidently conclude that the protected interests conception underlies the practice. If, however, it turned out that much of what is protected by the practice carries no such importance, while other things that are important are not protected, this would point to a deficit in the protected interests conception as a model explaining the practice.

The protected interests conception sits well with the tendency to recognize more rights, and to interpret existing rights more broadly. Take the *right to privacy*, whose scope has been growing continuously over the last decades. It arguably extends to such diverse things as abortion, sexual autonomy, and suicide; and it is striking that these actions are all very important from the perspective of the self-conceptions of the right-holders. Decisions whether or not to become a parent, in what sort of sexual (in particular, but not limited to, hetero- or homosexual) relationship to engage, or whether or not to end one's life, are crucial manifestations of a person's understanding of how to exercise his autonomy in order to live his life well. The growing recognition of these actions as constitutionally relevant is an indicator that the protected interests conception underlies much contemporary thinking in constitutional rights law. For example, Justice Sachs of the South African Constitutional Court has argued that the right to privacy has to be regarded:

> ...not simply as a negative right to occupy a private space free from government intrusion, but as a right to get on with your life, express your personality and make fundamental decisions about your intimate relationships without penalisation... [P]rivacy [must] be regarded as suggesting at least some responsibility on the State to promote conditions in which personal self-realisation can take place.[35]

The more traditional rights, such as the rights to physical integrity, freedom of expression, or freedom of religion also sit well with the

---

[35] *National Coalition of Gay and Lesbian Equality v. Minister of Justice*, 1999 (1) SA 6 (para. 116) (Sachs J).

protected interests conception. Part of the reason why the *right to physical integrity* is protected is that physical integrity is a precondition of an autonomous life. In addition to that, there is, however, an indisputable connection between physical integrity and one's self-conception. It may not seem as intuitively plausible as, for example, in the case of the right to sexual autonomy, where the claim 'This is how *I* choose to live my life!' carries great intuitive appeal. However, just imagine what kind of person one would have to be, and what self-conception one would have to hold, to be indifferent to what happens to one's body. The fact that almost all people are not indifferent in this way shows that we regard our physical integrity as an important element of our lives; and the fact that it may not spring to mind as the first thing to think of when fleshing out our priorities is due to two related facts: first, the fortunate fact that for most people in the Western world, control over their physical integrity is not under constant threat from government or others, and second, the uncontroversial nature of the prioritization of control over physical integrity: since basically everyone gives high preference to it, it is not a feature which we can rely on to demonstrate our individuality. Nevertheless it is clearly an instance of a highly prioritized good.

The latter argument shows an important link between the excluded reasons conception and the protected interests conception. I said above that while the excluded reasons conception fails to satisfactorily explain the practice, it can, however, explain many rights we regard as central, and I argued that this indicates that there is some truth in the theory. Here is the connection. Under the excluded reasons conception, an action will be protected if there exists the likelihood of the government restricting it for impermissible, in particular moralistic or paternalistic, reasons. For such a likelihood to exist, there must be substantial disagreement in the respective society about how to behave with regard to the activity in question, and such disagreement will only surface if one group regards the freedom as very important, whereas the government or majority regard it as very important for moralistic reasons that this freedom *not* exist. For example, the reason why societies have or had bitter disagreements about homosexual activity but not about whether one may scratch one's ear in public is that many people have strong feelings about the question of acceptable behaviour in sexual matters but not about the question of self-scratching in public. As an empirical matter, it seems plausible to assume that societies tend to have their most bitter disagreements with regard to individual behaviours which are of major importance, at least for the minority. This explains why the activities protected under the excluded reasons approach are usually of major importance for many people: if they weren't, there would presumably not be enough disagreement to acknowledge the likelihood of moralistic interference. So the excluded reasons conception captures *some* activities and personal resources which are of central importance for the self-conception of individuals, but it does not capture *all* such activities and resources because it has the additional criterion that there must exist the likelihood of moralistic or paternalistic interference. The protected interests conception leaves aside that additional criterion and focuses directly on the importance of the respective actions and personal resources for individuals.

The justification of the *right to freedom of expression* can be seen in its importance for individual speakers, for the general interest, or for democracy. Raz holds the view that the right acquires its special weight through its contribution to the general interest: he has famously argued that if he had to choose between living in a society which enjoys freedom of expression, but not enjoying the right himself, or enjoying the right in a society which does not have it, he would choose the first option.[36] Two points can be made in response to this. First, I harbour doubts as to whether Raz assesses the weight of the individual interests correctly in his account of freedom of expression. Raz compares the weight of a person's individual interest in freedom of expression with his interest in the fortune of his marriage or the state of repair of his house, and judges that the latter interests carry more weight for most people than the former.[37] Therefore, if given the choice, most people's personal interests would be better served by an intact marriage, a water-tight roof, and the absence of the right to speak their minds, than in the opposite situation. But that conclusion seems overstated to me. While Raz's account plausibly reflects some people's self-conceptions, for others, not having the right to speak their minds would not simply affect some isolated aspect of their well-being, but carry much bigger implications, namely a denial of their self-conception as *participators* in conversations and discussions taking place within their families, workplaces, social environment, and other communities, including, of course, political communities. And that may arguably seem worse than a failed marriage or a hole in the roof.

---

[36] Raz, *Ethics in the Public Domain* (new edition, Clarendon Press, 1995), 54.

[37] Ibid.

Be that as it may; my second point is that I have no objection to Raz's argument that rights, including constitutional rights, can gain additional weight if they serve the general interest. So in the case of the right to freedom of expression, it is arguable that the right is based on an autonomy interest of people for whom it is important to be free to speak their minds and interact with others through the exchange of ideas, and that the right also serves the general interest, which makes it even more important.

Furthermore, the right to freedom of expression, at least with regard to political speech, is also required by the value of democracy, quite independently of its contribution to personal autonomy or the general interest: collective self-government requires conditions where different view-points about the merits of policies can be exchanged freely. This democracy-related argument provides a further, independent justification of the right.[38] So my point is not that personal autonomy provides the *only* justification of the right to freedom of expression, but that it forms part of what gives the right its constitutional importance. This reliance on arguments relating to personal autonomy interests, the general interest, and democracy is also reflected in the jurisprudence of constitutional courts. The ECtHR, for example, holds that freedom of expression 'constitutes one of the essential foundations of a democratic society and one of the basic conditions for its progress and for each individual's self-fulfilment.'[39]

A parallel idea applies to the *right to freedom of demonstration*. Its connection to autonomy interests and the development of one's personality has been acknowledged by the German Federal Constitutional Court in the following passage:

> By announcing his opinion in physical presence, in public, and without the intermediation of the media, he also directly develops his personality. In their ideal form, demonstrations bring convictions to the fore collectively, with the participants, on the one hand, experiencing recognition and strengthening of their convictions, and on the other hand in the immediate sense of the word taking a position in relation to the outside world and bearing testimony to their view-point.[40]

The point of the *right to freedom of religion* is often seen in its peace-promoting effect. Since there is no agreement about the true religion in

---

[38] This issue, as well as the above point regarding the general interest, are dealt with in greater depth in Chapter 4, section III.

[39] *Lingens v. Austria* (1986) 8 EHRR 407, para. 41.

[40] BVerfGE 69, 315, 345.

most societies, and since religious disagreements tend to lead to unwelcome consequences such as violence and oppression of minorities, it is in the general interest to respect freedom of religion.[41] Again, such an understanding is not at odds with the account presented here. It is certainly arguable that its contribution to religious peace—which is in the general interest—makes the right to freedom of religion more important than it would be if its sole point were respect for personal autonomy. At the same time, however, it is obvious that freedom of religion protects an extremely important autonomy interest from the point of view of individuals: it is at the heart of most people's self-conceptions to decide about religious matters themselves, rather than to have religious views imposed on them.[42] This is captured in the ECtHR's statement that freedom of religion is 'one of the most vital elements that go to make up the identity of believers and their conception of life...'[43] The Court immediately goes on to stress the public good served by the right: '...but it is also a precious asset for atheists, agnostics, sceptics and the unconcerned. The pluralism indissociable from a democratic society, which has been dearly won over the centuries, depends on it.'[44] So again, the conception of autonomy and constitutional rights developed here finds support in the practice.

The South African Constitutional Court has acknowledged the nature of freedom of expression, freedom of demonstration, freedom of religion, and a number of other rights as protecting both autonomy interests and other values in the following sweeping statement:

> [Freedom of expression] is closely related to freedom of religion, belief and opinion (s 15), the right to dignity (s 10), as well as the right to freedom of association (s 18), the right to vote and to stand for public office (s 19) and the right to assembly (s 17)...The rights implicitly recognise the importance, *both for a democratic society and for individuals personally*, of the ability to form and express opinions, whether individually or collectively, even where those views are controversial.[45]

---

[41] Raz, *The Morality of Freedom* (Clarendon Press, 1986), 251–2.

[42] This may include deferring to some theoretical authority in religious matters—an expert, a priest, a book—but that is fully compatible with autonomy, indeed it is often a wise exercise of autonomy: see Raz 'Introduction', in Raz (ed.), *Authority* (New York University Press, 1990), 12.

[43] *Refah Partisi (Welfare Party) and Others v. Turkey* (2002) 35 EHRR 3, para. 49.

[44] Ibid.

[45] *South African National Defence Union v. Minister of Defence*, 1999 (4) SA 469, para. 8 (emphasis added).

It has been demonstrated that the rights which could be explained under the excluded reasons conception can also be justified under the protected interests conception. What about those rights with which the excluded reasons conception struggled? One particularly suitable example to demonstrate the connection between the practice and the protected interests conception is the *right to knowledge of one's family descent*: it is of great importance for the self-conceptions of some (not necessarily all) adopted persons to acquire knowledge about their family descent in order to be able to *form* or *develop* a self-conception which includes an element of 'where one is coming from'. This is exactly the angle from which the German Federal Constitutional Court has approached the matter:

> The right to the free development of one's personality and human dignity secure for every individual an autonomous area for the private arrangement of his affairs, in which he can develop and preserve his individuality. The understanding and development of one's personality is however closely connected with the knowledge of the factors which are constitutive of it. One of these is one's descent. It does not only determine the individual's genetic endowment and thus has an impact on his personality. Independently, it occupies a crucial position in the consciousness of the individual for the determination of his individuality and self-understanding... Independently of the degree of scientific knowledge, knowledge of one's descent offers the individual important links to the understanding and development of his personality. Therefore, the right of personality [allgemeines Persönlichkeitsrecht] includes also knowledge of one's descent.[46]

The ECtHR made substantially the same point, only shorter: persons have 'a vital interest, protected by the Convention, in receiving the information necessary to know and to understand their childhood and early development'[47]. Both statements underline the usefulness of the protected interests conception and the self-conception approach in understanding the practice.

With regard to the *right to data protection* and media intrusion into one's private life, for most of us it is important to control the flow of personal information between ourselves and the public; this is best explained as a desire to shape our social identity, which in turn is an important element of our self-conception. The ECtHR, while to my mind not dealing with the matter in a wholly satisfactory way, nevertheless made it clear that

---

[46] BVerfGE 79, 256, 268–9.

[47] *Gaskin v. United Kingdom* (1990) 12 EHRR 36, para. 49.

the reason for recognizing the protection of one's picture as covered by the right to privacy lies in the link between media intrusion and the right-holder's personal autonomy:

> The Court reiterates that the concept of private life extends to aspects relating to personal identity, such as a person's name, or a person's picture. Furthermore, private life, in the Court's view, includes a person's physical and psychological integrity; the guarantee afforded by Art. 8 of the Convention is primarily intended to ensure the development, without outside interference, of the personality of each individual in his relations with other human beings. There is therefore a zone of inter-action of a person with others, even in a public context, which may fall within the scope of 'private life' . . . In the present case there is no doubt that the publication by various German magazines of photos of the applicant in her daily life either on her own or with other people falls within the scope of her private life.[48]

Data protection has two dimensions: protection of one's data from the *public*, and protection of one's data from the *state*. The latter dimension has been termed the *right to informational self-determination* by the German Federal Constitutional Court. In its *Census* Judgment, the Court stressed the link between data protection and personal autonomy:

> A person who cannot overlook with sufficient clarity which information concerning him is known in specific areas of his social environment and who cannot somewhat estimate the knowledge of possible contact persons, can be substantially inhibited in his freedom to plan and to make decisions in self-determination . . . A person who is unsure about whether deviating activities will be noted down at any time and permanently saved, used, or passed on will try not to raise attention by engaging in such activities . . . This would not only affect the individual's opportunities to flourish but also the common good because self-determination is a basic condition of a free democratic polity which is based on the ability of its citizens to engage in activities and participate.[49]

From this the Court concluded that the right to informational self-determination 'guaranteed in principle the right of the individual person to decide autonomously about the release and use of his personal data',[50] stressing that this applied to *all* pieces of personal data: 'in times of automatic data processing there exists no "trivial" data anymore'.[51]

---

[48] *von Hannover v. Germany* (2005) 40 EHRR 1, para. 50–53.

[49] BVerfGE 65, 1, 42–3.   [50] Ibid., 43.   [51] Ibid., 45.

Interestingly, if this reasoning is correct, it follows that the main purpose of the right to informational self-determination is *not* that it protects an important element of our self-conceptions as such: it is not part of our self-conceptions to be seen by the state as unsuspicious so that the state leaves us alone; rather, its point is instrumental in that it is a *precondition* of our ability to live lives according to our self-conceptions: we would be constrained in our ability to live such lives if we had to fear that 'Big Brother' always watched us. So in spite of its nature as a negative vertical right, the right to informational self-determination belongs, just as socio-economic rights, to the group of rights which ensure the preconditions of autonomy.

The South African Constitutional Court has observed that 'property clauses are notoriously difficult to interpret',[52] and this difficulty is grounded in uncertainty of the purpose of the *right to property*: the question is why property should be protected as a constitutional right at all. By way of contrast, it is intuitively plausible to give a person control over his own body. But why should a person have control over 'his' property, or put differently, why should there be such a thing as private property at all, protected at the constitutional level? The reason cannot be that owning property is part of the self-conceptions of property owners: there is nothing wrong with that self-conception from a constitutional point of view, but it cannot explain why it should be respected more than that of people whose self-conception includes controlling their local parks or swimming pools. Nor can its justification be that property enables persons to live autonomous lives: if that were true, then a right to *have* property would be required. However, one important feature of the right to property is that it protects only the *enjoyment* of one's property; it does not give a right to *have* or to *acquire* property.[53] A further possible justification is that the right to property protects the fruit of the agent's labour; but while I am not unsympathetic to that line of argument, it doesn't work as a *general* explanation because quite often, people own property for which they have never laboured (e.g. they have inherited it), or which stands in no relation to the amount or quality of labour they have invested. More plausibly, the value in the right to property is that it protects a precondition of autonomy: property

---

[52] *First National Bank of SA Ltd t/a Wesbank v. Commissioner, South African Revenue Service; First National Bank of SA Ltd t/a Wesbank v. Minister of Finance*, 2002 (4) SA 768, para. 48 (Ackermann).

[53] Schermes, 'The international protection of the right to property', in Matscher and Petzold (eds.), *Protecting Human Rights: The European Dimension* (Carl Heymanns Verlag, 1990), 569.

facilitates the autonomous planning and conduct of the property owner's life; but it does so only if he has some security that his property rights will be respected in the future. Therefore, just as in the case of informational self-determination, the right to property, in spite of its negative character, belongs to the group of rights protecting the *preconditions* of autonomy.[54]

The right to *freedom of profession* also sits well with the protected interests conception: being able to choose and pursue one's profession is an important exercise of autonomy. One's profession plays an important part in quantitative terms with regard to the proportion of one's available time normally dedicated to it, but also in qualitative terms. When we ask ourselves questions such as: 'What kind of person am I?', or 'What kind of person do I want to be?', our profession will often play a prominent part in the answer. We choose our professions because of who we are and who we want to be; and conversely, we are who we are partly because of our professions, because they shape our identities and self-conceptions to such a considerable extent. The importance of our professions for our lives has entered everyday language, where we speak of our private and professional 'lives'. The rights to privacy and freedom of profession reflect this perceived dichotomy and protect the 'two lives' into which we divide our existence.[55]

The connection between freedom of profession and a person's self-conception has been acknowledged by the German Federal Constitutional Court in the following passage:

> The 'profession' has to be understood in relation to the human being's personality as a whole, which only fully achieves its form and completion in the individual person's devotion to an activity which is, for him, life

---

[54] This may seem like a contradiction of my statement in Chapter 2 where I argued that property should not be regarded as a precondition of autonomy. But the point in that chapter was that regarding *owning* property as a precondition of autonomy does not sufficiently well explain our intuition that even a light interference with the property of a very rich person should count as an interference. But regarding the facilitation of the planning of one's life as the point of protecting property can in fact explain this intuition because the protection of property rights will only have the effect of facilitating the planning of our lives if it is comprehensive.

[55] In reality, however, the 'two lives' are often not strictly separate. One way in which they overlap was strikingly pointed out by the ECtHR in *Niemitz*, where the Court regarded the search of a lawyer's office as an interference with the right to respect for private life and home (Art. 8), arguing that '[r]espect for private life must also comprise to a certain degree the right to establish and develop relationships with other human beings', and that 'it is in the course of their working lives that the majority of people have a significant, if not the greatest, opportunity of developing relationships with the outside world'. (*Niemitz v. Germany* [1993] 16 EHRR 97, para. 29).

task and livelihood, and through which at the same time he generates a contribution to the societal overall performance.[56]

In another decision, the Court wrote: 'Art. 12 (1) Basic Law concretizes the basic right to the free development of one's personality in the areas of individual achievement and securing of one's livelihood.'[57] Both passages use the familiar language of developing one's personality, which, as argued above, is closely related to respect for a person's self-conception.

IV. CONCLUSION

The discussion showed that the rights which are protected by the practice of constitutional rights law can be explained under the protected interests conception as being about or related to autonomy interests which carry a relatively high relevance from the perspective of the self-conception of the agent. Conversely, I cannot think of any activities or personal resources which stand a chance of surviving the justification stage[58] and which carry a high relevance for people but are not protected by constitutional rights. Taken together, these two observations justify the conclusion that the protected interests conception is superior to its rival, the excluded reasons conception, in explaining the set of rights widely acknowledged by the practice of constitutional rights law today.

---

[56] BVerfGE 50, 290, 362.

[57] BVerfGE 54, 301, 313.

[58] This qualification is necessary because for some people activities such as killing might be very important (e.g. for hitmen). As I will argue in the next chapter, while the limitation of such activities is of course justified and indeed required, it is correct to protect them at the prima facie stage. But even if they are not protected, no harm is done in light of the fact that they would never survive the justification stage.

4

The Right to Autonomy

This chapter completes Part I of this book by proposing a theory of the scope of constitutional rights. Its central claim, presented and defended in the first section, is that there exists a general right to personal autonomy, that is, a right to everything which, judged from the perspective of the agent's self-conception, is in his interest. To demonstrate this claim, the section first refines the protected interests conception discussed in Chapter 3 in order to develop a comprehensive conception of autonomy which is both coherent and fits the global model of constitutional rights. It concludes that *every* autonomy interest, including trivial interests and even autonomy interests in engaging in immoral activities, must be protected. The section then takes the step from a doctrine of autonomy to a theory of rights by defending the idea of a *right* to autonomy. The second section examines the implications of this conclusion for the interpretation of existing, and the design of new, constitutions. The final section deals with a separate issue, namely the idea that besides the personal autonomy of the right-holder, there might be further values justifying or lending special weight to constitutional rights, in particular the general interest and the value of democracy.

I. THE RIGHT TO AUTONOMY

This section proposes and defends the idea of a general right to personal autonomy. In a nutshell, it relies on two arguments to reach this conclusion. First, any attempt to limit the scope of rights to certain especially important autonomy interests will come at the price of incoherence of the underlying conception of autonomy; thus, the only way to avoid this incoherence is to include *all* autonomy interests in the scope of rights. Second, in order to defend the claim of a *right* to autonomy, one must abandon the idea that rights hold a special normative force (for example, that they act as trumps or side constraints); rather their point and purpose is to give the right-holder an entitlement to have his autonomy interests adequately protected at all times. He can demand a justification for any state act or omission affecting his ability to live his life according to his self-conception; and this justification will succeed only if the state measure denying him a certain protection is based on good reasons which show adequate respect for his autonomy interests.

1. The scope of rights: refining the protected interests conception of autonomy

a) Comprehensive or threshold model?

As was shown in the last chapter, civil and political rights protect (at least) all those autonomy interests which are of a certain importance. This section will ask a follow-up question which is important both in order to identify the breadth of the constitutional conception of autonomy and to further illuminate the phenomenon of rights inflation (the first feature of the global model of constitutional rights): is there a certain *threshold* in terms of the importance of an autonomy interest which must be met for it to qualify for protection by constitutional rights, or is *any* autonomy interest sufficient? Take the case of hobbies: collecting stamps, playing tennis, or riding in the woods. These hobbies do not display crucial life decisions such as whether or not to procreate, whom to choose as a partner or which profession to take up. They are nevertheless reasonably import-ant activities for the people engaging in them; their relevance is, broadly speaking, somewhere above, say, eating green ice cream, and somewhere below, say, choosing one's partner or profession. Two possibilities of addressing this issue present themselves. According to the *threshold model*, autonomy interests will only attract constitutional protection if they cross a specific threshold of importance. According to the *comprehensive model*, *any* autonomy interest, however trivial, will be sufficient.

The protected interests conception of autonomy must favour the comprehensive model for two reasons. First, the threshold conception would have to draw a line somewhere, stipulating that anything below the line falls foul of the necessary threshold and is therefore not pro-tected. However, it is hard to see how it could do so in a non-arbitrary way. Would the interest have to be of reasonable, average, high, or fundamental importance? What should be the criteria here? We might consider drawing the line in a pragmatic way, stipulating that only autonomy interests of, for example, at least 'high' importance qualify as protected. However, the threshold model must claim that there is a *principled* distinction separating interests from rights; therefore a merely pragmatic approach will not suffice. This leads to the second point. Under the logic of the protected interests conception, the relevant criterion must be that the interest in question is of some, however small, importance: as long as it has *some* importance, as is certainly the case with the pursuit of hobbies, *something would be lost* for autonomy if it were not protected at all. This provides a principled basis for including all autonomy interests and avoids arbitrary distinctions such as the pragmatic one discussed above.

One might object to this conclusion and argue that it is simplistic to assume that the threshold would have to be set at some level of importance, such as 'reasonable' or 'high' importance. Maybe the threshold points to a *qualitative* difference? The most promising attempt in this direction has been made by James Griffin in his book *On Human Rights*, and his discussion is of particular interest in the present context because Griffin's conception of human rights relies heavily on the value of personal autonomy (albeit under a slightly different terminology). He argues that the threshold can be derived from the idea of personhood:

> Human life is different from the life of other animals. We human beings have a conception of ourselves and of our past and future. We reflect and assess. We form pictures of what a good life would be . . . And we try to realise these pictures. This is what we mean by a distinctively *human* existence . . . And we value our status as human beings especially highly, often more highly than even our happiness. This status centres on our being agents – deliberating, assessing, choosing, and acting to make what we see as a good life for ourselves.
>
> Human rights can then be seen as protections of our human standing or, as I shall put it, our personhood. And one can break down the notion of personhood into clearer components by breaking down the notion of agency. To be an agent, in the fullest sense of which we are capable, one must (first) choose one's own path through life – that is, not be dominated or controlled by someone or something else (call it 'autonomy') . . . [And] (third) others must not forcibly stop one from pursuing what one sees as a worthwhile life (call this 'liberty').[1]

At another place Griffin tells us more about how demanding the right to liberty is:

> [L]iberty applies to the final stage of agency, namely to the pursuit of one's conception of a worthwhile life. By no means everything we aim at matters to that. Therefore, society will accept a person's claim to the

---

[1] Griffin, *On Human Rights* (Oxford University Press, 2008), 32–3.

protection of liberty only if the claim meets the material constraint that what is at stake is indeed conceivable as mattering to whether or not we function as normative agents.[2]

Griffin's idea is that 'personhood' functions both as the basis of human rights and as a limitation on their scope: only those interests which are important for personhood are protected as human rights. Personhood requires what Griffin calls autonomy and liberty (in my terminology, personal autonomy): basically, control over one's life. But it requires only that kind of control over one's life which is important for personhood. This, however, leaves open the question of what the test is for determining whether some instance of liberty (autonomy) is required for personhood. My suspicion is that it is simply 'importance'. For example, Griffin says later in the book that 'the domain of liberty is limited to what is *major enough* to count as part of the pursuit of a worthwhile life'.[3] At another place he defends a human right to gay marriage on the ground 'of its *centrality* to characteristic human conceptions of a worthwhile life'.[4] Thus, it seems that the threshold of personhood simply refers back to a sliding scale of importance: an interest that is 'major enough' or 'central' will acquire the status of a human right. But such a sliding scale cannot, as I have explained above, do the moral work. The threshold would have to be between 'not quite major enough' and 'barely major enough' or 'not quite central' and 'barely central'. But then, under Griffin's model, all that separates an interest which is just below from one which is just above the threshold is a small difference in terms of importance or centrality, and this small difference cannot justify the great normative significance that for proponents of threshold models comes with one of them being a simple interest and the other a human right. I believe that this is a general problem of threshold theories which is not limited to Griffin's particular account.[5] If that is true, then the only possible conclusion is that the threshold requirement should be dropped and it should be acknowledged that the scope of freedom protected by rights must extend to *everything which is in the interest of a person's autonomy.*

This conclusion sits well with the global model of constitutional rights and its trend towards rights inflation; and herein lies a further indicator of its correctness. However, someone might object that while such a

---

[2] Ibid., 167.

[3] Ibid., 234 (emphasis added).   [4] Ibid., 163 (emphasis added).

[5] Cf. Raz, 'Human Rights without Foundations', in Besson and Tasioulas (eds.), *The Philosophy of International Law* (Oxford University Press, 2010), 321, 326 with a similar point.

trend exists, it would be an overstatement to say that constitutional rights law generally protects *all* autonomy interests as rights. This is true insofar as the German idea of a constitutional right to freedom of action, which includes rights to go riding in the woods or feed pigeons in the park, still seems to be an outlier in constitutional rights law around the world. But it must be acknowledged that once we agree that the point of constitutional rights is to enable people to follow their projects, the inclusion of hobbies loses any flavour of absurdity. In fact, on this understanding, the only difference between the German approach and other, less generous approaches is that the German approach sets the threshold lower, or even sets aside any threshold, whereas other jurisdictions may still follow a threshold model. But the best explanation for this threshold lies *not* in a morally different conception of autonomy or rights, but in a simple pragmatic consideration, namely a sense that constitutional courts should, because of their limited resources, only deal with matters of a certain *importance*. This presents only a minor variation in the scope of rights adopted in different jurisdictions and leaves intact their moral core as being about protected autonomy interests comprehensively understood.

b) *Immoral and 'evil' activities*

The question of whether both liberty and rights, properly understood, include immoral or even 'evil'[6] activities such as, for example, murder, is a recurrent one in political theory.[7] The dispute is not about whether such activities can or cannot be prohibited—of course they can; in fact, taking into account the doctrine of positive obligations, usually they *must* be prohibited. Proponents of a wide understanding of rights include murder at the prima facie stage, but there is no doubt that there are reasons of sufficient weight in favour of a prohibition, in particular, the rights of the possible victims, which are taken into account at the justification stage. The point of the critics must be that personal autonomy is a value and that, therefore, if we protect murder as part of autonomy, we must be able to point to the value of doing that: we must find some value in protecting murder. Since in light of its evil

---

[6] The point of labelling the activities in question somewhat vaguely as 'evil' is to indicate that they are the sorts of activity which because of their extremely harmful and immoral nature nobody can possibly have a *definite* right to engage in.

[7] Cf. Berlin, 'Two Concepts of Liberty', in Berlin, *Liberty* (Oxford University Press, 2002), 166, 169; Dworkin, *Justice in Robes* (Harvard University Press, 2006), 112.

nature there is no such value, any attractive understanding of autonomy must exclude murder—or so it seems.

We must be careful, however, not to confuse two distinct issues. It does not follow from the fact that murder is worthless that it ought not to be protected as part of autonomy. If that logic were correct, then respect for autonomy could not possibly extend to respect for any worthless actions.[8] So we must not ask whether the action protected as part of autonomy (murder) has any value, but the slightly different question of whether *protecting* the action as part of autonomy serves any value. I argued in the last chapter that a key feature of the protected interests conception is its insistence on neutrality: it does not judge the ethical value of the projects people choose. This does not mean that 'anything goes': if someone chooses murder as his project, he should be punished because he violates the rights of others. But he should *not* be punished on the ground that he has chosen a worthless project. The same point is captured in Ronald Dworkin's distinction between ethics and morality: ethical questions are about how to live a good life, whereas moral questions concern the duties we owe to each other.[9] Autonomy, as understood here, is solely concerned with ethics in the Dworkinian sense: the murderer has to decide for himself whether murdering promotes or ruins the value of his life, and deciding that lies within his autonomy. In a community committed to personal freedom, judging the value of his projects is the agent's responsibility and not that of the state.

Thus, there are two possible reasons why the state might want to prohibit evil activities. The first is their ethical worthlessness; but, as explained above, judging ethical value is not the rightful concern of the state. The second is their immorality. This issue is indeed the concern of the state, but under the global model it is addressed at the justification stage, where the rights of others and relevant public interests are considered, and those rights reflect precisely the domain of morality in the

---

[8] Raz says that the ideal of autonomy requires only the availability of morally acceptable options (*The Morality of Freedom* [Clarendon Press, 1986], 381). This statement should however not be misunderstood as implying that respect for immoral choices may not be necessary. Raz says explicitly that coercion of a person who engages in a non-harmful activity is not permissible because it would violate the person's autonomy and express a relation of domination and an attitude of disrespect for the coerced individual (ibid., 418). In the context of his discussion of authority, he has also acknowledged that there are areas where it is more important to make one's own decision than to make the right decision ('The Problem of Authority: Revisiting the Service Conception', in Raz, *Between Authority and Interpretation* [Oxford University Press, 2009], 126, 137–9); and again, this will include worthless choices.

[9] Dworkin, *Is Democracy Possible Here? Principles for a New Political Debate* (Princeton University Press, 2006), 21.

Dworkinian sense. Adding a 'morality filter' for evil activities to the prima facie stage would lead to conducting the same inquiry at the prima facie stage *and* the justification stage, and would thus point to incoherence and structural confusion.

This explains the puzzle about murder and other 'evil' activities as part of autonomy and protected by rights. Whether or not an action is protected as part of one's autonomy and therefore also as a right is solely to be determined by whether that action carries any importance, however small, under the agent's self-conception. This understanding of autonomy and rights does, contrary to the objection raised above, serve a value: by adopting a neutral perspective towards the ethical value of the agent's choice it shows appropriate respect for his ethical responsibility.

c) Autonomy and horizontal effect, positive obligations, and socio-economic rights

The protected interests conception has no difficulty in explaining horizontal effect and positive obligations: what matters for it is that the agent's autonomy interests are adequately protected, not whether the government or a private party violates them. Thus, it does not only allow for but in fact requires the protection of a person's autonomy interests against their violation by private parties.

With regard to socio-economic rights, there is a general reluctance to include them among the set of enforceable constitutional rights. This reluctance is based on a couple of different concerns relating to both moral and institutional issues. At the institutional level, the main question is one about *institutional competence*: are courts well-equipped to decide claims about positive rights? The relevance of this question will be addressed in Chapter 5. Regarding the *moral structure* of rights, we need a theory which explains how extensive the scope of socio-economic rights should be. This is the topic of the present section.

One possible approach is to stipulate a *threshold*: everyone has a (prima facie) right to enough to live an autonomous life, but not more. For example, Griffin wonders how much is required by what he calls the human right to welfare, and concludes: 'the cut-off point is when the proximate necessary conditions for normative agency are met. This point will be higher than mere subsistence but lower than levels of well-being characteristic of rich contemporary societies.'[10]

---

[10] Griffin, *On Human Rights* (Oxford University Press, 2008), 183.

I am sceptical about this line of reasoning. The problem is that while there may be a minimum threshold below which a meaningfully autonomous life is not possible, for persons above the threshold it is still true that the more goods they have access to, the more autonomous they are. Consequently, just as in the case of negative rights, it is impossible to stipulate a threshold separating in a non-arbitrary way mere interests from human rights. For example, one can arguably live an autonomous life, having enjoyed only primary education; however, clearly one is more autonomous having enjoyed higher education. What follows from this? With regard to civil and political rights, I argued above that there is no reason to limit their scope at the prima facie stage; thus, even comparatively trivial activities such as horse-riding are protected by the protected interests conception. A corresponding approach should be adopted in the context of socio-economic rights: the scope of (prima facie) socio-economic rights extends to everything which is a precondition of the agent's autonomy. This does not pose a practical problem because eccentric claims—think of a right to air-conditioning—can easily be disposed of at the justification stage, pointing to the problem of limited resources.

This argument may seem rash. A critic might object that there is a relevant structural difference between negative rights and socio-economic rights, which can be explained in the following way. On the one hand, even a claim to a right to the most trivial activity—feeding birds in the park—can sometimes succeed, for example, when the state does not come forward with any substantive reasons for its restriction, or when the interference is not necessary to achieve the goal and therefore is in violation of the proportionality principle. On the other hand, claims to things such as air-conditioning, one might argue, will *never* succeed, simply by virtue of the fact that, contrary to the situation in the case of negative rights, the state *always* has a strong reason against the acknowledgement of such a (definite) right: the scarcity of resources. Dealing with the issue of limited resources requires a distributive theory, which is not the topic of this chapter;[11] but whatever theory is appropriate, it is obvious that the world and its resources being what they are, it will not endorse (definite) rights to many things which would make us more autonomous. Therefore, a critic might object that there is indeed a sound reason for denying hopeless claims the status as prima facie rights

---

[11] I discuss this issue in Chapter 6, section IV.2.

straight away in spite of the fact that fulfilling them may make people more autonomous: while the 'pure' doctrine of autonomy suggests the inclusion of a broad range of goods among the preconditions of auton-omy, a coherent conception of rights requires or at least allows for the exclusion of any prima facie rights which will *never* survive the justifica-tion stage.

This objection, however, fails for four reasons. First, what may seem like an eccentric claim today may not be eccentric tomorrow; for example, if a previously poor country becomes very rich, it is not unthinkable that at some point, a definite right to air-conditioning might come into existence. Second, even today and at least in wealthy countries it would often be possible to increase taxation in order to provide all citizens with certain goods, including even mundane things such as air-conditioning.[12] There may be good reasons not to do so, but in order to assess the strength of those reasons, a prima facie right to be provided with the respective goods must be acknowledged, in order to be able to assess the justifiability of its limitation at the justification stage. Third, even where a general entitlement of every person to receive particular goods, such as air-conditioning, may seem absurd, there may be situations where some people under specific circumstances could arguably have such an entitlement (for example, prisoners or patients in hospitals might have a definite right to air-conditioning under certain circumstances). Fourth, there is the problem of discrimination: the state may choose to provide something which is a precondition of autonomy to only some but not all. Again, in order to be able to assess the justifiability of the unequal treatment, a prima facie right to the respect-ive goods must be assumed.[13]

I do not dispute that there may be *pragmatic* considerations for confining the breadth of socio-economic rights in actual constitutions to fundamentally important goods, along the lines of the South African Constitution, for example, which is mainly concerned with housing, food, water, social security, health care, and education.[14] As in the case of negative rights, discussed above, those pragmatic reasons may include a need to use the limited resources of the constitutional court only for

---

[12] I am grateful to the anonymous reviewer for OUP for pointing this out to me.

[13] This problem can in most actual constitutions be resolved under a free-standing right to equality or non-discrimination. I address the relationship between autonomy-based rights and equality rights in Chapter 5, section V.

[14] Ss. 26, 27, 29 of the South African Constitution.

cases of a certain importance, or to avoid giving people false hopes about the (definite) rights that they enjoy. But at the level of a coherent conception of autonomy and rights, it must be maintained that everything which is a precondition of a person's autonomy must be protected; thus, the breadth of socio-economic rights cannot coherently be limited to certain fundamentally important interests.

d) Autonomy and positive options

Positive rights can serve two distinct purposes for people's autonomy: they can be about *autonomy* or about the *preconditions of autonomy*. Horizontal effect and protective duties are (mostly) autonomy-protecting: they ensure that individuals retain control over their actions and personal resources. Socio-economic rights, by way of contrast, are about the preconditions of autonomy. Access to food and water is not mainly about living an autonomous life: it is about *staying* alive, thus securing a necessary precondition of an autonomous life. Similarly, primary education is not mainly about living one's life now, but about enabling one to live one's life later. The distinction between autonomy-protecting and preconditions-protecting rights is not clear-cut: many people find inherent value in eating, drinking, education, having a home, or enjoying social security. However, this merely shows that for some rights there exist overlapping justifications.

Once we accept that on the basis of an autonomy-based approach there is no reason to limit the state to duties of non-interference at the outset, we must address the question of whether the protected interests conception requires the state to *create* options in order to enhance people's autonomy, and if so, how that can be reconciled with the practice of constitutional rights law which is mainly concerned with non-interference with the people's projects. Joseph Raz has shown that a purely negative understanding of autonomy as non-interference is not attractive. To illustrate his point, he invented the example of the Man in the Pit: a person falls down a pit and spends the rest of his life with his choices confined to questions such as whether to eat now or a bit later (there is enough food), sleep now or a bit later, scratch his ear, and so on.[15] The lesson to be learned from the example is that non-interference is not a sufficient condition of autonomy; rather, to be autonomous, a person must have *options* to choose from.

There are not many rights providing options to enhance one's autonomy that are recognized by constitutions; I shall refer to such rights as

---

[15]   Raz, *The Morality of Freedom* (Clarendon Press, 1986), 373–4.

option rights. One important exception is the widely recognized right to marry.[16] Interestingly, the example of marriage also features in Raz's book as one of his few explicit examples of valuable options.[17] Griffin, too, subscribes to the idea of seeing the right to marriage as a matter of human rights: he argues that while 'in general, we must simply accept, and build our lives from, the range of options with which fortune has endowed us',[18] there are exceptions to this rule, and the one example he gives is the availability of unions and the possibility to raise children for same-sex couples: 'This too, I believe, is an issue of liberty. No matter how many options there are already, this one, because of its centrality to characteristic human conceptions of a worthwhile life, must be added.'[19]

Which options does the protected interests conception of autonomy require? The answer is straightforward: just as in the case of negative rights and socio-economic rights, there is no coherent way to confine the breadth of options which are necessary for autonomy to certain especially important ones. It follows that the protected interests conception demands that every option which has some importance for the way in which a person wants to live her life must be protected. Just as in the case of socio-economic rights, this will not pose a practical problem: there will normally be sufficiently important reasons against the creation of a particular option. The first and most important point to note is that as in the case of socio-economic rights, in most cases the creation of options will require scarce public resources. Second, it is also important not to forget that the urgency of claims to be provided with a specific option will in many cases be greatly exaggerated. The general point here is that we should not think of a person's self-conception as necessarily requiring him to engage in a specific activity (such as tennis-playing or being a teacher in a primary school). Rather, our self-conceptions are about *what kind of a person* we are and want to be, and more often than not that self-image can be implemented through engagement in one of several different activities.[20] When a person claims that unless he is provided with one specific option his life will greatly suffer, we have every reason

---

[16] Art. 12 ECHR; Art. 6 of the German Basic Law; for the US: the US Supreme Court held in *Loving v. Virginia* that there is a fundamental right to marry as part of the right to privacy, *Loving v. Virginia* (1967) 388 U.S. 1.

[17] Raz, *The Morality of Freedom* (Clarendon Press, 1986), 161.

[18] Griffin, *On Human Rights* (Oxford University Press, 2008), 163.

[19] Ibid.

[20] Griffin (ibid., 162) makes essentially the same point.

to be suspicious because it is unlikely that any one option will be of such importance. Finally, even if, as I suggest, we accept that coherence demands the inclusion of all options required under a person's self-conception, there are good pragmatic reasons for not including too many option rights in actual constitutions, in particular in order to avoid creating false hopes and unrealistic expectations.

While it will often or usually be the case that a person has no definite right to be provided with a particular option, it is also important to see that there are situations where such entitlements may indeed exist. For healthy people, the absence of state interference normally leaves them enough options for an adequately autonomous life under their self-conceptions; however, this is often not the case for the elderly or the sick. Constitutional lawyers would certainly not be surprised if at some point a constitutional court recognized a constitutional obligation—maybe flowing from human dignity—to provide certain options to people who do not have the physical abilities to make use of the otherwise sufficient options available to them. Thus, it may not be sufficient from a constitutional point of view to secure only the precon-ditions of autonomy, as far as possible, for bedridden persons, that is, to feed them, give them medical treatment, and so on, if there are no meaningful options left to them. So it is certainly plausible to argue that for these people dignity requires the provision of at least some options so that they can give their lives some meaning and direction, within the limited abilities they retain. This is not the place to discuss this issue in detail; but the point is that there is not necessarily a gap between the protected interests conception and the practice: first, the protected interests conception does not demand the creation of innumerable options because of the limited importance of such options for the people's autonomy in most cases and the problem of scarcity of resources; furthermore there are sound pragmatic reasons for limiting the breadth of option rights in actual constitutions. Second, constitu-tional rights law could well be interpreted to demand the creation of options at least for those for whom there are no other meaningful options available to choose from.

2. *From autonomy to rights: the right to autonomy*

By arguing that there is indeed a constitutional *right* to everything which is in the interest of a person's autonomy, my approach seems to run into an obvious trap: it would seem that simply by virtue of the fact that something is important for my autonomy, it does not become the case that I have a right to it. For example, if it is the case that I enjoy feeding the birds in my local park,[21] it may follow that I have an autonomy interest in feeding the birds, but it may be an entirely different question whether I do indeed have a *right* to feed the birds. Consider Raz's famous account of rights:

> *Definition*: 'X has a right' if and only if X can have rights, and, other things being equal, an aspect of X's well-being (his interest) is a sufficient reason for holding some other person(s) to be under a duty.[22]

This is sometimes taken to mean that all one needs for a right to come into existence is an interest; but that is based on a misunderstanding. Rather, it must be the kind of interest *which grounds duties in others*. Thus, as Raz explains elsewhere, just because the love of my children is the most important thing to me, it does not follow that I have a right to it.[23] To get back to the example of feeding the birds, just by virtue of the fact that feeding the birds is of some importance to me, it does not follow that I have a right to it unless this interest can be shown to ground a duty of non-interference in the state.

As a preliminary point, the strategy of simply introducing a threshold of importance does not offer a way out of this problem. There would still remain the question of why, just because not starving to death is a fundamentally important interest, the state should be under a duty to provide food, or why, just because not being tortured is a fundamentally important interest, the state should be under a duty not to torture. To resolve the puzzle, we need a general account of the duties which the state owes to its citizens. I will propose such an account in Chapter 5, where I will argue that the point and purpose of state policies is to specify the spheres of autonomy of equal citizens. From this it follows that the state is under *a duty to ensure that the personal autonomy interests of each person are adequately protected at all times. This* is the duty which is grounded by the prima facie 'right to everything'. For example, the right to feed the birds grounds the state's duty to take the respective autonomy interest in bird feeding adequately into account in its policy-making; and this means that feeding the birds can only be regulated or prohibited if

---

[21] Cf. BVerfGE 54, 143 (*Pigeon-Feeding*).

[22] Raz, *The Morality of Freedom* (Clarendon Press, 1986), 166.

[23] Raz, 'Human Rights without Foundations', in Besson and Tasioulas (eds.), *The Philosophy of International Law* (Oxford University Press, 2010), 321, 325.

there are good reasons for this (for example the prevention of pollution) which are such that they justify the prohibition or regulation in spite of the fact that thereby the would-be bird feeder is denied the pursuit of this particular activity. This understanding of the relationship between rights and duties resolves the conceptual puzzle and explains why it is indeed coherent to accept a right to everything which is in the interest of a person's autonomy.

A further objection to this understanding of rights could be that it is in conflict with the widely accepted view that rights hold a special norma- tive force. If every autonomy interest is protected as a right, then it is obvious that rights cannot have a normative force comparable to, for example, trumps or side constraints. Thus, the conception of rights proposed here is a frontal attack on the dearly held belief of most philosophers, including Griffin whose view I discussed above, that human rights protect only a limited domain of certain especially import- ant interests, and that corresponding to their narrow scope they hold a special normative force. I will offer two further arguments, one negative and one positive, against that idea and in support of the view proposed here. The negative reason is the deficiency of the dominant view. If it were true that rights protected only a limited domain of interests which in turn led to and justified their special normative force, then we should expect someone to have successfully articulated the threshold by now; the inability to do so raises the suspicion that there is a fault in the theory. The second, positive reason can be explained in the following way. Human rights are commonly referred to as the rights which a person is entitled to simply by virtue of his or her humanity. Most would agree that the best interpretation of this very abstract idea has something to do with personal autonomy (Griffin would say, autonomy and lib- erty). But it does not follow that we should think about the point of autonomy as being provided with certain goods (in particular, free- doms), such as the freedoms to speak one's mind, choose one's partner, and follow one's religion. Under the global model, the main entitlement that a human being has with regard to how he lives his life *and* simply by virtue of being human is about being treated with a certain *attitude*: an attitude that *takes him seriously as a person with a life to live*, and that will therefore deny him the ability to live his life in a certain way only when there are *sufficiently strong reasons* for this. Applied to the case of hobbies such as collecting stamps, this means that we should not ask whether the freedom to collect stamps is indispensable for making a person a person. Rather, we should ask whether the state treats a person subject to its authority in a way which is in line with that person's status flowing from his humanity when it, for example, prohibits him the activity of collecting stamps; and this will be the case only when there are sufficiently strong reasons supporting the prohibition. Thus, the point of rights under the global model is not to single out certain especially important interests for heightened protection. Rather, it is to show a particular form of respect for persons by insisting that each and every state measure which affects a person's ability to live her life according to her self-conception can be justified *to her*.

One consequence of adopting this conception of rights is a shift of the focus of the analysis from the prima facie stage of rights ('Which instances of autonomy are important enough to count as a human right?') to the justification stage ('Are there good reasons for the interference with the protected interest?'); in this sense one could also speak of the right to autonomy as a 'right to justification':[24] any limitation of a person's autonomy triggers the duty of justification. It is precisely such a shift which has occurred under the global model of constitutional rights, where the prima facie stage of rights has been interpreted more and more broadly (leading to rights inflation) and the focus of the legal analysis has turned to the justification stage, asking whether the interference with the right is proportionate.

II. IMPLICATIONS FOR CONSTITUTIONAL DESIGN AND INTERPRETATION

The acknowledgment of a general right to personal autonomy has implications for the interpretation of existing, and the design of new, constitutions. With regard to the former, every plausible approach to constitutional interpretation must take the point or purpose of the respective constitution into account. It follows that if its set of rights is best explained by the protected interests conception of autonomy, then this fact must feature in its interpretation. This implies that its rights ought to be interpreted broadly in order to minimize gaps in the constitutional protection of personal autonomy. The argument is that (1) all things being equal, an interpretation of the constitution should be adopted which is in line with the general point or purpose of the

---

[24] On the idea of a 'right to justification' as the basic common ground of human rights see Forst, 'The Justification of Human Rights and the Basic Right to Justification: A Reflexive Approach', (2010) 120 *Ethics* 711.

constitution as a whole; (2) the constitution as a whole is best explained by a commitment to a comprehensive protection of personal autonomy; (3) therefore a prima facie right which is open to a broader or narrower interpretation should be interpreted broadly so as to include the respective personal autonomy interest at stake. Such a development can clearly be observed in constitutional rights adjudication, for example in the US Supreme Court's discovery of the right to privacy as part of a *procedural* clause,[25] or in the ECtHR's broad understanding of the right to *private* life as including, of all things, aspects of a person's *professional* life.[26] The right to privacy has a crucial role in constitutional rights adjudication as a *gap filler* which kicks in when some element of personal autonomy is worthy of constitutional protection but does not fit into one of the more traditional rights. Thus, the emergence of a broad approach to privacy provides a further indicator of the explanatory power of the claims defended here.

For framers of new constitutions, the idea of a comprehensive right to personal autonomy calls into question the necessity of a set of distinct constitutional rights. Nothing would be lost in theory by simply acknowledging one comprehensive prima facie right to personal autonomy instead. This approach would have at least three advantages over a long list of constitutional rights. First, it would serve intellectual clarity by focussing both the citizens' and the lawyers' attention on the point and purpose of constitutional rights, rather than having a long and often confusing list of different constitutional rights which, to make things worse, will often have individual limitation clauses contributing further to the wrong impression that constitutional rights law is inevitably a subject-matter of great technicality. It would therefore also help rebutting one of the objections to judicial review, namely that judicial review, by turning moral questions into legal ones, loads them with all sorts of legalistic baggage which obscures rather than illuminates the substantive issues at stake.[27] Second, it would abolish one of the regular and fruitless exercises plaguing constitutional rights law, namely the determination of the precise doctrinal boundaries between neighbouring rights, for example, the boundaries between the right to property and freedom of profession, or between freedom of expression and freedom of religion.

---

[25] *Griswold v. Connecticut* (1965) 381 U.S. 479 (concerning a state's prohibition of contraception for married couples).

[26] *Niemitz v. Germany* (1993) 16 EHRR 97, para. 29.

[27] Cf. Waldron, 'The Core of the Case against Judicial Review', (2005–6) 115 *Yale Law Journal* 1346, 1380–2.

Nothing would be lost: what matters is not whether a particular inter-ference with personal autonomy falls within right A or right B, but rather the fact that an interference with personal autonomy has taken place and the extent to which it affects a person's ability to live his life under his self-conception. Finally, a comprehensive right to autonomy would avoid the possibility of unjustifiable and unanticipated gaps, in part by deliber-ately releasing judges from the interpretative constraints imposed by detailed and sometimes unfortunately framed constitutional provisions.

But this raises the question of why constitutions, even relatively new ones such as the South African Constitution, continue to rely on lists of rights: it might seem that the account of rights proposed here must miss something important if its central claim does not resonate with the framers of constitutions. This objection can be split into two points. First, there is the question of why constitution makers, as a matter of psychological historical fact, have not been attracted to the idea of one comprehensive right to personal autonomy. The second and distinct question is whether they ought to be attracted to that idea.

Regarding the first point, the explanation is straightforward. The account presented here is largely novel and in conflict with many conventional views about rights; doubtless it is also controversial. At the level of theory, most people are attracted to a view of rights which I summarized under the label of the 'dominant narrative' in Chapter 1; and it is one element of the dominant narrative that rights are seen as having some special importance compared to mere interests. As such, it is not surprising that the framers of constitutions continue to stick to the dominant narrative when designing a new constitution and thus refuse to include, let alone exclusively rely on, a broad right to personal autonomy.

The more difficult question is whether on the basis of the account of rights advocated here, they ought, in the future, to design constitutions in a different way, with just one comprehensive right to personal autonomy. While this would have the advantages described above, on balance I would still argue in favour of a well-designed list of rights for the following reasons. First, a list of rights has the advantage that it can single out some particularly important aspects of personal autonomy, thus making it clear that interferences with these particularly important interests will require correspondingly solid justifications. A list thus avoids the misleading impression that all instances of a person's auton-omy receive the same level of protection. This does not of course imply that trivial interests should be excluded: they ought to be protected as part of a general right to liberty or privacy which is applicable only when none of the more specific rights is engaged. Second, for the reasons laid out above, a list of rights can pragmatically leave out those rights which will rarely or never survive the justification stage, thus avoiding to some extent unrealistic expectations. The final reason is maybe the most important one. A list of rights is much easier to understand for ordinary citizens than the simple stipulation of a general right to autonomy. One of the advantages of the protected interests conception is that, unlike the excluded reasons conception, it does not start with some abstract ideal of how to treat people but with a very down-to-earth account of what matters to people. Therefore, framers of constitutions can carry this philosophical advantage over to the level of constitutional design by constructing a comprehensive list of rights, each of which is specific enough to relate to actual grievances that citizens may suffer. For example, if a person is worried about the state collecting some of her personal data, she will find in the well-designed constitution a right to private life, possibly with an additional explanation that this includes a right to data protection.[28] If the state prohibits a demonstration in which he wishes to participate, he will find a right to freedom of assembly of which the right to demonstrate is a part. If the state prohibits a person from taking up a profession of his choice, he will find in the constitution a right to freedom of occupation. By being more specific than simply referring to 'personal autonomy' and providing more detail with regard to the various instances of autonomy protected, the constitution speaks to individual citizens at a level which makes it easier for them to assess the question of whether what has happened to them has constitutional significance as an interference with their autonomy which requires justification.

III. BEYOND PERSONAL AUTONOMY: THE LEGITIMACY OF DEMOCRACY, AND THE GENERAL INTEREST

The argument so far has established that an autonomy-based understanding of constitutional rights explains core features of the practice of constitutional rights law. This does not necessarily imply that the personal autonomy of the right-holder is the *only* value at stake in the justification of rights. In this section I will explore the possibilities, already hinted at in the last chapter, that for some rights there might

---

[28] See, for example, Art. 8 of the Charter of Fundamental Rights of the European Union.

exist an independent, overlapping justification flowing from the value of democracy and that rights might acquire additional weight by serving the general interest.

First, with regard to democracy, it is a well-established point in the theory of constitutional rights that the legitimacy of democratic decision-making requires the protection of certain rights.[29] By 'democracy' I mean here the *procedural* dimension of democracy; I shall leave open until Chapter 5 the question of whether there is a *substantive* dimension to it which requires that policies adopted by the majority must comply with certain substantive standards—such as showing equal concern and respect for every citizen[30]—in order to be considered truly democratic. It is certainly a highly plausible assumption that for the legitimacy of the procedures of a majoritarian process, there must be respect at least for the rights to vote, freedom of expression and freedom of association and maybe also freedom of assembly. These rights flow from overlapping justifications: for many people, their exercise—discussing politics, participating in a political party or a demonstration—is also part of their personal projects. In fact, democracy could not thrive unless there was appeal to many people in the idea of making it their personal project to participate in it in some form; so it is not a coincidence that the legitimacy conditions of democracy overlap with many people's personal autonomy interests. But analytically we can separate the two and hold that some rights flow from two independent justifications, namely personal autonomy and the legitimacy conditions of democracy.

Second, some rights which are based on personal autonomy interests may acquire extra weight by virtue of their contribution to the general interest. Joseph Raz has argued that many of our most cherished rights gain their weight through serving the general interest; his example concerning freedom of speech is that this right gains its fundamental importance not in light of its importance for the well-being of the right-holder, but because of its contribution to a common liberal culture which is achieved through the protection of the individual interests.[31] I will argue in the next chapter that what we sometimes loosely refer to as being in the general interest is in fact simply a different way of saying

---

[29] Cf. Dworkin, *Freedom's Law: The Moral Reading of the American Constitution* (Harvard University Press, 1996), 24–5; Ely, *Democracy and Distrust: A Theory of Judicial Review* (Harvard University Press, 1980), ch. 5.

[30] Dworkin, ibid., 25.

[31] Raz, *Ethics in the Public Domain: Essays in the Morality of Law and Politics* (new edition, Clarendon Press, 1995), 54–5. See also Chapter 3, section III.2.

that it serves everyone's autonomy interests; thus, it is important to note that under the approach proposed here, the reference to the general interest should not be understood as introducing a new value not related to autonomy but rather as meaning that a right may gain additional weight because of the autonomy interests of people other than the right-holder.

The general interest argument has to be distinguished from the democracy argument: the latter is not about the general interest (although some, including Raz, would argue that democracy is justified in light of the fact that adopting democratic procedures furthers a community's interest because it leads to better policies compared to non-democratic alternatives), but about the *legitimacy* of a procedure; and the value of the procedure is at least partly independent of the *results* achieved through the use of this procedure. In other words, most proponents of democracy believe in democracy not only because it leads to better policies but (also) because they find intrinsic value in the idea of a people governing itself.

Both ideas—rights as flowing from the legitimacy conditions of democracy and rights as gaining additional weight because of their importance for the general interest—are commonly employed by constitutional courts, even though those courts do not always distinguish precisely between interest-based arguments relating to the general interest and legitimacy arguments relating to democracy. I pointed out in the last chapter that the ECtHR regards freedom of expression as 'one of the essential foundations' of 'a democratic society' (this is the democracy argument), 'one of the basic conditions of its progress' (this is the general interest component: it is in the general interest of a society to enjoy progress), and also as one of the basic conditions 'for each individual's self-fulfilment' (this is the personal autonomy component). The German Federal Constitutional Court has made a statement similar in this respect:

> The basic right to freedom of expression, the most immediate aspect of the human personality in society, is one of the most precious rights of man . . . It is absolutely essential to a free and democratic state, for it alone permits that constant spiritual interaction, the conflict of opinion, which is its vital element.[32]

---

[32] BVerfGE 7, 198, 208 (*Lüth*); English translation from the website of the University of Texas School of Law, http://www.utexas.edu/law/academics/centers/transnational/work_new/ [copyright: Basil Markesinis].

In its case law on freedom of association, the ECtHR has stressed the importance of that right for the values of social cohesion and pluralism:

> While in the context of Article 11 the Court has often referred to the essential role played by political parties in ensuring pluralism and democracy, associations formed for other purposes, including those proclaiming or teaching religion, are also important to the proper functioning of democracy. For pluralism is also built on the genuine recognition of, and respect for, diversity and the dynamics of cultural traditions, ethnic and cultural identities, religious beliefs, artistic, literary and socio-economic ideas and concepts. The harmonious interaction of persons and groups with varied identities is essential for achieving social cohesion. It is only natural that, where a civil society functions in a healthy manner, the participation of citizens in the democratic process is to a large extent achieved through belonging to associations in which they may integrate with each other and pursue common objectives collectively.[33]

As laid out in Chapter 3, the ECtHR regards the right to freedom of religion as important for pluralism which in turn is 'indissociable' from a democratic society. The German Federal Constitutional Court derives from the right to freedom of religion the requirement of state neutrality in religious matters by pointing to the need of the state being 'a home to all citizens',[34] which in turn is important for 'religious peace' in society[35]—another example of referring to the general interest: it is in the general interest of a society to enjoy religious peace. Regarding the freedom of assembly, the democracy justification has been explicitly acknowledged by the Court, which calls assemblies 'essential elements of democratic openness'[36]. It goes on to state:

> In the literature, the stabilising function of freedom of assembly for the representative system is correctly described to the effect that it permits the dissatisfied to publicly bring forward and discharge their dissatisfaction and critique and that it functions as a necessary condition of a political early-warning system which highlights potential for disruption and makes visible deficits in integration and thus also enables corrections of the official policies.[37]

The argument here seems to be that freedom of demonstration, while maybe not essential for the legitimacy of democracy as such, improves

---

[33] *Moscow Branch of the Salvation Army v. Russia* (2007) 44 EHRR 46, para. 61.

[34] '*Staat als Heimstatt aller Staatsbürger*': BVerfGE 108, 282, 299.   [35] Ibid., 300.

[36] BVerfGE 69, 315, 344.   [37] Ibid., 347.

the processes of democracy in that it makes policy-makers aware of dissatisfaction among the citizenry and thus increases their responsiveness to the interests of the people they are representing.

The above statements by constitutional courts explain an intuition widely shared, namely that some rights have an importance which cannot be accounted for by exclusively relying on the interests of the right-holder. Whether or to what extent it follows that an interference with these rights will be harder to justify is, of course, a different question. I will argue in Chapter 6 that for the case of hate speech, contrary to some views especially of American origin, the fact that the right to freedom of expression is partly justified by the value of democracy does not require a modification of the standards determining the conditions under which a limitation of the right is justified. The main difference between rights justified exclusively on personal autonomy grounds and rights justified partly by the procedural dimension of democracy is that in the case of the latter, the state may more often be obligated to provide resources in order to enable the right-holder to engage in the activity protected by the right. For example, the fact that the state is obligated to enable demonstrations to take place (which requires the spending of scarce resources) cannot be explained by exclusively relying on the autonomy interests of those demonstrating; otherwise a group of persons enjoying expensive opera performances would also be entitled to the receipt of state funding for opera. Rather, the reason why the state must spend resources to enable the demonstrators to pursue their project of demonstrating but probably need not spend resources to enable opera lovers to attend opera performances lies in the fact that the right to freedom of demonstration is partly justified by the value of democracy, whereas the right to go to the opera is not. But apart from this issue, the argument in this book will largely proceed on the basis that the main justification of constitutional rights lies in the value of the personal autonomy of the right-holder, while keeping the role of democracy and the general interest in mind and coming back to it when appropriate.

IV. CONCLUSION

While the argument in the preceding sections and chapters has been long, its central claim is quite straightforward: constitutional rights comprehensively protect the freedom of the right-holder to conduct his life according to his self-conception. The two crucial steps towards this conclusion are the broad understanding of autonomy and the acknowledgement of a *right* to autonomy. The combined effect is that any state action or omission which affects a person's ability to conduct his life according to his self-conception interferes with a constitutional right and thus triggers the duty of *justification*: to be legitimate, the state policy which denies the right-holder some element of control over his life must *take his autonomy interests adequately into account*. What this implies is the subject-matter of the second part of this book.

PART II
THE STRUCTURE OF JUSTIFICATION

Towards a Theory of Balancing and Proportionality: The Point and Purpose of Judicial Review

I. INTRODUCTION

The most important tools employed by the global model in order to assess the justifiability of an interference with a constitutional right are the doctrines of balancing and proportionality. As indicated by their names, the doctrine of balancing requires competing values to be 'balanced' and the principle of proportionality prohibits state measures which are 'disproportionate'; but the problem is that these doctrines, because of the high level of abstraction at which they are formulated, offer no immediate guidance as to what makes a measure disproportionate or how to conduct the balancing. In order to understand them properly, we must interpret them in the light of coherent theories of the *standard* and, inseparable from this, the *point and purpose* of judicial review under the global model. Therefore, this chapter will engage in a philosophical inquiry about the point and purpose of constitutional judicial review. In doing so, it will remain faithful to the reconstructive approach of this book: it will take the features of constitutional rights, so far as they have emerged in the previous chapters, as a given and ask which theory of judicial review fits these specific features *and* is morally coherent.

Such a theory must reflect attractive conceptions of constitutional rights, the value of democracy and the value of the separation of powers. With regard to democracy, it must find a reply to the objection that judicial review is undemocratic because it gives unelected judges the power to strike down laws passed by a democratically elected legislature. With regard to the separation of powers, it must offer a response to the charge that judges and courts are institutionally poorly equipped to protect rights, or in any case less well equipped than legislatures, and that this raises problems for the legitimacy of judicial review. Therefore the relationship between constitutional rights, democracy, and the separation of powers will be at the centre of this chapter. It will begin with the relationship between constitutional rights and democracy (sections II–V) and assess the institutional questions in a second step (section VI).

II. PERSONAL AND POLITICAL AUTONOMY

The moral ideal of democracy is the people ruling themselves: they are the authors of the laws which bind them. Thus, democracy is about *autonomy* and in some ways similar to personal autonomy: at the political level, the people, collectively, are the authors of their laws; and at the individual level, each person is the author of his or her life. In order to stress this parallel between personal autonomy and democracy, I shall refer to the moral ideal of democracy as *political autonomy*. The political community as a whole exercises its political autonomy. At the level of the individual citizen, every citizen is entitled to *participate* adequately in the community's political autonomy.[1] The two kinds of autonomy, personal and political, reflect our different roles as individual persons, giving our lives meaning and direction, on the one hand, and as citizens, participating in elections and other democratic procedures in order to co-determine the political direction of the country, on the other hand. Rather than being passive recipients of other people's or bodies' directives, they empower us to become active (co-)shapers of our personal lives and the life of our political community.

The following sections will examine the relationship between personal and political autonomy. Speaking of personal and political autonomy, as opposed to constitutional rights and democracy, has the advantage of laying bare the moral ideals at stake and making it clear that the argument at this stage is not about institutional considerations (which will be dealt with in section VI below). It will turn out that institutional considerations do of course play a role in a theory of constitutional rights, but a smaller one than is often assumed in Anglo-American discourse; in other words: the step from a theory of the relationship between personal and political autonomy to a theory of

---

[1] On the right to participation, cf. Waldron, *Law and Disagreement* (Oxford University Press, 1999), ch. 11.

the relationship between, in particular, courts and legislatures is much smaller than often assumed. As will be demonstrated, the moral ideals are in the driving seat and institutional design by and large ought to follow the moral ideals, making the courts responsible for ensuring that the elected branches remain within their sphere of political autonomy and thus do not violate the personal autonomy of the citizens.

III. THREE DESIDERATA

As a starting point for the inquiry, I shall present three *desiderata* which a sound theory of the relationship between personal and political autonomy ought to satisfy. In section IV, I will discuss different theories of the point and purpose of judicial review in light of the extent to which they comply with these desiderata.

1. The theory must provide a meaningful role for personal autonomy

The argument in the last chapters has established that under the global model, constitutional rights comprehensively protect the autonomy interests of individuals. Therefore, it is evident that a theory which searches for a justification of this practice must accord a prominent, meaningful place to personal autonomy.

2. It must provide a meaningful role for political autonomy

All the discussion of constitutional rights and personal autonomy in the previous chapters must not lead to an underestimation of the undisputed importance of democracy or political autonomy. Surely any theory of political autonomy and democracy must endorse their being about deciding, collectively, questions of great *importance*, thus shaping the character of the political community in fundamental ways. This involves the existence of *genuine choice* on the side of the decision-makers. If it turned out that respecting personal autonomy imposed such constraints on political autonomy that, while political decision-makers were still required to make important decisions, the content of these decisions was predetermined by considerations relating to personal autonomy and did not leave any meaningful element of choice to the decision-makers, this would point to a serious flaw in the theory.

3. It must integrate personal and political autonomy in an attractive way

To understand this desideratum, imagine the following, straightforward argument claiming to resolve the puzzle of the relationship between personal and political autonomy. It is important, the argument goes, that the people enjoy political autonomy and rule themselves through democratic procedures. It is also important, however, that each person enjoys personal autonomy and rules himself. Since sometimes we cannot have both at the same time, the argument continues, we must make compromises. When the two values of political and personal autonomy clash, we must balance them so that neither of them takes complete priority at the cost of the other. So, as a result, we should, for example, conclude that when there is merely a 'light' violation of personal autonomy, political autonomy takes precedence; however in case of a 'grave' violation, personal autonomy takes precedence. We thereby ensure that the core of personal autonomy is protected, but that at the same time meaningful political self-government exists.[2]

I do not want to discuss this view in depth here, but rather use it to illustrate the necessity of the integration requirement. The balancing approach is based on the undefended assumption that political and personal autonomy clash. However, before concluding that there is a clash of values we must be careful to make sure that we have the right understanding of the two values at stake; we must investigate the possibility of an *integrated account* which shows the two values—personal and political autonomy—in harmony rather than conflict.[3] Only if we cannot come up with such an account are we justified in assuming that there is a genuine clash of values.

IV. THE RELATIONSHIP BETWEEN PERSONAL AND POLITICAL AUTONOMY

1. 'Political autonomy takes precedence'

The view discussed in this section claims that political autonomy takes precedence over personal autonomy. It integrates political and personal autonomy in a peculiar way: it need not deny the importance of personal

---

[2] Cf. Sager, 'The Domain of Constitutional Justice', in Alexander (ed.), *Constitutionalism: Philosophical Foundations* (Cambridge University Press, 1998), 235, 248–9: constitutional justice should narrow its focus to extreme and rather clear breaches of political justice, partly because of a concern for democracy.

[3] On the issue of clashes of values, see Dworkin, *Justice in Robes* (Harvard University Press, 2006), ch. 4; Dworkin, *Justice for Hedgehogs* (Harvard University Press, 2011), 118–120.

autonomy—it may even hold that the wise exercise of political autonomy will consist in creating conditions where the people enjoy personal
autonomy. However, it creates a hierarchical order between the two
values by insisting that freedom, properly understood, means first and
foremost the freedom of political participation, and that the freedom to
advance one's personal projects is protected only insofar as it is recognized under the scheme of policies flowing from the community's
exercise of its political autonomy.

As a means of identifying a conception of political autonomy which
will help to justify judicial review under the global model, we can
quickly dispose of this approach: it violates the first desideratum by
not giving adequate protection to personal autonomy. Its natural mate
in the world of constitutional design is undoubtedly a UK-style sovereign
legislature. However, apart from this approach not fitting the practice of
judicial review, it fails also on grounds of philosophical attractiveness;
and as its failure is instructive, I would like to press the matter further.
There is something to be said for this view under conditions of *unanim-
ity*, with everyone consenting to policies which thereby become reflections of the general will. Nothing seems wrong with a community of
equals first deciding unanimously upon a scheme of justice, and then
holding every member to be bound by it; in fact it would be absurd for
someone first to agree to be bound and then to claim that the law
violated his personal autonomy and should not be enforced. Obviously,
however, in the real world unanimous decision-making is not practical
because it would usually lead to political stagnation. Therefore, beautiful
as the image of the general will may be, it is insufficiently close to
majoritarian decision-making, which is the only practicable way for a
community to exercise its political autonomy.

Under conditions of majority-voting, it is not plausible to understand
political autonomy as limitless and trumping personal autonomy. That
approach would imply, for example, that if the political community
decided to inflict genocide on a part of the population, it would be
morally entitled to do so: it falls within its political autonomy which
trumps the personal autonomy of the victims. Such a broad understanding of political autonomy must be unattractive. Note again that from this
it does not necessarily follow that one should endorse constitutional
judicial review; my argument is not about institutions at this stage. It
may, for example, be possible to defend traditional UK-style conceptions
of parliamentary sovereignty by reference to the idea that legislatures are
better than courts in adequately protecting personal autonomy. All I am

saying is that an understanding of political autonomy which regards the community as *morally entitled* to do anything it likes to its members *just because it so chooses* must be deficient.

Here lies an important difference between the self-determination of individual persons and that of political communities. As I have argued in previous chapters, individual persons are (prima facie) entitled to choose and to act upon their self-conceptions, i.e. the goals towards which they strive, and the state must not judge their goals. In contrast, a political community does not have such an entitlement: it cannot legitimately choose, for example, to prize the infliction of genocide on some of its members. In contrast to individual persons, the goal of its activities is fixed: at the most abstract level, it must be a value such as justice, the common good, or possibly a combination of different values (for example freedom, equality, solidarity). At this stage, I am not concerned with deciding which value or set of values exactly it is that communities must realize; rather, my point is only to illustrate that there must be some value or set of values constraining the policies that political communities can legitimately adopt. At the very least, a community cannot claim to act within its political autonomy if it acts in a way *which cannot be defended as a* bona fide *attempt at these values*.

This has implications for the right to participation. Since this right is derivative of the community's political autonomy, its content is limited in exactly the same way as political autonomy: it means, at most, the right to participate in shaping a *bona fide* conception of the value or values which the political community must pursue. In particular, an individual's right to participate is *not* about trying to get the most out of the political process for herself, at the cost of the legitimate interests of others. Of course, some democratic theorists have argued exactly this: that the value of democracy lies in the fact that legislatures are a suitable forum to take the partisan interests of everyone into account. This argument obviously does not paint a very flattering picture of the ways in which people think about political questions, and some would refute it as not only unflattering but inaccurate in its description of how people actually reason in their political roles.[4] Be that as it may, this approach is not necessarily at odds with the account given above. The theorists defending it will either not see the value of democracy in political self-government (they might see it, for example, in advancing the happiness or the well-being of the people);

---

[4] Cf. Waldron, *Law and Disagreement* (Oxford University Press, 1999), 221–2.

or if they do, they must regard counting the partisan interests of everyone as the arrangement most likely to lead to the adoption of adequate policies (the idea being that if everyone's interests are taken into account on an equal basis, the result is likely to be adequate in terms of realizing the values which political communities ought to pursue). They would, in other words, certainly not think that there was much value in democracy if it regularly led to results which could not be regarded as *bona fide* attempts at the relevant value(s). If that is true, then while this argument allows the people to be partisan and ignore the relevant values on an individual basis, it does so because it has in advance come to the conclusion that this procedure is actually likely to promote the realization of these very values.

2. *'Personal autonomy takes precedence to the extent that its protection is necessary for the legitimacy of the processes of political autonomy'*

One way of integrating personal and political autonomy is the idea that for legitimate democratic decisions, certain procedural conditions must be satisfied. The best-known proponent of this approach is John Hart Ely, who argued in his book *Democracy and Distrust* that constitutional rights ought to be process-perfecting, i.e. they should be concerned 'on the one hand, with procedural fairness in the resolution of individual disputes (process writ small), and on the other, with what might capaciously be designated process writ large—with ensuring broad participation in the processes and distributions of government.'[5]

I discussed this basic idea in Chapter 4,[6] where I considered and accepted the idea that for some rights—including the freedoms of expression, association and assembly—there exist overlapping justifications based on personal autonomy *and* the legitimacy conditions of the procedures of democracy. The question to be addressed here is whether it is possible to interpret the *entire* set of rights protected under the global model as required for the procedural legitimacy of democracy. This, however, is a hopeless task. Ely's theory seeks to limit the breadth of constitutional rights, not to expand the American understanding to the even broader one prevalent under the global model, which, as I argued in the previous chapter, is best understood as including a right to everything which is in the interest of a person's autonomy. The furthest

---

[5] Ely, *Democracy and Distrust: A Theory of Judicial Review* (Harvard University Press, 1980), 87.

[6] Chapter 4, section III.

Ely is willing to go is to award some protection to minorities.[7] While it is already doubtful whether this can be justified under a *procedural* approach,[8] under the global model *everyone's* autonomy interests are protected, not only those of minorities or people at risk of suffering discrimination. Thus, while the procedural legitimacy approach may provide an overlapping justification for some rights, it cannot even come close to explaining the breadth of the protection offered by constitutional rights today. It must therefore be rejected as unhelpful for an understanding of the point and purpose of judicial review under the global model.

3. 'Political autonomy ends where personal autonomy begins'

A popular account of the relationship between democracy and human rights is the following: 'Democracy in the sense of majoritarian decision-making is legitimate only when it does not violate human rights'.[9] The problem with this approach is that while it presents itself as an integrated account of democracy and human rights (democracy ends where human rights begin), the integration is only rhetorical because it does not show the substantive link between the two concepts. What makes it the case that democracy ends where human rights begin? What are the values at stake? A refined version of the idea can be formulated by replacing 'democracy' with 'political autonomy' and 'human rights' with 'personal autonomy'. The revised statement reads: 'Political autonomy ends where personal autonomy begins'. On one interpretation of this statement, it divides issues by subject-matter and claims that some issues properly fall into the domain of personal autonomy, and others fall into the sphere of political autonomy. For example, giving a political speech or choosing an intimate partner are issues that fall into the sphere of personal autonomy and are therefore no-go zones for the political community; whereas building a new road or deciding about economic policies are issues that fall into the sphere of political autonomy. Its claim for respecting the integration desideratum is more plausible now: rather

---

[7] Ely, *Democracy and Distrust: A Theory of Judicial Review* (Harvard University Press, 1980), ch. 6.

[8] Sager, 'The Domain of Constitutional Justice', in Alexander (ed.), *Constitutionalism: Philosophical Foundations* (Cambridge University Press, 1998), 235, 246–7.

[9] See, for example, Fleming's characterization of constitutional democracies: 'A constitutional democracy is a system in which a constitution imposes limits on the content of legislation: to be valid, a law must be consistent with fundamental rights and liberties embodied in the constitution.' (*Securing Constitutional Democracy: The Case of Autonomy* [Chicago University Press, 2006], 77).

than speaking of two concepts (democracy and human rights) which on the surface seem to have nothing to do with each other, it links both concepts to the same ideal, namely self-determination. To be a comprehensively self-determining person, one has to be personally autonomous in one's private sphere and participate adequately in the political self-determination of one's political community. Both kinds of self-determination have their respective spheres which can and must be delineated from each other according to the subject-matter at stake.

So while there is an attempt at integration, the question is whether it is an attractive one. The argument rests on the premise that we can separate the two spheres of autonomy in such a way that each issue will fall into one of them. I explained in Chapter 1 that the domain of constitutional justice has constantly grown over recent decades. In the old days, when people thought, following what I called the 'dominant narrative', that constitutional rights applied only vertically and imposed only negative duties on the state, there was naturally a part of policy-making reserved for political autonomy where rights had no normative impact: the entire area of private law, and that part of public law which did not interfere with the negative liberty protected by constitutional rights. But the situation has changed. Under the global model with its commitment to negative and positive obligations as well as vertical and horizontal effect, constitutional rights apply in the context of both actions and omissions and both private and public law. The state has to ensure adequate protection of personal autonomy; and since almost *all* policies affect the personal autonomy of *someone*, it is not possible to delineate a sphere of political autonomy which is unaffected by the demands of personal autonomy. The consequence is that the idea of the separation of personal and political autonomy into two spheres collapses.

4. *The 'total constitution'?*

The preceding sections point to the main challenge for a theory of judicial review which fits the global model of constitutional rights. Metaphorically speaking, it is tempting to regard the domain of policy-making as a cake, and then to cut out one piece of the cake (constitutional rights) and remove it from politics. That piece could be the area of policy-making which is concerned with the preconditions of the legitimacy of the democratic process (above, section 2), or a specific, limited personal sphere (section 3). However, this image, intuitively appealing as it may be, is not compatible with the broad, autonomy-based understanding of rights employed by the global model. Rather, under the global model, constitutional rights affect the whole domain of policy-making. In other words, the entire cake is about constitutional rights.

Mattias Kumm has recently put forward a theory of judicial review which whole-heartedly embraces this proposition.[10] His approach can be summarized as follows.[11]

(1) Kumm argues that in the enlightenment tradition, rights were not perceived to cover only a limited—and certainly not a negative—domain.

> Indeed, the core task of democratic intervention in a true republic was to delimitate the respective spheres of liberty between individuals in a way that takes them seriously as equals and does so in a way that best furthers the general interest and allows for the meaningful exercise of those liberties. In this way democracy was conceived not only as rights-based, but as having as its appropriate subject matter the delimitation and specification of rights. Legislation, such as the enactment of the *Code Civil*, was rights specification and implementation.[12]

(2) What is new in post-WWII constitutionalism is not this broad under-standing of rights, but the supervisory role of the judiciary. Courts engage in what Kumm calls 'Socratic contestation'. They challenge the authorities in order to establish whether their acts are justifiable. Their role is not to assess whether the public authorities have found the 'one right answer', but rather to police whether the authorities have come up with a *reasonable* way of specifying the rights and duties of free and equal citizens.[13]

(3) This understanding of the role of courts connects to an attractive conception of democracy. The ideal of democracy is the *consent* of the governed, not *majorities*. Since actual consent is impossible to achieve in the real world, there are two surrogates that need to cumulatively be fulfilled in order for law to be constitutionally legitimate. Firstly and

---

[10] Kumm, 'The Idea of Socratic Contestation and the Right to Justification: The Point of Rights-Based Proportionality Review', (2010) 4 *Law & Ethics of Human Rights* 141; Kumm, 'Institutionalising Socratic Contestation: The Rationalist Human Rights Paradigm, Legitimate Authority and the Point of Judicial Review', (2007) 1 *European Journal of Legal Studies*.

[11] The following account does not discuss all strands of Kumm's argument; in particular, I will not deal with his argument that once the step from direct democracy to representative democracy is taken, there is no 'issue of deep principle' which would 'condemn judicial review, but not electoral representation'. Furthermore, my account will not rely on the idea of public reason, not because I consider that idea unattractive but because it is not necessary for my overall argument.

[12] Kumm, 'Institutionalising Socratic Contestation: The Rationalist Human Rights Paradigm, Legitimate Authority and the Point of Judicial Review', (2007) 1 *European Journal of Legal Studies*, 23.

[13] Ibid., 23–4.

procedurally, there must be a majoritarian decision-making process. Secondly and outcome-oriented, the outcome must plausibly qualify as a collective judgment of reason about what the commitment to rights translates into under the concrete circumstances: the result must be justifiable such that even those who disagree with it could reasonably accept it. In other words, even those burdened most heavily by the act in question must be able to interpret it as a reasonable attempt at specifying what the people owe to each other as free and equal citizens.[14]

a) Politics as oriented towards the specification of the spheres of autonomy of equal citizens

Kumm rejects the idea that rights cover only a limited domain of politics and claims, strikingly, that all of politics is about specifying the rights of free and equal citizens. This claim obviously makes sense only on the broadest possible understanding of rights. Kumm observes the tendency of contemporary constitutional rights discourse to include 'all kinds of liberty interests' in the catalogue of rights. In other places, he speaks of rights being affected whenever a person's 'interests' are engaged. I will examine these two related claims in reverse order, starting with the broad understanding of rights, and then asking whether Kumm is correct in claiming that all of politics is about rights specification. In short, I agree with the core of Kumm's argument, but think that it can be stated more precisely.

My reconstructive account as developed in the last chapters has defended rights as based on autonomy interests of individuals. When Kumm speaks of 'liberty interests' or, most often, simply 'interests', he must have in mind what I have called, more precisely, I think, autonomy interests. The term 'interests' is used in multiple ways in the theoretical literature. For example, Joseph Raz connects a person's interests to his or her well-being. So, for example, someone might argue that it is in a person's interest to read the Bible. Such a claim makes sense under an approach which connects interests to well-being, but it is surely not an understanding of interests which has a legitimate place in constitutional rights discourse. The constitutional right to freedom of religion protects an individual's *autonomy* interest in choosing and pursuing a (in the sense of: any) religion, but it is neutral with regard to the value of reading the Bible for a person's well-being. More generally speaking, rights do not

---

[14] Ibid., 27–9; Kumm, 'The Idea of Socratic Contestation and the Right to Justification: The Point of Rights-Based Proportionality Review', (2010) 4 *Law & Ethics of Human Rights* 141, 168–70.

enable people to live objectively good lives, but they enable people to act upon their ('subjective') self-conceptions of what a good life requires; this is captured by referring to the relevant interests as 'autonomy' interests.

The next question is whether Kumm is right that all of politics is about rights specification. I have argued above that under the global model there is no area of policy-making which remains unaffected by constitutional rights. Kumm's claim goes one step further: he says that policy-making is not only affected by constitutional rights, but that all policy-making *is* rights specification. I will analyse this claim in two steps. First, I will argue that, with certain qualifications, all state policy is aimed at securing the conditions of personal autonomy. Let me start with the qualification: the point and purpose of political autonomy, insofar as it relates to *the duties the political community owes to its members*, is to secure the conditions of personal autonomy. Political communities have other duties as well. First, they owe duties to other political communities; for example, Britain may owe duties to Iraq. Second, they owe duties to persons who are not members of the political community: for example, foreign immigrants or individuals living in other political communities. Third, they arguably owe duties to future generations. Fourth, there may be duties to animals or duties to preserve the environment; and these duties may be justified independently of the importance of animals or the environment for the personal autonomy of the people. Finally, there are duties which, one might say, the political community owes to itself (rather than to citizens individually): political self-government requires a legal system, political institutions, political infrastructure, a bureaucracy, staff, and so on. At this point, however, I am only concerned with the duties the political community owes to its members individually; I will therefore ignore the other duties in the remainder of the chapter and indeed the book.

With this qualification out of the way, the question is whether all state policy is about securing the conditions of autonomy. Take the example of choosing an economic policy. Political communities choose economic policies in order to serve the interests of their members. We may speak of good economic policies being in the 'public' interest; but that is just a short form for saying that they are in the interest of the people. To be more precise, they are pursued in order to serve people's *autonomy* interests: the very point of good economic policies is to lead to prosperity; and the reason prosperity is valued is that it enables people to take control of their own lives. When a very poor society reaches a modest level of prosperity, this may imply, for example, that the people do not have to constantly fight for physical survival. When a relatively wealthy society reaches an even higher level of prosperity, this means that the people will have even more resources to command; they have even more or more appealing options to choose from and thus more or better opportunities to give their lives meaning and direction. In both scenarios, the value in increased prosperity lies in its being instrumentally valuable for autonomy.

The general conclusion towards which I am steering is that the point and purpose of state policies is to enable the people to give their lives meaning and direction. Let me go through some other examples. The reason that many states maintain systems of health care lies in a concern for people's health which is a precondition of an autonomous life, as well as, partly, an element of it (control over one's body). The reason that states provide welfare (for example a social minimum) to unemployed persons is, first, to enable them to stay physically alive and healthy, which is a precondition of an autonomous life, and second, to enable them to some extent to give their lives meaning and direction even in the absence of the resources and increased opportunities which normally come with employment. The reason that states provide education is to enable people to live autonomous lives, or to increase the options they have later in life. The reason states maintain infrastructure (streets, public transport, etc.) is that this provides people with facilities which enable them to pursue their projects. The provision of public parks provides people with facilities for recreation and the enjoyment of nature. Policies are also often aimed at securing and realizing a beneficial social environment. Politicians care, for example, about creating or maintaining a sense of mutual respect, or a social climate without the presence of fear (of loss of one's job; of crime; of loss of status more generally). All these goals are autonomy-related. We should not think of autonomy as being exclusively about creating specific options which a person can then choose or reject. Rather, autonomy is more broadly about being able to give one's life meaning and direction, which takes place in a social context; and some social contexts are more beneficial than others in this respect. If all this is true, then we can generalize from the examples and conclude that *political autonomy is aimed at securing the conditions of personal autonomy.*

Second, while all state action is aimed at securing the conditions of personal autonomy, the design of policies ought not to be guided exclusively by autonomy-related considerations, but rather by a concern for the autonomy *of equals*: everyone's autonomy interests must be considered as equally important. Note that this is different from the narrower concern for 'equal autonomy'. Some might argue that the only way to treat people as equals with regard to their autonomy is to make them equally autonomous; but others will disagree and claim that treating people as equals with regard to their autonomy requires, for example, that people who invest more effort command more resources and enjoy a higher degree of autonomy as a result. I do not have to decide here which of the various possible interpretations of the equality principle is preferable; in fact it will turn out below that this is largely a question for the legislature to decide. At this stage, what matters is that the state should be concerned with the autonomy of equals, and that this has to be distinguished from the follow-up question of how the equality provision is best interpreted.

The equality principle is necessary in order to resolve *conflicts* between people's autonomy interests. Under the broad understanding of autonomy advocated here, it is clear that there will often be clashes between the autonomy interests of two or more persons: for example, there will be clashes between the autonomy interests of people who want to host parties with loud music in the middle of the night and the interests of their neighbours who want to sleep. The political community must devise a scheme which resolves such conflicts of autonomy interests, and the guiding principle must be to devise the scheme in a way which treats everyone's autonomy interests as equally important. The task of the political community is to devise a comprehensive scheme which *specifies the spheres of autonomy of its members in a way which respects their status as equals*. This is a reinterpretation of Kumm's formula of treating people as free and equal. It reinterprets the freedom part, in line with the reconstructive account of the last chapters, as positive freedom or autonomy, and connects equality to autonomy by insisting that the role of equality is to guide the resolution of conflicts of autonomy interests.

b) No independent value of well-being

The view that there is no need for any values except for autonomy and equality may seem extreme and one-sided to some who take a more pluralistic understanding of the values to be promoted by states. Cécile Fabre has argued that states have a responsibility not only for autonomy but also for a distinct value of *well-being*.

> [W]e do not only give a wheelchair to the disabled, we also relieve their physical pain, even when doing so does not increase their autonomy. But

there are other examples. Think about hunger. What we find unbearable when we watch images from Somalia, Ethiopia, from any country devastated by famine is not only the fact that these people are unable to be autonomous agents—in fact it is not generally the first thing we think of. Rather, it is the realization that they suffer horribly. Relieving hunger is also a matter of relieving this suffering. Equally, we do not want to give shelter or housing to homeless people only because without a home they cannot enjoy freedom and privacy and are therefore seriously restricted in the plans they can make for their lives, but also because they suffer from cold and exhaustion.[15]

I disagree with Fabre's argument and will focus on her example of relieving pain to prove my point. Fabre has in mind that someone may be in pain but the pain may not hinder her from pursuing her projects. So relieving her from the pain does not, under this logic, promote autonomy. However, almost everyone, when pain kicks in, immediately makes it her project—often her primary project—to get rid of the pain. Therefore, by relieving her pain, we assist her in succeeding in her project; and therefore, we have assisted her in living an autonomous life. As I have argued above, it is a mistake to regard autonomy as primarily concerning the ability to choose or reject certain options. It is *also* that, but it is broader: autonomy is about *being able to live one's life*; and the presence of pain makes a huge difference to the life one lives (even if it does not affect the options one can pursue).

Another way of making the same point is this. Under the approach defended here, the only difference between well-being and autonomy is that well-being concerns the interests of an agent, judged from an objective perspective, whereas autonomy interests concern the interests of an agent, judged from the ('subjective') perspective of his self-conception. When it comes to relieving pain, pain is almost always undesirable both from the subjective perspective of the agent and from an objective perspective: it is bad both from a well-being perspective and from a self-conception perspective. Therefore, there is no incoherence in defending the relief of pain under an autonomy-based approach.

To this argument one may object that while it is possible to pull the relief of pain under the umbrella of autonomy, this may distort the real concern and motivation of the state. Again, I disagree. Not only is it possible to think about Fabre's example in terms of autonomy; it is

---

[15] Fabre, *Social Rights Under the Constitution: Government and the Decent Life* (Oxford University Press, 2000), 20.

actually unattractive to think about it in terms of well-being. If we agreed that the state's role was to improve well-being detached from autonomy, this would imply that there was at least a prima facie case for the state to relieve pain (thus increasing well-being) even if the agent did not want to be relieved of the pain (e.g. she is a masochist): after all, the assumption is that relieving people of pain serves their well-being. To be sure, this concern for well-being might be outweighed by an independent concern for autonomy; but the fact remains that a responsibility for well-being generates a prima facie reason for action for the state to promote well-being, including cases where the agent autonomously rejects the action. This reasoning does not, however, correspond to how we think about these issues. Rather, it is common ground that respect for a person's autonomy requires not interfering with his body unless he consents: there is no balancing between his well-being and his autonomy. So the state action must be justified on autonomy grounds, not on well-being grounds. The reason why we say that the state should relieve pain, and why this is sometimes confused with a concern for well-being, is that in almost all cases, people desperately want to be relieved of pain. But in those few cases where they do not want to be so relieved, the state should not interfere. Fabre says that what we find unbearable about pictures of starving people is to see these people suffering. But we do not generally find pictures of suffering people unbearable. Many will have seen the pictures of people in some parts of Indonesia and the Philippines who have themselves crucified for a limited time at Easter. These people presumably experience extreme pain, but we do not find it unbearable to watch them, at least not in the same way as pictures of starving people; and the reason for this is that they are realizing their projects: they *want* to suffer, temporarily, in the same way that Jesus suffered. The general point is that we do not care about people suffering as such; we care, and rightly so, about people who suffer against their will. Therefore, our concern is for autonomy and not well-being.

There are several possible objections to the rejection of well-being as a legitimate state concern, which I will briefly address. First, there is the case of people incapable of leading autonomous lives, for example those who are senile or comatose, and it seems natural for the state, in these cases, to be concerned with their well-being rather than their autonomy. Fabre again:

> Furthermore, taking well-being into account enables us to make sense of the fact that we assign rights to beings who belong to the human species but who do not have the potential for developing into autonomous

persons, or who have lost their autonomy and sometimes even the potential for ever regaining it: people in deep coma, severely mentally handicapped people, and so on. They may not be autonomous, but they still belong to our species, and this, I think, is a reason for relieving their suffering, as a matter of right.[16]

This is true, to an extent, but it is not the whole truth. I agree with Fabre that there are duties towards people who have lost their capacity for autonomy and who will sometimes not even notice any longer what happens to them. These duties cannot easily be explained in terms of autonomy; rather, they seem to be based on some other value—Fabre says it is well-being; I would argue that intuitively, 'dignity' may fit better. So it may be necessary to introduce another value—well-being or dignity—for those who do not possess the capacity for autonomy. I am not convinced however that we can use this example to drive home the point that we should therefore also be concerned with the well-being of persons *capable* of autonomy. On the contrary, I believe that our inter-pretation of what dignity requires in the case of persons not capable of autonomy must rely heavily on autonomy and not, as Fabre would have it, well-being. Take the following example. Pete has smoked all his life, and at an old age becomes senile so that he is incapable of making autonomous decisions (but his senility is unrelated to the smoking). His wife Sarah nurses him. She argues that she has always, correctly, been of the view that smoking was harmful for Pete's well-being; and given that she is now in charge of his well-being, she withdraws his cigarettes. There is something wrong with her reasoning. If we respect a person's choice to smoke while he is autonomous, then once he loses the capacity for an autonomous life, we cannot just reverse his lifestyle into whatever serves his well-being. Rather, even in the light of his incapacity for autonomy, we must respect a person's personality to the greatest pos-sible extent—we must treat him with dignity—and therefore Pete should, all things being equal, still have his cigarettes. The example shows that what looks like a concern for the well-being of persons incapable of autonomy is really, often or possibly always, a concern for the *hypothetical autonomy* of this person. A concern for the well-being of a person comes in, for lack of any other guidance, only when there is no identifiable hypothetical will: we then conclude that the closest we can come to an appreciation of the hypothetical will of the person is to

---

[16] Ibid., 21.

assume that he or she would want whatever serves his or her well-being. So rather than it being the case that we need the idea of well-being to understand the duties we have to people capable of autonomy, it is the reverse: we need the idea of autonomy to understand the duties we have to people who are no longer capable of autonomy.

Second, there is the issue of paternalism. Examples of paternalistic laws arguably include prohibitions or regulations of drug use (including alcohol and tobacco), seatbelt laws, and consumer protection laws. The objection might be that the autonomy-based theory proposed here must reject any paternalism and is therefore out of touch with widely held beliefs about permissible state activity. This is not how I want it to be understood, however. The objection would be correct if we thought about paternalism in the following way: 'Sometimes people make autonomous decisions which are harmful to themselves. So when considering whether the state can stop them from harming themselves, it should balance autonomy against well-being. Depending on which value takes priority in the specific circumstances of the case, paternalistic measures may be justified.' Under this approach, there would indeed be an independent value of well-being, to be considered alongside the value of autonomy. This is, however, exactly *not* the way in which almost all of the relevant literature proceeds, and rightly so. The mainstream arguments for paternalism (as well as those, obviously, against) focus on autonomy-related reasons. One line of argument is to justify paternalism when it is maximizing freedom (read: autonomy), the idea being that it is permissible to force a person to give up a little bit of freedom now in order for her to enjoy much more freedom in the future.[17] Another, to my mind more promising, line of reasoning is to screen the decision of the agent for possible deficiencies which make it less than fully autonomous, and therefore, again, to base an interference with his autonomy on a concern for autonomy.[18] My own view, largely following John Kleinig, is that paternalism cannot be justified if it imposes a set of values on a person which that person rejects; it can sometimes be justified, however, when it aims to realize the person's *own* values.[19] What all these arguments have in common is that they

---

[17] Regan, 'Paternalism, Freedom, Identity, and Commitment', in Sartorius (ed.), *Paternalism* (University of Minnesota Press, 1983), 113.

[18] Feinberg, *The Moral Limits of the Criminal Law, v. 3: Harm to Self* (Oxford University Press, 1986).

[19] Kleinig, *Paternalism* (Manchester University Press, 1983); Möller, *Paternalismus und Persönlichkeitsrecht* (Duncker & Humblot, 2005).

insist that the only value that can possibly justify paternalism is a concern for the agent's freedom or autonomy. In other words, there is no independent concern for well-being to be balanced against autonomy, even in the domain of permissible paternalism.

Third, one might argue that limiting the state's legitimate concern to autonomy and equality neglects some crucial 'communitarian' values in favour of an 'atomistic individualism'. This is, of course, a debate that has been ongoing for a while,[20] and I have no intentions of resolving it. Suffice it to say that a concern for personal autonomy is compatible with a broad variety of arguments promoting 'community values', as long as a case can be made that realizing these community values plausibly adds value to the lives of the people, judged on the basis of their own self-conceptions. In fact, given that it is uncontroversially true that it is ethically important to be an active member of various communities, it would be plainly irresponsible for the state not to be concerned with the conditions in which people can engage with others in various forms. Thus, some form of 'community politics' is not only compatible with personal autonomy but presumably required by it. From the autonomy perspective, the only form of 'community politics' which is flatly out of bounds is one which imposes on people a set of values, community-related or otherwise, which they reject under their self-conceptions. Community centres, public sports facilities, parks, pools, concert houses and opera houses have in common that they not only expand the options that people have, but also give them opportunities to socialize and form communities; and they are valued by the people for these reasons. Policies creating the possibilities for parents to stay at home while raising children, or alternatively to continue working, not only enhance autonomy by giving people options but also by facilitating family life and thereby making good and close relations within one's family easier to achieve and uphold—something that almost everyone very much wants. A decent government trying to set up policies which create the conditions of autonomy on an equal basis will keep such considerations prominently in mind.

c) The reasonableness standard

The thesis that all state policy is about specifying constitutional rights seems to lead to the conclusion that constitutional rights completely determine all state policy, and that therefore the legislature must in each

---

[20] For an overview cf. Mulhall and Swift, *Liberals and Communitarians* (2nd edition, Blackwell Publishers, 1996).

and every case specify constitutional rights in the one right, constitutionally predetermined way. The practical consequence of this would, of course, be unacceptable: the legislature would come up with a policy; it would be challenged in court, and the constitutional court would either conclude that the legislature found the one right answer—thus upholding the policy—or that it did not find the one right answer. In the latter case, the court would send the matter back to the legislature to try again; and the new policy would again be challenged. This procedure would be repeated until the legislature had finally found the one right answer for specifying constitutional rights. To shorten the process, the constitutional court could just as well tell the legislature straight away what the one right answer was: after all, since all other answers are wrong and constitutionally illegitimate, the idea of the democratic legislature designing policies is only a farce under this model anyway. De facto, all political power would reside with the constitutional court. It is obvious that there must be something wrong with this model. It clearly violates the second desideratum because it does not leave any, let alone any important, role for the legislature. It is flatly incompatible with our understanding of democracy as a form of government where the people or their representatives debate and face genuine choice with regard to a broad range of important issues.

There are a few possible ways out of this dilemma, some of which I have discussed and rejected before. For example, limiting the domain of constitutional justice to negative freedom from the state would arguably leave large portions of policy-making unaffected by constitutional rights; but this would come at the cost of incoherence because an account of freedom as negative and vertical is morally unattractive. Another approach would be to protect as constitutional rights only *very important* autonomy interests, rather than the ever-broadening range of interests protected as a result of rights inflation under the global model. This approach, however, would lead to a situation where all the important questions are predetermined by constitutional rights (and thus eventually decided by the constitutional court), whereas the not-so-important questions (feeding birds in parks; riding in the woods, etc.) are left to the legislature. This would violate the second desideratum as well: surely any attractive account of democracy must insist that legislatures will decide more than just the unimportant questions (such as the regulation of bird-feeding), while leaving the important questions to the constitutional court.

Kumm's thesis points to a coherent solution: while all acts of public authorities specify constitutional rights, the constitutional court reviews these acts only under a reasonableness standard. So while the legislature and the constitutional court deal with exactly the same subject-matter, different standards apply to them: the legislature has the primary task of specifying the spheres of autonomy of equals in the correct way, and the constitutional court engages in a ('Socratic') review as to whether the approach chosen by the legislature is reasonable under the circumstances.

Does this model conform to the three desiderata? It respects the second desideratum because it insists on the primary responsibility of the legislature to design policies in all areas, including 'issues of high principle',[21] in other words: very *important* issues. It also awards the legislature a genuine *choice* with regard to the issues at stake, namely a choice between different reasonable solutions. It therefore reserves a meaningful, important and comprehensive role for the legislature.

What about the first desideratum, namely adequate protection of personal autonomy? The keyword here is 'adequate'. Kumm's approach does not demand that the spheres of autonomy of the people be specified in the 'correct' way; rather, 'reasonable' protection suffices. Can this be sustained?

Kumm's argument centres on the conditions of legitimacy under conditions of reasonable disagreement:

> The outcome must plausibly qualify as a *collective judgment of reason* about what the commitment to rights of citizens translates into under the concrete circumstances addressed by the legislation. Even if it is not necessary for everyone to *actually* agree with the results, the result must be justifiable in terms that those who disagree with it *might reasonably accept*.[22]

While this statement has some intuitive plausibility, it is partly question-begging. Why does the legitimacy of an act depend on grounds that might be reasonably accepted by the losing side, as opposed to grounds which provide the one right answer under the circumstances? Why should the losing side accept the burdens that come with an act which does not represent the right answer in the situation at hand?

Kumm's answer focuses on the notion of reasonable disagreement (his work is in part a response to and critique of Jeremy Waldron's and

---

[21] Waldron, *Law and Disagreement* (Oxford University Press, 1999), 213.

[22] Kumm, 'The Idea of Socratic Contestation and the Right to Justification: The Point of Rights-Based Proportionality Review', (2010) 4 *Law & Ethics of Human Rights* 141, 168 (emphasis in the original).

Richard Bellamy's arguments against judicial review, which rely heavily on the notion of reasonable disagreement). He argues at one point, quoting a court's imaginary reply to an unsuccessful claimant:

> Given the fact of reasonable disagreement on the issue and the corollary margin of appreciation/deference that courts appropriately accord electorally accountable political institutions under the circumstances, it remains a possibility that public authorities were wrong and you are right and that public authorities should have acted otherwise. But our institutional role as a court is not to guarantee that public authorities have found *the one right answer* to the question they have addressed. Our task is *to police the boundaries of the reasonable . . .* [23]

He explains further:

> Note how this understanding of the role of courts acknowledges that there is reasonable disagreement and that reasonable disagreement is best resolved using the political process. But it also insists that not all winners of political battles and not all disagreements, even in mature democracies, are reasonable. Often they are not. [24]

One interpretation of this statement is to read it as being about institutional competence (courts are good at policing the reasonable, rather than finding the one right answer); but that line of reasoning does not sit well with Kumm's overall argument which at this stage is about moral legitimacy, not institutional competence. Rather, he accepts Waldron's claim that there will be disagreement about rights issues and that often the disagreement will be reasonable. Where this is so, it is appropriate to let the elected branches have the final word even if their solution does not represent the one right answer.

This argument is not yet sufficient. It is true that often reasonable people will disagree in good faith about how to specify the spheres of autonomy of equals. However, as has been pointed out by Joseph Raz and Aileen Kavanagh, while we will often be unable to resolve reasonable disagreement regarding a specific policy question, we often have reason to trust certain people or certain procedures to be comparatively more likely to find the one right answer. [25] Imagine it turned out at some point that overall, courts are more likely than legislatures to find the one

---

[23] Ibid., 169.

[24] Ibid.

[25] Raz, 'Disagreement in Politics', (1998) 43 *American Journal of Jurisprudence* 25, 46; Kavanagh, 'Participation and Judicial Review: A Reply to Jeremy Waldron', (2003) 22 *Law and Philosophy* 451, 466–7.

right answer to the question of how best to specify the citizens' spheres of autonomy. It seems to follow, under Kumm's argument, that this would imply that from then on courts, rather than legislatures, should design policies. We are back to a variant of our old question: why should an act of a public authority which imposes a burden on someone be legitimate if it has not been reached by the procedure which is most likely to produce the one right answer?

I believe that the solution to the problem lies in a straightforward moral necessity. Given that it is supremely important that legitimate political self-government be possible (second desideratum), we are forced to accord the elected branches some leeway in their decision-making. Imagine a person wondering if he should accept as legitimate a legislative decision which imposes a burden on him. Proponents of the view that political autonomy takes precedence over personal autonomy in all cases would argue that the act is legitimate simply by virtue of the fact that a vote took place in the legislature. As I argued above, a majority vote cannot be sufficient, however; if it were, then even a majority vote to authorize a genocide would be legitimate; and that must be wrong. At the other extreme, someone might argue that a legislative decision is legitimate only if it identifies the one right answer to the problem at hand. Obviously, being a conscientious citizen, our person could normally not be sure that he was right in assuming that the legislature had failed to find the one right answer. But leaving that issue aside, if this extreme approach were correct, then hardly any policy could ever confidently claim to be legitimate, and that is normatively unacceptable for someone who believes in political self-government. So the answer *must* lie somewhere in the middle. A reasonableness standard is appropriate because, on the one hand, under normal conditions there is no reason to require anything *less* than reasonable solutions from the political process.[26] On the other hand, it seems inappropriate to require *more* than reasonableness: I cannot identify any intermediate standard between the reasonable and the correct. Any standard which requires more than reasonable results will demand the correct (the one right) result, and that is normatively unacceptable for the reasons given above.

Thus, the reinterpretation of Kumm's model proposed here respects the first two desiderata. What about the third? Does it integrate personal and political autonomy in an attractive way? Its main claim is that

---

[26] For a qualification of this statement in cases where the issues are extremely complex, see Chapter 6, section IV.2.

personal and political autonomy are not two separable spheres but deal with the same subject-matter, namely the specification of the spheres of autonomy of equal citizens. Thus, it does not present the two values as clashing but rather in harmony: political autonomy is in the service of personal autonomy. A critic might object, however, that this integration represents exactly the same kind of lame compromise which the third desideratum was supposed to prevent: political autonomy is limited in order to ensure that personal autonomy is adequately protected, and personal autonomy is protected to a smaller degree than possible (because no correct, only reasonable solutions are required) in order not to limit political autonomy too much. This conclusion would how-ever be rash. First, political autonomy is not limited in order to make it compatible with personal autonomy; rather, it turns out that the very point and purpose of political autonomy is to secure the conditions of personal autonomy. So there is no compromise, but rather a specifica-tion of the content of political autonomy. Second, with regard to personal autonomy, there is in fact a (limited) compromise. Someone might complain that she is less autonomous under the reasonableness approach than she would be under a scheme insisting on the one correct specification of her sphere of autonomy, or a scheme employing the procedures most likely to lead to correct policies. As I have argued above, this simply is a pill that has to be swallowed in the interest of democracy. As long as we insist on a democratic system with meaningful debate and real choice, there is no alternative to accepting this point.

d) Conclusion: an integrated account of constitutional rights and democracy
The upshot of the above discussion is that political autonomy is about the specification of the spheres of autonomy of equal citizens; and that an exercise of political autonomy is legitimate if it specifies the spheres of autonomy of equal citizens in a reasonable, as opposed to the one correct, way. From here it is only a small step to attractive conceptions of democracy and constitutional rights: democracy is about making majority decisions which reflect reasonable ways of specifying the spheres of autonomy of equal citizens; and constitutional rights give each citizen an entitlement to the effect that a policy which affects his personal autonomy must be based on a scheme which specifies his sphere of autonomy in a reasonable way. The doctrinal structure through which this is achieved is the acknowledgement of a general right to autonomy: any interference with this right triggers the need for

justification, and this justification will succeed if the policy in question is legitimate in the sense just described.

V. ADDENDUM: THE RIGHT TO EQUALITY

The previous section introduced the *value* of equality into the theory of rights proposed here, and this allows us to derive some conclusions about the *right* to equality, the discussion of which I postponed earlier in the book.[27] The argument of this section will be that under the standard developed above—according to which constitutional legitimacy requires that policies reflect reasonable specifications of the spheres of autonomy of equal citizens—a separate right to equality is not needed: all cases which could be constructed as involving a violation of the right to equality will also involve a violation of the right to autonomy. Thus, while it is not incoherent to accept a right to equality, it does not add anything to the protection offered by the right to autonomy.

Often, it simply does not matter whether one approaches a rights issue from an autonomy perspective or an equality perspective. Take the example of *Smith and Grady v. United Kingdom*,[28] where the ECtHR decided that the dismissal of members of the armed forces on the ground of their homosexuality violated their right to private life under Article 8 ECHR. While the ECtHR constructed this case as involving an unjustified interference with the (autonomy-based) right to private life, it would have been equally possible to resolve the case on equality grounds as being about unjustified discrimination on the grounds of sexual orientation. Let me refer to two further examples. A law banning hate speech can be seen as an interference with the right to freedom of expression or alternatively as discrimination on the grounds of political conviction (people whose political views, if expressed, would amount to hate speech, are limited in their freedom whereas other people can freely express their respective views). Banning headscarves in the public sphere can be regarded as an interference with Muslim women's rights to freedom of religion or alternatively as an unequal treatment on the basis of religious belief (or, if all religious symbols are banned, as unequal treatment of religious believers compared to non-believers).

The above examples already indicate that regarding autonomy-based and equality-based rights as two sets of rights with distinct standards

---

[27] See Chapter 2, section III.

[28] *Smith and Grady v. United Kingdom* (2000) 29 EHRR 493.

would be misleading. But my claim that equality rights are not needed goes further than this: it argues that all cases which raise equality issues can be resolved under an autonomy-based approach, and that therefore having a separate right to equality does not add anything to the protection afforded under the autonomy-based theory of rights proposed here. This can be demonstrated in the following way. Any claim to a violation of the right to equality is necessarily concerned with an instance of unequal treatment in relation to something which we might call X. For example, in *Smith and Grady*, X would stand for 'being eligible to serve in the army': in relation to being eligible to serve in the army, homosexual people are treated differently from heterosexuals. The question would then be what kind of thing must X be for it to be the case that an unequal treatment in relation to it engages the right to equality. The straightforward answer is that an unequal treatment in relation to X is relevant if X is something which matters to people; something which has some importance for the ways in which they conduct their lives. But that is, of course, precisely what is protected by the conception of personal autonomy advocated in this book. Given that there is a general right to autonomy, it follows that there is also a right to X: thus, any unequal treatment with regard to X will necessarily also constitute an interference with an autonomy-based constitutional right, triggering the need for justification. Under the approach developed above, this justification will succeed if the policy in question is based on a reasonable specification of the spheres of autonomy of equal citizens. An unjustifiably discriminatory policy violates this standard: it does not adequately specify the spheres of autonomy of *equal* citizens. Thus, all constitutionally relevant considerations will be addressed at the justification stage of the autonomy-based right to X; a separate argument relating to a right to equality is unnecessary.

As an example, take the *Brown* case, where the US Supreme Court decided that racial segregation in public schools violates the Equal Protection Clause of the Fourteenth Amendment of the US Constitution.[29] Intuitively, most people would regard this as a paradigm case on the right to non-discrimination. However, it can also be constructed as being about an autonomy-related right. The policy at stake specifies the spheres of autonomy of students as they relate to their education: in other words, it specifies the right to education, and given that there is

---

[29] *Brown v. Board of Education* (1954) 347 U.S. 483.

plainly no morally valid reason supporting segregation, it does so in a way which is unreasonable. Thus, *Brown* could just as well be regarded as a case involving a violation of the right to education.

The conclusion that the right to equality is not needed must be qualified in three ways. First, where a constitution does not include a general right to autonomy, a separate right to equality will have a role to play to fill the gap resulting from the incomplete protection of autonomy. Thus, in *Brown*, there was no alternative to constructing the case as being about discrimination because the US constitution does not contain a right to education. My argument is simply that under the theory of rights proposed in this book, a separate right to equality is not needed; it is not that equality rights cannot play a useful role under particular constitutions which depart from the conception of rights proposed here. To the extent that a particular constitution does not acknowledge a general right to autonomy, the resulting gap can indeed be filled at least partly by a separate right to equality: it comes into play when the state chooses to provide a good to some of its citizens, access to which is not protected by a constitutional right, but does so in a discriminatory way—as was precisely the case in *Brown*.

Second, there is the special issue of the coherence of a policy. Often, the state chooses a policy which in isolation may be justifiable but whose fault is that it treats others in similar circumstances differently. For example, it may be justifiable (reasonable) to ban religious symbols in public universities, and it may also be justifiable to allow them. However, presumably coherence requires that either all religious symbols are allowed or all are prohibited. Unless there are special reasons justifying the difference in treatment, a policy which bans only the religious symbols of one particular religion—say, Muslim headscarves—but not those of other religions—Christian crosses—will be discriminatory. This is a scenario which can in principle be resolved without recourse to a right to equality: an incoherent policy does not specify the sphere of autonomy of the affected right-holder in a reasonable way. In the example, a policy banning only headscarves but not crosses would interfere with the right to freedom of religion of Muslim women wanting to wear headscarves; and given its incoherence, it would not specify the spheres of autonomy of the affected women in a reasonable way; thus there would be a violation of the right to freedom of religion. But while it is possible to pull this issue under the umbrella of autonomy-based rights, the principle of proportionality as it has developed in legal practice is not well-equipped to deal with this issue because it does not contain a separate 'coherence stage' in addition to the other four stages.[30] As long as this remains the case, the right to equality has a role to play with regard to the issue of coherence.

The third way in which it may be necessary to qualify the statement that a separate right to equality is not needed is that arguably such a right has a useful rhetorical function because invoking it can sometimes direct attention to the most problematic aspect of a policy (again, *Brown* is a good example). This may be true.[31] My point in this section should not be understood as in any way critical of the right to equality as such, its possible rhetorical usefulness or its usefulness under particular constitutions or in the context of particular doctrines. All I am arguing is that under the theory of rights advocated here it is not necessary in the sense that the protection that a right-holder is entitled to under the right to equality is also available under the general right to autonomy.

VI. THE INSTITUTIONAL DIMENSION

1. The separation of powers

The conceptions of constitutional rights and democracy proposed in section IV above translate into an institutional arrangement under which the elected branches design and execute policies and the courts scrutinize whether the elected branches have acted within their political autonomy, i.e. whether they have come forward with reasonable ways of specifying the spheres of autonomy of equals. The question to be addressed in this section is whether this division of labour between the elected branches and the judiciary is compatible with an attractive conception of the separation of powers. Under a common understanding, this doctrine requires that tasks ought to be assigned to that institution which is best capable of dealing with them.[32] Thus, if constitutional legitimacy requires the protection of constitutional rights, then the institutional arrangement that ought to be chosen is the one which is most

---

[30] On the different stages of the proportionality test, see Chapter 7.

[31] There is, however, also a downside to this: invoking the right to equality can sometimes make a policy seem highly problematic when its reasonableness is in fact relatively straightforward. Some cases of policies involving affirmative action may fall into this category. Here, invoking the right to equality by focussing attention on the fact that the respective policy distinguishes, for example, on the basis of race detracts the attention from the important issue, namely that often policies involving an element of affirmative action will be entirely reasonable (if not correct).

[32] As a paradigmatic statement see Barber, 'Prelude to the Separation of Powers', (2001) 60 *Cambridge Law Journal* 59: 'The essence . . . of separation of powers lies in . . . the matching of tasks to those bodies best suited to execute them. The core of the doctrine is . . . efficiency.'

likely to lead to policies which respect rights. It follows that judicial review is justified only if and to the extent that it leads to an improvement in the protection of rights over other institutional arrangements.

Until fairly recently, the above argument was uncontested: even staunch defenders of judicial review such as Ronald Dworkin[33] accepted that the justifiability of judicial review rested on its ability to improve the overall level of rights protection; consequently much work was invested in examining the comparative strengths of courts and, in particular, legislatures. It should be noted, however, that more recently, the question has become controversial: an emerging view in the literature denies that institutional competence is the key to the institutional question. Alon Harel and Tsvi Kahana have criticized the competence-focussed approaches as misguided and have put forward an intriguing argument to the effect that there is a 'right to a hearing' before a court in situations where the claimant can make a plausible case that his rights have been violated, and that the justification of that right is at least partly independent of the quality of the resulting judicial decision.[34] Kumm's argument is more modest, but falls into the same category. He claims that there ought to be a system of judicial review even if it were 'less obvious that outcomes are improved'.[35] For him, the commitment to legislatures and courts reflects democracy's commitment to majority decision-making and providing plausible justifications; and he finds value in this symmetry, speaking of '*archetypal expressions*' of basic liberal-democratic constitutional commitments'.[36]

I will not take sides in this emerging discussion here for two reasons. First, it would be a mistake to think that, even if the authors who object to the focus on outcomes were correct, outcomes would not matter. Rather, they should be understood as saying that outcomes are not the only thing that matters: if it turned out that courts were manifestly ill-equipped to adjudicate constitutional rights claims, their defence of judicial review would collapse. Second, I believe that even on the traditional competence-based

---

[33] Dworkin, *Freedom's Law: The Moral Reading of the American Constitution* (Harvard University Press, 1996), 34: 'I see no alternative but to use a result-driven rather than a procedure-driven standard for deciding [the institutional questions]. The best institutional structure is the one best calculated to produce the best answers to the essentially moral question of what the democratic conditions actually are, and to secure stable compliance with those conditions.'

[34] Harel and Kahana, 'The Easy Core Case for Judicial Review', (2010) 2 *Journal of Legal Analysis* 227.

[35] Kumm, 'The Idea of Socratic Contestation and the Right to Justification: The Point of Rights-Based Proportionality Review', (2010) 4 *Law & Ethics of Human Rights* 141, 171.

[36] Ibid. (emphasis in the original).

grounds one can make a plausible case for the involvement of courts. My interest at this stage is not to examine comprehensively the arguments for and against the relevance of institutional considerations, or for and against the institutional competence of courts. Rather, my ambition is to make a *plausible*, albeit not conclusive, case for the institutional appropriateness of having courts involved in the adjudication of constitutional rights on the basis of the reconstructive account which has emerged in this and the previous chapters. The reason for this limitation lies in the reconstructive nature of the theory of rights proposed here. To repeat, the goal of this book is not to design the best possible theory of rights or judicial review, but to propose a theory which is coherent and fits the global model. Thus, if it turned out that it would not only be problematic but straightforwardly absurd to think that courts could perform the kind of review advocated here, this would throw doubts on the correctness of my reconstructive account: it would seem unlikely that a theory of rights which is, for example, far too complex to be applied by courts could be the best possible reconstruction of the global model which, after all, relies heavily on the involvement of courts. But if a plausible case can be made for the institutional competence of courts, then this leaves the reconstructive account proposed here undamaged.

The following assessment of the institutional competence of courts will proceed on the basis of the assumption of a *well-designed* court. Thus, importantly, my argument will *not* be that *any* court, just by virtue of its being a court, will be comparatively good at adjudicating constitutional rights claims. Obviously, much turns on the specific design of the court in question: in particular the various procedural rules; but also the rules governing its composition, the appointment of judges, the length of their tenure, and so on.[37] Therefore, all I am purporting to demonstrate is that it is plausible to believe that a *well-designed* court will be institutionally competent to deal satisfactorily with constitutional rights claims.

The authority and respect that constitutional courts adjudicating rights claims have gained around the world in recent decades indicate that on the whole, courts seem to have fulfilled their task reasonably well. Two preliminary points have to be made. First, it has to be noted that the practice of constitutional rights adjudication is a relatively recent phenomenon, and it is too early to tell whether it is based on an institutional arrangement which is likely to continue to produce the

---

[37] Ibid., 171–2.

well-respected results which, on the whole, it seems to have produced so far. Second, when analysing the practice in terms of whether it has in fact improved the outcomes, we must not make the mistake committed by some critics of judicial review, namely deriving general conclusions from a few carefully selected examples. Nobody can deny that there are instances where courts get it wrong and legislatures get it right. Kumm observes correctly that the one example Waldron chose in his recent article on judicial review, namely contrasting the US Supreme Court's decision in *Roe v. Wade* with the debates on abortion legislation in the British House of Commons,[38] does not even come close to providing a comprehensive analysis of the ability of courts to engage in judicial review.[39] In fact, the helpfulness of much of the scholarly discussion of the merits of judicial review is limited anyway because it usually refers to the experiences in the US, which is unfortunate because US constitutional rights jurisprudence seems to be an outlier in the spectrum of constitutional rights adjudication around the world.[40]

Any argument about the institutional competence of courts must start with an account of their *task*: unless we know the courts' task, we cannot assess whether they are likely to be good or bad at it. Remember that courts assess policies not with regard to whether they represent the one right answer to the problem of how to specify the spheres of autonomy of equals, but whether they represent a plausible or reasonable way of doing so. So what courts do is at the same time *similar to* and *different from* policy-making: it is *similar* in that it deals with the same subject-matter: both legislatures and courts deal with the subject-matter of the specification of the spheres of autonomy of equal citizens. It is *different* in that courts do not set up policies but assess the strength of reasons supporting a policy decision made by the elected branches. This is something we are familiar with in many different areas of life: artists and art critics deal with the same subject-matter (art), but they need different capabilities: the former's emphasis is on creativity, the latter's on analysis. Politicians and political journalists, too, deal with the same subject-matter (politics), but again, they need different abilities to carry out their tasks successfully, with the former being more active and pragmatic—identifying and tackling new problems, being receptive and

---

[38] Waldron, The Core of the Case Against Judicial Review, (2005–6) 115 *Yale Law Journal* 1346, 1384–5.

[39] Kumm, 'Institutionalising Socratic Contestation: The Rationalist Human Rights Paradigm, Legitimate Authority and the Point of Judicial Review', (2007) 1 *European Journal of Legal Studies*, 18.

[40] See Chapter 1, section IV.

responsive to changing circumstances and needs—and the latter being more reactive and, again, analytical. But while it would never occur to anyone to criticize an art critic for not being a good artist, or to criticize a political journalist for not being a good politician, judges are often criticized for not being good policy designers. This criticism, which often refers to their supposed lack of expertise, rests on weak ground because it fails to appreciate the important difference between policy-making and policy reviewing.

Let us examine the issue of expertise in more depth in order to assess whether or to what extent the criticism might be justified. Doubtless one needs *empirical expertise* in the subject-matter at stake in order to competently design or review policies, but equally doubtless, this particular expertise is not the whole story: it must be complemented with *moral expertise*. In order to develop this point, let me start with the kinds of expertise needed by policy makers before turning to that needed by policy reviewers. To *make* policies, one must engage in a two-step process. First, one must collect all the relevant data; including data about likely conse-quences of different policies. To do this well, one mainly needs empirical expertise in the respective subject-matter. Second, one must develop a scheme which, given the data identified in step one, is best in terms of specifying the spheres of autonomy of everyone; and this requires moral expertise. For example, a head teacher who has to design the school's policy regarding the wearing of religious symbols[41] will need empirical expertise about the religious backgrounds of the students and the likely consequences of adopting one scheme or the other. She will need some-thing else as well, however: an idea of how to design a policy which, based on her expert knowledge and understanding of the situation, specifies the spheres of autonomy of the pupils and everyone else in a justifiable way. She might make mistakes with regard to both issues: she might get the expert knowledge wrong for whatever reason—for example, insufficient experience or lack of intelligence—and/or she might get the policy design wrong for a number of reasons—for example, she could hold discriminatory views about some religions; or, while not holding such views, she might just be a poor policy-maker who, with the best of intentions, designs incoherent policies.

To an extent, a policy *reviewer* will carry out a task that is similar to that of a policy maker. An ideal policy reviewer must normally have the same

---

[41] See *R (SB) v. Governors of Denbigh High School* (2006) UKHL 15.

empirical expertise as a policy maker because often (not always) the question of whether a policy is reasonable will depend on the data on which it is based. It seems plausible to assume that the elected branches will normally have more empirical expertise than judges in this regard. From this it does not follow, however, that judges should always unquestioningly accept the data presented to them. First, many policy decisions rest on evidence that is readily and easily accessible to everyone, and which a judge is capable of acquiring very quickly. Second, to the extent that the relevant expert knowledge is unclear or controversial, well-designed procedural rules must enable courts to invite independent experts to testify before the court. Finally, they can assess the appropriateness of the *procedures* by means of which the policy makers have acquired the relevant data. So while it may sometimes be impossible for judges to fully understand and assess all the relevant data, and while this may lead to some degree of justified deference where the reasonableness of the policy in question depends on this data, judges will still have an important role in policy review, even with regard to the identification of the relevant data.

Regarding their moral expertise, here the situation of a policy reviewer is in some respects *different* from and in some respects *easier* than that of policy makers. It is *different* in that his task is less creative and active, and more analytical and reactive. While the policy maker has to engage in the often complex task of designing policies which specify the spheres of autonomy of everyone on an equal basis, the policy reviewer analyses the proposed policy and screens it for possible mistakes. It is *easier* in that the policy reviewer is not under the burden of having to find out whether the best possible answer to the problem at hand has been chosen, but that he must only satisfy himself of the reasonableness of the answer. It is with regard to this second stage that judges can plausibly be regarded as having exactly the right kind of moral expertise because question-asking, pressing others for justifications for their actions, and assessing the reasonableness of the reasons given, are among the core qualities of a capable judge. This moral expertise is often overlooked by the critics of the competence of judges, but it is just as important as the empirical expertise needed for the identification of the relevant data.

2. Deference

The above account of the institutional competence of courts leads straightforwardly to a theory of deference. Just like an analysis of the institutional competence of courts, a theory of the appropriate degree of deference must rest on a distinction between empirical and moral questions: as has been pointed out, to engage in policy review, a court must, first, understand the empirical issues, and must, second, assess whether the policy, on the basis of the empirical facts, represents a reasonable specification of the sphere of autonomy of the right-holder. With regard to the *empirical* stage, deference may be appropriate to the extent that the court is institutionally incapable of acquiring the relevant knowledge even with the help of independent experts; however, as has been pointed out, even then the court can assess the *procedures* by means of which the original decision-maker has acquired the facts. With regard to the *moral* stage, deference will normally be inappropriate for two reasons. First, there is normally no need for it, given that, as has been argued above, holding public authorities to account by critically examining the reasonableness of their acts is something which capable judges are well equipped to do. Second, if as a matter of constitutional law courts are entrusted with the task of deciding questions of constitutional legitimacy (and only then does any issue of deference arise), then it is hard to see why the fact that in a given case a judge might be incapable of fulfilling her task adequately should be relevant: the normal procedure must be the same as in any other legal case: she simply has to decide the case to the best of her abilities. While I wish to leave open the question of whether special considerations might apply in morally exceptionally difficult cases, a constitutional court would abdicate its constitutional role and responsibility if it *routinely* refused to interpret constitutional rights provisions, determine their normative content and apply this standard to the facts of the case before it.

To avoid a misunderstanding: when I say that deference with regard to the moral issues is inappropriate, this must not be confused with claiming that the court should engage in a correctness review. The job of the court with regard to the moral issues is to decide, without any deference, whether the policy is in the realm of the reasonable. As has been demonstrated above,[42] the reasonableness requirement is part and parcel of the moral substance of constitutional rights: if it were not, then all policy questions would be determined by constitutional rights and there would not be any room left for democratic decision-making. Thus, when a court decides that a policy, while possibly not correct, is nevertheless reasonable and therefore not in violation of constitutional rights,

---

[42] Section IV.4.c.

it does not apply any deference; rather it fully decides, without any deference, that the policy in question respects the moral requirements of constitutional rights and is therefore constitutionally legitimate.

VII. CONCLUSION

This chapter has proposed a theory of the point and purpose of judicial review which is morally coherent and fits the global model of constitutional rights. It argues that a policy, to be constitutionally legitimate, must specify the spheres of autonomy of equal citizens in a reasonable, as opposed to the one correct, way. Thus, a person's constitutional rights will be violated if a policy which imposes a burden on her cannot be defended as reasonable. This understanding of constitutional rights fits the global model with its extremely broad understanding of prima facie rights. It also reflects attractive conceptions of the values of democracy and the separation of powers. Democracy demands not only, procedurally, that the policy has been passed by a majority, but also, substantively, that it is such that it could be accepted by the person who carries the greatest burden of the policy, and this will be the case if the policy represents a reasonable specification of the spheres of autonomy of equal citizens. The principle of the separation of powers as it is conventionally understood requires that powers be distributed in a way which makes each respective branch institutionally competent in dealing with the task assigned to it; the chapter has made a plausible case for the assumption that well designed courts working under well designed procedural rules will indeed be capable of performing the specific kind of judicial review required by the global model.

The conclusion of this chapter provides only a first step towards a theory of the justification stage of constitutional rights. Its main claim regarding the specification of the spheres of autonomy of equal citizens operates at a high level of abstraction and must be interpreted further in order to derive from it more concrete propositions. The next chapters will take up this task and demonstrate that it can be refined into a set of coherent and attractive tests: the doctrines of balancing and proportionality.

6

Balancing

I. INTRODUCTION

The doctrine of balancing holds a central position in the global model of constitutional rights. It occupies the final and often decisive stage of the proportionality test, where it is used to resolve a conflict between a right and a competing right or public interest. Furthermore, in situations where the proportionality test is not used, courts often resort directly to balancing to determine the permissible limitations of rights.[1] But in spite of its undisputed practical importance, the doctrine is still under-theorized. What does it mean to say that the respective rights or interests have to be 'balanced'? This chapter provides two answers to this question, one negative and the other positive. First and negatively, it demonstrates that, contrary to some views, balancing neither refers to utilitarianism or consequentialism, nor to a mechanical exercise of quantification. Rather, at the most general level balancing ought to be understood in the sense of 'balancing all the relevant moral considerations'. Second and positively, the chapter makes proposals for the specific kinds of moral argument that are appropriate in different contexts. It will turn out that this is an enterprise of considerable complexity; and this reflects and exposes the complexity that hides under the convenient doctrinal label of balancing.

The theory of balancing to be developed here takes as its starting point the conclusions of the previous chapters. Chapters 2–4 dealt with the prima facie scope of constitutional rights, and thus focussed exclusively on the respective right-holder and her autonomy interests, ignoring the autonomy interests of others. Chapter 5 then addressed the issue of the relationship between the spheres of autonomy of different people: every person's right to autonomy is limited by the equal right of

---

[1] Consider for example the 'fair balance' test which the ECtHR applies in the case of positive obligations.

everyone else; and the task of policies is to specify each person's sphere of autonomy in line with her status as an equal. This chapter will identify as the core problem for this specification the issue of *conflicts of autonomy interests*. It is clear that under the expansive understanding of autonomy proposed in the first part of this book, there will often be such conflicts. Constitutional rights law recommends that in order to resolve them, the relevant rights or autonomy interests are to be '*balanced*'. Thus, in providing a theory of balancing, this chapter also develops an account of *the moral structure of personal autonomy in conditions of conflict*.

II. CONFLICTS OF AUTONOMY INTERESTS

The issue of conflicts of autonomy interests is not only relevant for but at the very heart of the global model and the theory of rights proposed here. Under the global model, at the final stage of the proportionality test (the balancing stage) the right is 'balanced' against the competing right or public interest. Thus, constitutional law acknowledges the centrality of conflict by reserving the most important stage of its core doctrinal tool for the resolution of conflicts. The issue of conflicts of autonomy interests is also at the heart of the reasonableness test proposed in Chapter 5: the specification of the spheres of autonomy of equals is problematic only because of conflict of interests. If a single person lives on an island isolated from the rest of the world, there is no conflict and the sphere of autonomy of this one person simply consists of what he is able to do with his life. It is only when a second person joins him that the need for a specification of the two people's spheres of autonomy arises because now the two compete for the same resources; the problem of conflict has arisen and requires a resolution. *Conflict of autonomy interests is the source of the necessity of specifying the spheres of autonomy of equals.*

Most cases of conflicts of autonomy interests are straightforward. If the state prohibits a demonstration on the grounds of a danger of it turning violent, there is a conflict between the autonomy interests of those who want to demonstrate and those who might be harmed by the resulting violence. If the state sets up a scheme which takes money from the rich and uses it to provide housing for the poor, then the conflict is between the property of the rich[2] (property being of instrumental value

---

[2] This way of posing the conflict serves its purpose; but it is slightly simplistic because it assumes that it is correct to say that the rich 'own' the resources before the redistribution is carried out; cf. Murphy and

for leading an autonomous life) and the interest in housing the poor (having housing being partly a precondition and partly an aspect of an autonomous life). If the state allows night flights which lead to noise pollution and disturb people's sleep,[3] there is a conflict of interests between the economic interest in night flights and the interest in good sleep of the affected people.

We often speak of something being in the *public* or *general* interest. This is really only a short form of saying that it serves everyone's autonomy interests. Both policy-making and constitutional rights are exclusively concerned with the specification of the spheres of autonomy of equals; therefore there is no room for public interests except in their instrumental value for the personal autonomy of equals. So we might say that it is in the public interest to have a strong army; but what we mean by this is that in terms of the control that a person has over her life, everyone benefits from the security that comes with a strong army. Similarly, in Chapter 4 I accepted the point that some constitutional rights may derive some of their importance from their contribution to the general interest, and I cited as an example the ECtHR's view that freedom of expression contributed to a democratic society's 'progress', with progress being in the general interest. But the reason that progress is in the general interest is that it serves autonomy: we value precisely that kind of progress which enables people to take control of their lives (even) better.

Public interest questions are often at the core of constitutional rights problems: think of the problem of whether there is a public interest in secularism which clashes with a student's autonomy interest in wearing a religious symbol in a public university;[4] or the problem of whether there is a public interest in the preservation of life which clashes with a pregnant woman's autonomy interest in having an abortion or a terminally ill person's autonomy interest in a dignified death.[5] The first step to the resolution of cases involving 'public' interests is to determine to what extent the respective 'public' interests are really personal autonomy interests.

Nagel, *The Myth of Ownership* (Oxford University Press, 2002), 8. But the point which is important here is that a particular resource will, after the redistribution has taken place, be controlled by either the rich person or the poor person, and it is this interest in controlling this particular resource which is the source of the conflict: both the rich and the poor person have an autonomy-related interest in it; only one of them will get it; thus there is a conflict.

[3] *Hatton v. United Kingdom* (2003) 37 EHRR 28.

[4] *Şahin v. Turkey* (2007) 44 EHRR 5, para. 114.

[5] Cf. *Cruzan v. Director, Missouri Department of Health* (1990) 110 S.Ct. 2841, 2853, recognizing an 'unqualified interest in the preservation of human life'.

III. BALANCING

1. *Four concepts of balancing*

The global model of constitutional rights recommends that in the case of a conflict between a right and another right or a public interest, *balancing* is the appropriate method to determine which right or interest takes priority. But what does that mean? Balancing is a concept often used not only in constitutional rights law and moral philosophy but also in everyday language, and this popularity already indicates that it is a particularly *useful* concept. This section will show that part of what makes it useful is its flexibility: balancing can mean very different things. The following four kinds or concepts of balancing are reconstructions of different ways in which the term can meaningfully be used. They point not to completely separate meanings; rather, each concept includes the previous one(s) but is broader; thus the four kinds of balancing can be imagined as four concentric circles.

The first and narrowest concept simply puts the two (or more) competing autonomy interests on an imaginary set of scales; and their respective weight is determined, in accordance with the approach developed in Chapter 3, with reference to their importance from the perspective of the self-conceptions of the agents. One might call this kind of balancing a 'utilitarianism of autonomy interests' (parallel to Nozick's 'utilitarianism of rights'[6]) or 'autonomy maximization': the controlling factor is the weight of the respective autonomy interests, which is determined with reference to the perspective of the agent whose autonomy is at stake; and preference is given to the weightier autonomy interest. I shall refer to this kind of balancing as *autonomy maximization*.

The second kind of balancing is slightly broader. It still works with the image of scales, but it does not necessarily determine the weight of the respective autonomy interests exclusively with regard to their importance for the self-conceptions of the agents; rather, it acknowledges that there may be moral reasons which require the adjustment of the weight ascribed to an autonomy interest. I shall call this kind of balancing *interest balancing*. I cannot provide a complete typology of all possible kinds of reason which make such adjustments necessary, but I will give three examples. The first is where a person's *prior behaviour* makes him wholly or partly *responsible* for the situation in which he finds himself. Take the case of Joe and Jill, who allowed the tabloids exclusive and comprehensive coverage of their

---

[6] Nozick, *Anarchy, State, and Utopia* (Basil Blackwell, 1974), 28.

marriage, which is in line with their self-conceptions as people who like to share good news with the world but keep bad news private. A year later they divorce, again under great media interest, and Joe is upset by the media coverage of this. Joe's autonomy interest in keeping the divorce private is relatively weighty because it is an important part of his self-conception to keep bad news private. But it would be plausible to argue that the weight one should attach to this interest should not be exclusively determined by the importance of this aspect of his privacy for his self-conception; rather there should be another relevant factor: the weight of Joe's interest in privacy is reduced (though not necessarily to zero) because of his previous choice to expose and thus direct public attention to his marriage.

The second example—*competition harm*—is taken from Ronald Dworkin who explains it in the following way:

> We live our lives mostly like swimmers in separate demarcated lanes. One swimmer gets the blue ribbon or the job or the lover or the house on the hill that another wants ... [E]ach person may concentrate on swimming his own race without concern for the fact that if he wins, another person must therefore lose. That inevitable kind of harm to others is, as the old Roman lawyers put it, *damnum sine injuria*. It is part of our personal responsibility – it is what makes our separate responsibilities personal – that we accept the inevitability and permissibility of competition harm.[7]

Thus, if you open a shop next to mine and as a consequence I lose many customers, then this greatly affects my control over my life: I can no longer make profit in the same way as before. Now I might argue that this poses a conflict of autonomy interests: your interest in earning a living versus mine; that this conflict should be resolved by balancing the competing interests; and that therefore we should ask which of us needs his shop more urgently. But that would obviously be wrong; and Dworkin's idea of competition harm explains why we should adjust the weight of my autonomy interest to 'zero': it is part of my personal responsibility to accept competition and any harm to my autonomy flowing from it.

I will just briefly mention the third example—*ethical disapproval*—but will postpone its full discussion until the next chapter. Sometimes people have autonomy interests which come into existence only because of their ethical disapproval of another person's lifestyle. The classic case is that a homophobic person might feel uncomfortable about having to

---

[7] Dworkin, *Justice for Hedgehogs* (Harvard University Press, 2011), 287–8 (emphasis in the original).

work with gays or lesbians (for example as part of his employment). As I will argue in the next chapter, while the homophobic person's autonomy interest in not having to deal with homosexuals may be genuine— he may suffer genuine discomfort if he must work with them—it ought not to be accorded any weight under an interest balancing approach: in a community committed to personal freedom, the harm to one's autonomy which rests merely on disapproval of another person's lifestyle cannot be a morally relevant consideration to be balanced against the other person's autonomy interests.

My third understanding of balancing—*formal balancing*—no longer works with the image of scales; thus the balancing metaphor is somewhat misleading. But it is still about balancing in the sense that none of the two (or more) competing interests takes unconditional priority; thus, there is a trade-off between the two interests and it is plausible to say that the right way to resolve the conflict is 'to strike a balance'. But in contrast to interest balancing, under formal balancing the conflict between the two autonomy interests is resolved by recourse to a moral argument which may be wholly or partly *insensitive* to the weights of the two interests at stake. For example, let us stipulate that, as some argue, torture would be permissible in the 'ticking bomb case' if the police could thereby save at least, say, one thousand lives. This would be a case in which, while autonomy maximization and interest balancing (the first two forms of balancing) would not be adequate, formal balancing would apply: even if torturing one person for the sake of ten others is impermissible, when we increase the number of lives to be saved, eventually the balance will tilt in favour of allowing torture and saving the many lives; in this sense there is a trade-off between the terrorist's interest in not being tortured and the possible victims' rights to life, and it is plausible to say that there is a balance to be struck between the two.[8]

The fourth kind of balancing—*balancing as reasoning*—regards balancing simply as a matter of assessing the relative strength of reasons. We

---

[8] The difference between interest balancing and formal balancing is that under an interest balancing approach, all that counts is the agent's interest in a particular aspect of his autonomy (X), whereas under formal balancing what matters is not only X but also the *means* used to achieve the protection of X. In the example, it is a relevant consideration that the means to protect the lives of the innocent people is torture. This cannot be captured by interest balancing: the interest of the innocent people in their lives is independent of whether or not torture must be used to protect them; but of course the fact that torture must be used to save them is relevant for the question of whether it is permissible to protect their lives. Thus, interest balancing cannot capture the moral complexity and formal balancing, which allows for the inclusion of the additional argument regarding the means used to protect the interests at stake, is required.

sometimes say that we need to 'balance' all the morally relevant considerations, and what we mean by that is that we have to develop a moral argument. Thus, balancing as reasoning applies in *all* cases of conflicts: it is always correct to say that a conflict of autonomy interests has to be resolved in line with a sound moral argument. Even in the case of an absolute prohibition of torture we could still say that we have to 'balance' the reasons for and against torture and conclude that it is impermissible. Balancing then is a synonym for practical reasoning.

2. Implications for balancing in constitutional rights law

Can the above four concepts of balancing be of assistance in determining the proper meaning of balancing in constitutional rights law? A preliminary point to note is that the choice is not between any of the concepts in isolation, such as between concept 1 (autonomy maximization) and concept 3 (formal balancing). Rather we have to keep in mind that the four concepts relate to each other in the fashion of four concentric circles: each one includes the previous ones. Thus, balancing as reasoning is *always* appropriate: it simply directs us to moral argument in order to resolve the conflict. In those relatively few cases where one interest takes unconditional priority (such as arguably in the case of a conflict between freedom from torture and security), balancing as reasoning is indeed the only applicable kind of balancing. In all other cases, formal balancing applies as well: the correct moral argument requires a trade-off between the two values. In those cases of formal balancing where the trade-off operates such that all that matters is the importance of the respective interests, interest balancing, too, is appropriate. Thus, in those cases the appropriate balancing is at the same time balancing as reasoning, which takes the form of formal balancing, which is to be conducted as interest balancing. Finally, where, additionally, the importance of the respective interests is precisely the importance of those interests from the perspectives of the self-conceptions of the agents, autonomy maximization applies together with balancing as reasoning, formal balancing and interest balancing.

It follows that the correct starting point into an investigation of what kind of balancing is appropriate in constitutional rights law must be balancing as reasoning; in other words: the idea of balancing does not without further argument give us guidance other than that a moral argument about the correct balance between the competing values has to be made. There is no 'default' in favour of, say, balancing as autonomy maximization or interest balancing. If in a given case one or more of the other kinds of balancing is appropriate, then this is itself a conclusion of a moral argument: for example, the moral argument might lead to the (intermediate) conclusion that the two autonomy interests ought to be placed on the scales under an interest balancing approach.

3. The simpleton and his critic

The above discussion allows us to see both the appeal and the danger of recurring to the language of balancing. Its appeal is that one never makes a mistake when saying that in order to resolve a conflict of interests, one needs to engage in balancing: as shown above, balancing as reasoning is always appropriate. Its danger, however, is to make the mistake of equating balancing with autonomy maximization or one of the other, narrower kinds of balancing and to argue that balancing necessarily refers to a simple utilitarian or mechanical exercise of quantification. This mistaken approach could be taken in two directions. First, a simple-minded defender of constitutional rights law under the global model could try to rely on it to show the appeal of constitutional rights law by pointing to the fact that it is very easy to apply: all that has to be done is to perform a simple utilitarian or mechanical balancing act! Second, a critic could respond to the simpleton and use the mistaken equation of balancing with simple aggregation or mechanical quantification to make his case for the worthlessness of the doctrine of balancing: his point would be that since it is obvious that reasoning with rights must be much more complex than that, balancing does not do justice to the moral complexities involved in reasoning with rights.

But the truth is that both the simple-minded fan of the global model and his critic are wrong. The former is wrong because he uncritically subscribes to the simplistic approach to balancing where the only viable approach will be much more complex; and the latter is wrong because he attacks a straw man, namely an unattractive and over-simplistic account of balancing. The correct approach is to acknowledge that at the most general level, balancing simply points to the need to resolve a conflict of autonomy interests in line with moral principles. We must abandon the idea that balancing could offer a 'shortcut' to moral truth and engage in the difficult work of developing a set of moral principles which can provide guidance in the resolution of such conflicts. This is the task of the next section.

IV. RESOLVING CONFLICTS OF AUTONOMY INTERESTS

The upshot of the previous sections is that the idea of balancing does not offer us further guidance as to the proper resolution of conflicts of autonomy interests except in that it directs us to develop a moral argument about the correct 'balance' between the two values at stake. It follows that we have to take a step back and start afresh, focussing on the conclusions drawn earlier, namely that the point and purpose of policies is to specify the spheres of autonomy of equal citizens, and that at the heart of this specification lies the problem of conflicts of autonomy interests.

The proposition that policies are about the specification of the spheres of autonomy of equal citizens must be fleshed out further for our purposes. Can we give an account of what policies are trying to achieve? What are the problems they are trying to tackle? I wish to propose the following model which identifies three goals that policies can legitimately pursue in order to set up a system which specifies the citizens' spheres of autonomy adequately. My claim is not that those three goals are the *only* goals pursued by policies, but that, taken together, they form a large part of the set of legitimate goals. Each goal is a response to a problem which arises from the citizens' entitlement to have their spheres of autonomy specified in line with their status as equals. The *first* kind of policy, which is the most important one in constitutional rights law from a practical point of view, is about *regulation of harmful behaviour*. Generally speaking, it regulates situations where one person wants to engage, or is suspected of planning to engage, in some kind of behaviour which affects, or whose permissibility has an impact on, another person's autonomy. Core examples include prohibitions of murder and theft; a legal system which allowed those activities would fail to adequately protect the autonomy of those affected by the harmful acts of others. Examples closer to the practice of constitutional rights law are the regulation of clashes between freedom of the press and privacy rights; or the permissibility of killing or imposing other harm on the autonomy of someone suspected of posing a threat to others. The *second* kind of policy is *redistributive*: it redistributes resources in line with a plausible conception of equality. The problem that it addresses is that without some measure of redistribution there will exist inequalities between the citizens which may not be compatible with their status as equals. For example, if some people in the community are very rich and others do not even have access to the most basic goods to enable them to live an autonomous life, then without a policy addressing this inequality the spheres of autonomy of the poor will not have been specified in line with their status as equals. The *third* kind of policy is about *providing public goods and services*. This kind of policy is a response to the insight that the state can often greatly enhance people's autonomy by providing certain goods which are funded by all and available to all, such as infrastructure or arguably health services.

Each of these three kinds of policies—regulating harmful behaviour, redistributive, and providing public goods and services—resolves a conflict of interests; and thus some kind of balancing is appropriate. By developing a moral argument about the proper structure of the resolution of those conflicts, the following sections will also clarify what kind of balancing is appropriate in what scenario. The conclusion will be that in most cases, formal balancing but not interest balancing is required: a moral argument has to be made which is more complex than simply putting the respective interests on the scales, adjusting the weights and comparing them. However, in some cases interest balancing and occasionally even autonomy maximization will be appropriate. Thus, the following sections will illuminate the idea of balancing in constitutional rights law in an indirect way: not by starting with an exploration of the meaning of balancing, conducted independently of the moral argument about the specification of the spheres of autonomy of equal citizens, but rather by going back and forth between the four concepts of balancing and the moral argument, constantly asking which kind of balancing is appropriate in the respective situation in order to resolve the conflict in a morally sound way.

1. *Regulating harmful behaviour*

This section deals with the regulation by the state of the position of one person (or group of persons) vis-à-vis another. Core examples of such regulation are the prohibition of certain forms of harmful or dangerous behaviour, often but not necessarily under threat of punishment, such as the prohibitions of murder or theft, or the regulation of driving at excessive speed and other dangerous activities. Most problems in constitutional rights law, at least with regard to civil and political rights, are about the proper regulation of harmful behaviour.[9] Can a woman

---

[9] By behaviour I mean both acts and omissions. Most problems in the practice of constitutional rights law are about acts; the relevance of omissions is largely limited to the issue of conscientious objection, discussed below.

choose abortion at the cost (if it is a cost) of the life of the fetus? Can a person demand assistance with her plan to commit suicide when the permissibility of assisted suicide might lead to other persons being killed by their relatives or bullied into committing suicide? Can a person engage in racist speech if this is harmful to the targeted minority? Can a demonstration be prohibited if there is the risk that a counter-demonstration would lead to violence? Can the state allow night flights if they affect the ability of the residents living near the airport to sleep at night?

All the questions above point to conflicts of autonomy interests; and unsurprisingly, the answer that constitutional law would give to the resolution of these conflicts is to 'balance' the competing interests. We already know from the previous sections that this answer is technically correct because it is certainly true to say that the respective conflicts of interests must be resolved in line with a sound moral argument; thus, balancing as reasoning will apply. But it is a possibility worth exploring—indeed it is quite plausible to assume—that at least in some cases of conflict one or more of the other forms of balancing will apply as well. My argument in this section will be that while interest balancing is sometimes appropriate, in most cases we are presented with the necessity of formal balancing but not interest balancing. This means that while none of the two interests takes unconditional priority, the moral argument as to which interest takes priority in a concrete example will not normally lead to the conclusion that all that matters is the importance of the two interests at stake. This section will argue that the key to resolving conflicts concerning the regulation of harmful behaviour lies not in the weights of the respective interests at stake but in the *specific relationship* which the activity in question creates between the agent and other persons.

a) Regulating behaviour which harms others in a way which uses them as a means for the agent's projects

The general principle
The first of several kinds of relationship between the agent and those harmed is where the latter are *used as a means* for the purposes of the agent. The *Transplant Case*, widely discussed in moral theory in debates about consequentialism versus deontology, serves to illustrate the point. Five people need organs to survive; and the only way to save them is to kill one healthy person and use his organs to save the five. Should this be permissible? The case illustrates the danger of unreflective use of the language of 'balancing': there is a conflict between the interests of five

people in their lives and the interest of one person in his life; and in constitutional rights terminology, to resolve this conflict we need to 'balance' the interests at stake. Interest balancing would indicate that the right answer is to kill the one to save the five: five lives must outweigh one life! Yet our intuitions rebel against this conclusion. Now, one might say that the reason why we are so opposed to the idea of killing lies in slippery slope arguments of various kinds (allowing the killings undermines people's trust in doctors; it is a rule that could be abused; etc.); or that interest balancing must include, for example, the long-term side effects of permitting the killing in this case; and that this might justify the conclusion of prohibiting the killing of the one. But we can immunize the example against these objections by stipulating that nobody would ever find out. Even now, it seems that it must be impermissible to kill the one in order to save the five, and this shows that the real problem lies deeper.

In fact, the example shows the intellectual poverty of interest balancing: this method simply has no potential to grasp and resolve the morally problematic aspect of the *Transplant Case*. What is it that makes it wrong to kill the one, and is there a general conclusion to be drawn? In the philosophical literature several principles have been proposed to deal with this and similar cases. The most famous but slightly dated one is the *doctrine of double effect* according to which there is a relevant distinction between harm that is intended and harm that is merely foreseen. In the *Transplant Case*, the harm to the victim is intended since removing his organs and thus harming him is a necessary step on the way to saving the five. Other authors rely on the impermissibility of using people as a means, which is determined as an objective matter independently of (subjective) states of minds (such as whether or not the agent had a particular intention). What using people as a means involves has been nicely explained by Alec Walen in his distinction between enablers and disablers.[10] To explain his point, it is helpful to look at the famous *Trolley Problem*:[11] suppose a trolley is heading towards a group of five people. It is going to kill them unless it is redirected to a second track where it will kill one person instead. Is it morally permissible or required to redirect the trolley? Compare this case to the *Fat Man Case*: again, a trolley is heading towards the five, but this time the only

---

[10] Walen, 'Doing, Allowing, and Disabling: Some Principles Governing Deontological Restrictions', (1995) 80 *Philosophical Studies* 183.

[11] Kamm, *Morality, Mortality. Volume II: Rights, Duties, and Status* (Oxford University Press, 1996), ch. 6; Thomson, 'The Trolley Problem', (1985) 94 *Yale Law Journal* 1395.

way to stop it is to take a fat man and throw him onto the tracks. The trolley will crash into the man and come to a halt; the fat man will die but the five will remain uninjured. In both cases one has the option of preventing five from being killed by killing one; yet most people would be prepared to redirect the trolley in the first case but not to throw the fat man onto the tracks in the second case. Walen's distinction can be explained with regard to these two cases. In the first scenario, it would doubtless be permissible (or required) to redirect the trolley if there were no person on the other track. The claim of the one person on that track is therefore that his being on the track should *disable* the otherwise permissible rescue action. By way of contrast, in the *Fat Man Case*, the fat man is instrumental to the success of the rescue action. He is being *used as a means* to stop the trolley and thus *enable* the rescue action.[12] One could also say: in the original *Trolley Case*, the one on the second track is the *problem*; whereas in the *Fat Man Case*, the fat man is the *solution*.[13]

I am not yet concerned with what should happen in the case of disablers; but there seems to be a consensus that killing enablers—using people's lives (without their consent) as the solution to a problem—is wrong (except possibly in extreme cases). But there is no reason to limit the appeal of this principle to cases of killing. Rather, the general point is that it must normally be impermissible to harm another person in a way which uses his personal resources[14]—his life, body parts, property, liberty—in the pursuit of one's projects (without the other's consent).

This conclusion must be qualified in two ways. The first concerns *accommodation*; but I will postpone the discussion of this concept until the next section because it is more relevant with regard to the cases discussed there. The second qualification concerns cases of an *extreme disparity between benefit and sacrifice*. Mattias Kumm, who has subscribed to Walen's distinction between enablers and disablers and introduced it to constitutional rights theory,[15] gives as an example a law that requires a passer-by to suffer minor inconveniences to aid another person in serious distress.[16] Requiring a passer-by to make a phone call to request

---

[12] Walen, 'Doing, Allowing, and Disabling: Some Principles Governing Deontological Restrictions', (1995) 80 *Philosophical Studies* 183, 195–9.

[13] I am grateful to my colleague Jo Braithwaite for proposing this elegant formulation.

[14] For my usage of this term see Chapter 2, section II.

[15] Kumm, 'Political Liberalism and the Structure of Rights: On the Place and Limits of the Proportionality Requirement', in Pavlakos (ed.), *Law, Rights and Discourse: The Legal Philosophy of Robert Alexy* (Hart Publishing, 2007), 131, 154.

[16] Ibid., 163.

an ambulance in order to save a person who has just suffered a heart attack seems permissible in spite of the fact that this also uses the passer-by as a means. But this does not show that using people as a means is generally permissible: in terms of the interests at stake, it is clear that having to make a phone call is only a minor interference with a person's autonomy, whereas the importance of the autonomy interest of the other person is great (life is at stake). It would probably not be permissible to require a person to invest days of work to rescue a complete stranger in spite of the fact that on an interest balancing approach, days of work still count for much less than a life. And it would surely be impermissible to require a person to sacrifice an arm or a leg to save a complete stranger, again, in spite of the fact that an arm is less important than a life. So what justifies the legal duty to call an ambulance in an emergency is that while this uses the coerced person as a means, there is an extreme disparity between sacrifice and goal. If this is correct, then, given that there is no unconditional ban on such behaviour, formal balancing (but not interest balancing) applies to the case of using people as a means. The conclusion of the above argument is the following general principle: *with the exception of extreme cases and possibly of cases requiring accommodation, the state is justified in denying, and indeed is required to deny, one person the pursuit of his project if this would involve harming others (without their consent) in a way which uses them as a means.*

Application to constitutional rights law

Does the principle formulated above help to illuminate aspects of constitutional rights law? It is certainly relevant in the sense that it has such a strong intuitive grasp on us that most cases are entirely uncontroversial and for this reason alone do not come up in the case law. Take again the example of the *Transplant Case*. If interest balancing were correct, then forcing people to make organ donations, in fact killing them to use all their organs, would not only be permissible; it would even be required, in light of the fact that the good done outweighs the harm so clearly: the state would violate its positive obligation towards people in need of organs if it did not kill healthy people in order to use their organs to save a greater number. But the fact that we do not seriously consider such policies shows that we are already committed to rejecting an interest balancing approach and accepting the prohibition of harming others in a way which uses them as a means.

The clearest example of a constitutional right which can be explained by the prohibition of using others as a means is the prohibition of slavery.[17] A slaveholder uses the liberty of his slaves as a means to his own ends, and it is exactly this specific relationship which makes slavery impermissible. Its prohibition would be required even if it could be demonstrated that on the whole, a society which endorses slavery would be better off than one without slavery (for example, because it might turn out that slavery is very efficient and leads to economic advantages which outweigh, on an interest balancing approach, the harm to the autonomy of the slaves). While theoretically the prohibition of using others as a means is not absolute but can be overcome in extreme cases, it is implausible to assume that such an extreme case could ever occur in the case of slavery because, first, unlike in the example regarding the duty to call an ambulance, the harm imposed on the autonomy of a slave is so enormous, and, second, the institution of slavery is by its nature not something that can plausibly be set up for a short time in order to address an emergency but, where it exists, is usually a long-term structural feature of the way in which a given society is organized. It follows that the prohibition of slavery, which is absolute as a matter of law, is also absolute as a matter of morality. While in a technical sense, it is possible to speak of the need to strike a balance between the interests of the would-be slaves and those of the would-be slaveholders, and therefore 'balancing as reasoning' applies, formal balancing is not applicable because for all practical purposes one of the two interests takes unconditional priority.

There exist less extreme cases involving the claim of one party to be entitled, as a matter of right, to harm the other party in a way which uses it as a means. The first *von Hannover* case is one such example.[18] Princess Caroline of Monaco had been followed by paparazzi for a long time, who had taken pictures of her and sold them to tabloids and gossip magazines which then published them. The European Court decided that Germany had violated its positive obligation under Article 8 of the Convention (the right to private life) by not protecting Caroline from such activities. To arrive at this result, the Court 'balanced' the right to freedom of the press against Caroline's right to private life, concluding that as long as the publications did not contribute to a discussion of general interest, the right to private life took priority.

Under an interest balancing approach it is not clear that this is the right outcome. After all, on the one side of the scales, there is Caroline's interest

---

[17] See, for example, Art. 4(1) ECHR.

[18] *von Hannover v. Germany* (2005) 40 EHRR 1.

in privacy; but on the other side, there are the interests of thousands of people who derive pleasure from reading gossip about celebrities illustrated by unauthorized pictures. But interest balancing is not appropriate in this case because it involves the journalists harming Caroline and using her as a means to their ends. The interest protected under Article 8 ECHR is the right to control one's public image, which is an aspect of a person's identity (the social identity, namely the way in which a person sees himself through the eyes of others).[19] This right is obviously not absolute and it may be necessary to qualify it for information which the public has a right to receive, in particular for reasons related to democracy and the marketplace of ideas. If one concludes, as the European Court did to my mind correctly, that these qualifications do not apply in Caroline's case (because the reported facts were not capable of contributing to a debate of general interest),[20] then what the paparazzi did was simply to take away from Caroline something she was entitled to control—aspects of her social identity—and sell it for profit. This is no different in principle from taking another person's property or body parts in order to sell them for profit. It involves harming and using what rightfully belongs to the other as a means for one's own ends, and this is normally impermissible. It would be wrong to try to resolve the conflict of interests by engaging in an exercise of interest balancing between Caroline's, the journalists' and the readers' interests (and as mentioned, it is not at all clear what the outcome of that balancing process would be). Rather, the correct way of balancing is formal balancing: while there is no absolute prohibition on using others as a means—if for some reason one could save lives by publishing a private picture of Caroline's, then the outcome might be different—such behaviour can only be justified in extreme circumstances.

Another case to be considered here is the *Aviation Security Act* case which concerns a German law which gave permission to the Minister of Defence to order the shooting down of a hijacked plane in a 9/11 scenario.[21] The German Federal Constitutional Court argued that this violated the right to

---

[19] Möller, *Paternalismus und Persönlichkeitsrecht* (Duncker & Humblot, 2005), 84–8.

[20] In a second *von Hannover* case, decided by the Grand Chamber, von Hannover lost because it was held that the reporting of her being on holiday while her father, Prince Rainier of Monaco, was seriously ill, could reasonably have been held by the German courts to contribute to a debate of general interest; see *von Hannover v. Germany (no. 2)*, Application nos. 40660/08 and 60641/08.

[21] BVerfGE 115, 118 (*Aviation Security Act*). For a discussion of the case, see my 'On Treating Persons as Ends: The German Aviation Security Act, Human Dignity, and the Federal Constitutional Court', (2006) *Public Law* 457. For a further analysis of the moral problems, see my 'The Right to Life Between Absolute and Proportional Protection', in Bronitt, Gani and Hufnagel (eds.), *Shooting to Kill: Socio-Legal Perspectives on the Use of Lethal Force* (Hart Publishing, 2012).

life in conjunction with the human dignity of the innocent passengers aboard the plane. Balancing the lives of the innocent passengers against the lives of those who would die were the terrorist plot to succeed was impermissible because it would, according to the Court, amount to using the passengers as a means to the rescue action, and this was absolutely prohibited. So here we have the rare case where a court explicitly resorts to the idea of the prohibition of using others as a means and declares a law unconstitutional on this ground. Had the Court been correct in its assumption that shooting down the plane would use the innocent passengers aboard as a means, it would indeed, according to the argument developed above, have followed that interest balancing (in this case counting and comparing numbers of lives to be saved) would have been impermissible. The problem is that, in fact, shooting down the plane would *not* involve using the innocent passengers as a means because those passengers are disablers: their presence would not enable the rescue action in the way in which the presence of the fat man enables the rescue action in the *Fat Man Case.*[22] In other words, the passengers would be the problem for, not the solution to, the rescue action. While this part of the reasoning of the Court is mistaken, it does not follow without further argument that the outcome of the case is also wrong; interest balancing might be misguided in the case of disablers as well (I will say more about this below). But we could modify the case and say that the terrorists threatened to direct the plane into a building containing many innocent people unless one specific innocent person on the ground (say, the hijacker's ex-girlfriend) was killed by the state. Such a killing would have involved using the ex-girlfriend as an enabler (or as the solution to the problem), and that would have been impermissible.

b) Regulating behaviour which harms others (without using them as a means)

The harm principle
One of the reasons why the doctrine of double effect has lost favour more recently is that it cannot capture some of the cases which involve the imposition of harm on some which is not intended but merely foreseen, but which still seems impermissible. Philippa Foot came up with the following example: suppose you could perform an operation to save five lives, but the gas used for the operation would seep into a neighbouring

---

[22] Möller, 'The Right to Life Between Absolute and Proportional Protection', in Bronitt, Gani and Hufnagel (eds.), *Shooting to Kill: Socio-Legal Perspectives on the Use of Lethal Force* (Hart Publishing, 2012).

room where it would kill one (*Operation Case*). It seems impermissible to perform the operation in spite of the fact that the one is not being used as a means and his death is not intended either.[23] Another case which illustrates the point is the *Car Case*: a person is rushing to the hospital to save five people, foreseeing that he will run over and kill one person on the road.[24] Again, this seems impermissible in spite of the fact that the one person on the road is not being used as a means (he is a disabler).

I will argue below that for most practical purposes of constitutional rights law, it is correct to say that the state is normally justified in stopping a person from imposing harm on others in the pursuit of his projects. But before making that argument, I must add a disclaimer: moral philosophers have come up with various cases in which it does indeed seem permissible to impose such harm. However, those cases are of what one could call a more 'academic' nature for which there will be few real life examples (however, there are some; see the discussion of the *Aviation Security Act* case further below). One such case is the original *Trolley Case*, discussed above, where it seems permissible to redirect the trolley from the five to the one. For most practical purposes, however, it is true to say that it is impermissible to impose harm on some in order to save the many. The parallel I want to draw for conflicts of interests and constitutional rights law is that *the state is normally justified in prohibiting an agent's activity which, while not using another person as a means, imposes harm or risk of harm on others, even if the gain that the agent can derive for his autonomy outweighs the harm to the autonomy of the others.* In other words, interest balancing will be inadequate for scenarios where the imposition of harm on others (while not using them as a means) is at stake. For lack of a better name, and in spite of the philosophical baggage that comes with it, I shall call this principle the *harm principle*.

The harm principle has intuitive appeal. It reflects the widely held view that when we go about our business, we normally have to do so without harming others. Taken together with the prohibition of harming others in a way which uses them as a means (which is a subset of harming others: harming them *in a particular way*), it thus expresses an important limit of a person's entitlement to pursue her projects.

---

[23] Cited according to Kamm, *Morality, Mortality. Volume II: Rights, Duties, and Status* (Oxford University Press, 1996), 151.

[24] Foot, *Moral Dilemmas* (Oxford University Press, 2002), 81. The formulation used here derives from Kamm, *Intricate Ethics: Rights, Responsibilities, and Permissible Harm* (Oxford University Press, 2007), 22.

To be sure, the cases discussed in philosophy are different from my harm principle in several ways, and these differences require at least three modifications. *First*, they are about agents saving *others*, not saving their *own* lives. But we can easily modify the examples of the *Car Case* and the *Operation Case* to accommodate this. It would surely be impermissible for an agent to drive to the hospital to save his own life if this involved driving over another person who would as a consequence lose a leg; and it would be equally impermissible for an agent to perform a life-saving operation on himself if this involved using a gas that would seep under the door and seriously injure another person. We may consider, following certain developments in criminal law, to hold such actors to be excused under certain circumstances, but we would not regard their behaviour as justified, i.e. the morally right thing to do.

The *second* way in which the philosophical cases are different and more limited than the harm principle is that I intend the harm principle to apply to all kinds of harming others, not only killings. There is no principled reason—pertaining specifically to the importance of life or the evil of killing—to restrict the appeal of the harm principle to instances of killing. However, for cases other than killings the harm principle as stated above must be qualified in two ways. First, just as in the case of using others as a means, it has to be qualified for cases of extreme disparity between harm and benefit. Suppose that a person is being rushed to hospital, but to save him in time the driver has to drive over an expensive vase which will be smashed. It seems clear that driving over the vase is permissible; but parallel to the case involving the phone call to save an injured person, this is not the case because the interest in saving the injured person outweighs the interest of the vase owner in his property. If interest balancing were the appropriate standard, then it would even be permissible to drive over another person's legs, necessitating amputation, in order to save an injured person, and that seems impermissible. Rather, the point is that there is a great disparity in importance between the two interests at stake. So just as in the case of using others as a means, formal balancing but not interest balancing applies: there is no unconditional prohibition; rather, a moral argument has to be made which allows trade-offs without, however, endorsing interest balancing.

Second, in cases where values other than lives are at stake, the harm principle must be qualified for reasons of *accommodation*. Accommodation is a concept which is often used in constitutional rights law, in particular, but not only, with regard to religious exemptions. It can be defined as a social practice in which agents absorb some of the costs of others' behaviour.[25] This definition brings to the fore the key problem with accommodation, namely that it requires others to pay (part of) the price of the agent's pursuit of her projects. This seems unjust, and the harm principle as formulated so far protects people against this injustice by prohibiting activities which harm others and thus impose a cost on them. Nevertheless practices of accommodation are widespread and widely accepted. The concept is maybe most widely employed in the context of religiously motivated activities, such as drug use for religious purposes or the religious duty to wear special clothing. However, it is often used in other areas as well, for example with regard to rules accommodating parents caring for their children or children caring for their parents (by giving them leave, the cost of which is carried either by co-workers or the employer); or issues relating to health care such as the accommodation by the health care system of smokers or drinkers (instead of holding them responsible for their harmful habits, they receive treatment which is ultimately paid for by everyone who contributes to health care costs).[26]

While most people support some accommodation at least in some cases, as far as I can see, its theoretical justification seems to be unclear. It seems likely that there are several and partly overlapping justifications. One very general idea of why accommodation is sometimes justified lies in the idea of social cooperation. Seana Shiffrin explains this, highly convincingly to my mind, in the following way. Once we move towards a system of social cooperation, many choices which were purely self-regarding before (such as heavy drinking, or following certain religious practices regarded as eccentric by the majority) suddenly become other-regarding because of the intertwined nature of our lives in conditions of close social cooperation. Accommodation can then be seen as a response to this which helps to adequately preserve our autonomy.[27] Another idea is to regard some accommodation as a response to the needs of minorities: when the majority organizes the social practices of a community around their own ideas of the good life (for example, a Christian majority will make Sunday the day of rest), accommodation becomes necessary to serve adequately the needs of those in the minority in order

---

[25] Shiffrin, 'Egalitarianism, Choice-Sensitivity, and Accommodation', in Wallace, Pettit, Scheffler, and Smith (eds.), *Reason and Value* (Clarendon Press, 2004), 270, 275. Shiffrin adds: '... even if this behaviour is voluntary and the cost-absorption is not necessary in order to achieve luck-insensitivity'.

[26] Ibid., 276–84.

[27] Ibid., 285.

to prevent a situation where for them leading their lives according to their ideals becomes disproportionately difficult. Furthermore, sometimes accommodation may be seen to serve public goods; for example accommodating certain needs of parents may be justified because children are 'public goods' in that they are necessary for society's survival; or the accommodation of certain religious practices may be beneficial because religion may have certain positive effects.[28] Finally, some regard accommodation, especially of religious people, as justified because they question the voluntariness of the religious person's choice, so that accommodating the religious becomes similar to accommodating, for example, disabled people.[29]

My concern at this stage is not to offer a comprehensive theory of the circumstances under which and the extent to which accommodation is permissible or required. Rather, I want to develop the proper *structure* of an argument about conflicts of interests in constitutional rights law, and in particular I want to show that interest balancing is often inadequate. In a case where one person harms another in the pursuit of his project, the proper structure is as follows: the 'default' position is that the pursuit of the project is *impermissible*, irrespective of the relative weights of the competing interests. However, this must be qualified by permitting the pursuit of the project in cases of *extreme disparity* between the relative weights of the autonomy interests and in cases where *accommodation* is required. Thus, interest balancing is inappropriate; rather, formal balancing applies.

The *third* and final aspect in which real life policies will depart from the philosophical discussions is that policies will often respond not to the threat of a definite harm, but to *risks* of harm. Contrary to the example about rushing an injured person to hospital, in real life we often do not know in advance whether a risky activity such as driving will lead to some harm. We regulate driving and other dangerous activities because they create risks; sometimes we know that statistically speaking, the risks will materialize in a certain percentage of the cases. The principles developed above again need some modification for risks as opposed to definite harms. Clearly we hold driving to be permissible in spite of the fact that it creates risks for others, and the justification for this permissibility must be connected to our intuition that accepting the general principle of not harming others for the case of risks would stifle autonomous activity too much. I cannot develop a comprehensive solution to

---

[28] Ibid., 277–8.
[29] Ibid., 280–1.

the problem of creating risks here, but it seems worth pointing out that in contrast to the imposition of harms on others, in the case of risks we are even willing to accept, under certain circumstances, the risk of harm to life, and we do so even though we know that for statistical reasons, the risk will materialize in some cases (as in the case of driving).

Application to constitutional rights law

The harm principle helps shed light on the practice of constitutional rights law. My first example is hate speech. Some hate speech properly falls into the category of harming others in a way which uses them as a means, discussed in the previous section. Hate speech uses the victim as a means if the speaker has made it his project to derive pleasure or satisfaction or feelings of self-worth from the humiliation of the other. In that case, hate speech amounts to using the other person for one's own purposes much in the same way as using another's property. I am not sure whether all hate speech is of this kind, i.e. that the speaker tries to lift himself up at the cost of the victim. The issue does not matter in the end because even if the speaker does not use his victim, hate speech should be impermissible because it imposes harm on the other person. The speaker pursues his project (of insulting others) by denying the other's equal importance; and people have an important autonomy interest in their recognition as equals, or at least the absence of denial of their equal importance. He thus enlarges his own proper share at the cost of others, and this is normally, according to the harm principle, impermissible. Interest balancing would be inadequate to resolve the conflict between the autonomy interest of the speaker and the victim.

Note that there is an additional complexity here. Some argue that special considerations apply to freedom of speech because of its importance for democracy, and that freedom of speech requires that we tolerate verbal abuse in the interest of democracy, or that at least we have to tolerate it to a greater extent than we tolerate harmful activities which are not speech. Such an argument is compatible with the theory proposed in this book because I accept the general point that special considerations may apply to those rights which are grounded not only in personal autonomy but additionally required by democracy.[30] However, I do not believe that it is correct as a matter of substance because there is a relevant difference between proposing *political ideas* and attacking the

---

[30] See Chapter 4, section III.

dignity of persons; and democracy requires only the former but not the latter. It is true that there is sometimes a grey area (take the slogans 'Deport all Muslims!' / '... foreigners!' / '... homosexuals!', which express a political idea but may also be seen as using this only as a cover for insulting certain groups), and in such cases the delineation of attacks on ideas and attacks on persons will be difficult. But this difficulty and the existence of hard cases do not affect the general point that we should perceive of democracy as requiring that the people and their representatives discuss the future direction of the country, not as permitting abuse and insult. Democracy is therefore fully compatible with normal rules of civilized conversation and general rules of decent behaviour (including the harm principle). The same constraints on harming others apply both in the context of rights which are required by democracy and in the context of rights grounded purely in personal autonomy.

My second example in this section concerns the famous case of *Hatton v. United Kingdom*.[31] The UK government had allowed night flights at Heathrow airport, and residents living in the vicinity of the airport complained that the flights, especially in the early morning hours, disturbed their sleep and thus violated their right to private life under Article 8 ECHR. Given the importance of sleep for a person's ability to lead his life, the Court was correct to hold that Article 8 ECHR was engaged. The crucial question was whether the policy struck a 'fair balance' between the interests of good sleep and the economic well-being of the country. The Grand Chamber decided eventually that the interference was justified, paying special regard to the fact that the residents could sell their houses, which curiously had not lost value since the introduction of the new policy, and move to other areas with less noise pollution.

This is yet another case resolved by the respective court by referring to 'balancing', and again, autonomy maximization or interest balancing cannot have been meant by that: it is obvious that on the basis of those approaches, the interests of the residents would clearly have lost out, given that allowing night flights presumably led to considerable economic benefits including the creation of new jobs and additional tax revenue, which could be used for all sorts of beneficial purposes such as building new hospitals or schools. One can only understand why the case made it to the Grand Chamber of the ECtHR by acknowledging that the

---

[31] *Hatton v. United Kingdom* (2003) 37 EHRR 28.

case involves the beneficiary of a policy (for reasons of simplicity referred to as Heathrow airport) imposing harm on others (the residents). This is a situation in which according to the harm principle the interests of the harmed persons normally prevail: normally we have to arrange our affairs so that we do not impose harm on others in the pursuit of our projects. But as has been explained above, this principle is limited by the principle of accommodation: where many people live together closely, the imposition of certain nuisances must sometimes be accepted in order not to stifle autonomous activity too much. So we all have to put up with a certain measure of noise, smell, ugliness and other pollution imposed on us by others. It is clear that in economically developed countries, there will be some important industries which produce a certain measure of pollution, and such pollution will unavoidably hit some harder than others. But it would be inappropriate to declare all such pollution a violation of constitutional rights just because it imposes a harm on some (that would bring economic development in some areas to a halt), just as it would be inappropriate to hold all such pollution to be acceptable as long as it can be justified on autonomy-maximizing grounds. The truth must lie somewhere in the middle between these extremes. This explains why the *Hatton* case was a hard case at all, and why—especially in light of the fact that the residents could move away without financial loss—it was probably correctly decided in spite of the fact that it involved a situation where one actor imposed harm on others.

The third example is about abortion. Let us stipulate that the fetus is morally a person or of equal status to a person and that the fact that the fetus needs the support of the pregnant woman for its physical survival is morally irrelevant.[32] Both stipulations are, of course, central to any comprehensive argument about abortion; it is not my concern here, however, to resolve the abortion debate, but rather to show the relevance of the harm principle to one of its aspects. On the assumption that the fetus is a person or enjoys equal status to a person, it seems clear that there is no interest balancing between the right to life of the fetus (which, as a person, it enjoys) and the right to self-determination of the woman. Plainly, we cannot be justified in killing other people in pursuit of our self-determination: according to the harm principle, we normally have to conduct our affairs such that we do not impose harm on others. So if there is a right to abortion, it cannot be defended on the

---

[32] For an argument to the contrary, cf. Thomson, 'A Defense of Abortion', (1971) 1 *Philosophy & Public Affairs* 47.

ground that the right to self-determination of the woman is in the concrete circumstances more important than the right to life of the fetus. Rather, any such defence must challenge the stipulations I made in the beginning. It is therefore not surprising that the US Supreme Court, in holding that there was indeed a right to abortion, first concluded that constitutionally the fetus was *not* a person.[33] Even the German Federal Constitutional Court, holding that in principle abortion must be outlawed, explicitly left open the question of whether the fetus enjoys the right to life but held that in any event the 'value' expressed by that right applies to the fetus.[34] Again, this is strategically plausible because had the Court concluded that the fetus was indeed a right-holder, it could hardly have left the door for abortion open with regard to the so-called 'social indication' (situations of stress and conflict within the family of the pregnant woman): clearly just the fact that I am stressed or in a situation of conflict cannot, under the harm principle, justify my violating the right to life of another person.

Finally, let me present two cases which seemingly fall under the harm principle but which on a closer look turn out to be structurally different in important ways. In the 'gays in the army' case of *Smith and Grady v. United Kingdom*,[35] the UK had administratively discharged soldiers from its armed forces after it had turned out that they were homosexual. It justified this by pointing, in particular, to the risk of tensions between heterosexual and homosexual members of the armed forces, which would affect morale and unit cohesion and therefore ultimately oper-ational effectiveness and national security. The ECtHR regarded the dismissals as interferences with Article 8 ECHR (the right to private and family life). Applying the proportionality test, it accepted that some difficulties of the kind envisaged by the British authorities could arise when homosexual soldiers were allowed to serve; it held, however, the privacy interest of the affected soldiers to be weightier in the concrete circumstances than the public interest in national security.

---

[33] *Roe v. Wade* (1973) 410 U.S. 113, 156–8.

[34] BVerfGE 39, 1, 41 (*First Abortion Judgment*): 'On the other hand, the question disputed in the present proceeding as well as in judicial opinions and in scientific literature whether the one about to be born himself is a bearer of the fundamental right or, on account of a lesser capacity to possess legal and fundamental rights, is "only" protected in his right to life by the objective norms of the constitution need not be decided here.' (Translation by Robert E. Jonas and John D. Gorby in *The John Marshall Journal of Practice and Procedure* (Vol. 9, 605): http://groups.csail.mit.edu/mac/users/rauch/nvp/german/german_abortion_decision2.html).

[35] *Smith and Grady v. United Kingdom* (2000) 29 EHRR 493.

This is a puzzling result: isn't it odd that the privacy interests of relatively few affected soldiers should outweigh a national security interest (read: lives and physical integrity at stake) of a country of 60 million? Interest balancing would indicate at the very best a draw (in which case the policy would have been within the UK's margin of appreciation), and more likely a balance in favour of national security. After all, the point and purpose of armies is to win wars, and the last thing one wants in the case of a war is the army to work less than optimally because of internal tensions between different groups of soldiers. Therefore, any erring should be on the side of national security—or so it seems.

However, interest balancing is not always adequate; the starting point must be to determine the relationship between the different agents. But this only seems to lead to a deepening of the puzzle. Under a policy allowing gays to serve in the army, the group burdened by the policy is the British people (who will be less secure when homosexuals are allowed to serve), and the beneficiaries are the homosexual soldiers. The homosexual soldiers, by serving in the army, contribute to a situation that makes the British people less secure. This seems to be a case where the harm principle applies with the consequence that it is permissible to stop (i.e. dismiss) the homosexual soldiers.

But this conclusion would be premature. The crux of this issue lies in the relationship between heterosexual soldiers, homosexual soldiers and the population. The real cause of the problem was not the presence of the homosexual soldiers, but the behaviour of (some of) their heterosexual colleagues because the latter did not want to work together with homosexuals. Thus, the responsibility for the problem lay with (some of) the heterosexual soldiers: only because they violated their duties (or were anticipated to violate their duties if the policy were changed) of working together smoothly with a group of colleagues they did not like did the problem for national security arise. So the relationship between the three groups was that the response to the problem (decline in national security) was to limit the freedom not of those who by their misbehaviour were about to cause the harm (some of the heterosexual soldiers) but that of an entirely innocent group (the homosexual soldiers). This must normally be impermissible, and the case was therefore rightly decided in favour of the homosexual soldiers. The result could only have been different in the case of a great disparity between the interests of the affected soldiers and the national security interest. But since, as the Court observed, other armies in Europe had integrated homosexuals and the UK itself had integrated women and ethnic minorities; and given that no significant problems had been reported, such a disparity seemed far-fetched.

The other case which warns against a mechanical application of the harm principle is the *Aviation Security Act* case. I argued above that contrary to the view of the German Federal Constitutional Court, shooting down a hijacked plane which is about to be used as a terrorist weapon does not use the innocent passengers aboard the plane as a means. It would however obviously impose a harm—loss of life—on them, and according to the harm principle this is normally prohibited. Therefore, it seems that we ought to conclude that the Court arrived at the right solution, even if by incorrect reasoning. There is, however, an additional complexity. Consider Frances Kamm's hypothetical *Grenade Case*: a runaway trolley will kill five people unless we explode a grenade that will kill an innocent bystander as a side effect.[36] Kamm argues it would be impermissible to explode the grenade. There is a remarkable parallel between the *Grenade Case* and the *Aviation Security Act* case. However, one important difference between them is that in the *Aviation Security Act* case, the passengers are part of the weapon, and I wonder whether the real reason for the permissibility of balancing lives in the *Aviation Security Act* case flows from that fact. I cannot resolve the issue here; rather, I just want to point out that the classifications I offer in this chapter should not be taken to exhaust the endless variations existing in the moral universe.

c) Regulating behaviour which is not harmful to others but whose legal permissibility would lead to harm to others

This scenario is slightly but crucially different from the one discussed in the previous section. A certain behaviour may be prohibited because of the risk of abuse in case of it being permitted. I shall present two examples to illustrate and analyse this scenario, starting with the *Pretty* case.[37] Ms Pretty suffered from motor neurone disease and wanted her husband, who was supportive of the plan, to assist her in committing suicide when her situation became unbearable and she would no longer be able to carry out her plan without help. The ECtHR correctly, if in slightly twisted language, held that her wish was covered by the right to private life (Article 8 of the Convention). It however denied her the definite right on the ground that making assisted suicide legal could lead

---

[36] Kamm, *Morality, Mortality. Volume II: Rights, Duties, and Status* (Oxford University Press, 1996), 151.

[37] *Pretty v. United Kingdom* (2002) 35 EHHR 1.

to abuse by others (who might kill old or ill relatives, claiming that they assisted them with their suicide, or might bully them into committing suicide).[38] Let us assume that the empirical assumptions about this risk are correct. Then Ms Pretty demanded that a legal regime be installed which, while serving her interest—in fact a fundamentally important interest of hers, namely dying with dignity—would lead to the risk for others of being killed without their consent or of them being bullied into committing suicide. However, and this distinguishes this case from the cases discussed in the last section, it is not Ms Pretty's (or her husband's) action that creates the harm or the risk thereof to others. Rather, the harm is caused by the legal regime that allows people in Ms Pretty's situation to receive assistance in committing suicide. This difference is morally relevant: if assisted suicide were permitted, any abuse flowing from this could not be attributed to Ms Pretty. She and others in comparable situations would be the beneficiaries of the legal situation; the victims of abuse would be burdened by the legal situation; but there is nothing to establish a special relationship between the two groups. It would be misleading to say that Ms Pretty, had she won her case in time, could have realized her wish to die with dignity 'at the cost' of the lives of others, thus shifting the cost of her project on to others: whether or not she would eventually have received assistance with her suicide would not at all have affected the situation of those burdened by the permissive legal regime (who would have been abused or killed or bullied into suicide independently of Ms Pretty's actions). It is therefore more adequate to say that in the scenario discussed here, the state has a choice between two policy options, both of which will have beneficial consequences for some and harmful ones for other people, but that neither policy establishes a special relationship between the respective groups. This is why I believe that in this case interest balancing is indeed appropriate: where the state, regulating harmful or risky behaviour, is faced with two policy options with costs and benefits, and where neither of the options creates a special relationship between the persons affected by it, it should choose the option which on the whole does the best job of allowing the people to live their lives according to their self-conceptions.

To illustrate this further, let us stipulate that the risk of becoming fatally ill and needing assistance with one's project of dying with dignity and the risk of being killed by one's relatives if assisted suicide were legal

---

[38] Ibid., para. 74.

are exactly the same; so in a given society both cases would happen equally often, depending on whether assisted suicide was permissible or not. It would seem that in this situation, whether or not assisted suicide ought to be permissible would depend upon whether an undignified death or being killed by one's relatives is worse (judged from the perspectives of the self-conceptions of the people); thus interest balancing (and possibly even autonomy maximization[39]) would indeed be adequate. The question becomes more complex if the two risks are not equally high. Let us stipulate that being killed by one's relatives is worse than being denied a dignified death, but also less likely. I am not sure that performing a simple mathematical calculation (the evil that could happen to one, multiplied by its probability) would do justice to the issue; in particular because it might be reasonable to avoid a slightly worse evil even if it is much less likely to happen. So the weights of the respective interests might have to be adjusted by including further considerations. I will not resolve this issue here; the goal of this section is merely to point out the moral structure which an argument about the *Pretty* case, or more generally arguments about cases where one person relies on a legal rule which as a side effect leads to harm to others, ought to take. Further complications will arise when applying the moral principles to the facts of the case: there are, of course, open empirical questions, in particular with regard to the seriousness of the risk of abuse. There is also the question of how to determine the respective weights of the autonomy interests of not being bullied into suicide and being denied a death with dignity (I will say something about the problem of incommensurability below). Finally, the case gets even more complex because it might be necessary to consider further policy options which would eliminate or reduce the risk while enabling terminally ill people to die with dignity (such as certain safety procedures involving physicians).[40]

The use of certain prohibited drugs for religious purposes is another example falling into this category. The respective cases have in common that a certain drug is generally prohibited and a religious believer who

---

[39] Relying on considerations of personal responsibility, one might consider whether in a situation where an individual has through his own fault brought himself into a situation where he now requires assistance with his plan to commit suicide, the weight to be attached to his interest is reduced. But first, that was not the case in *Pretty*, and second, even if it had been, such an argument would seem rather heartless; presumably we would accommodate terminally ill people in such situations (just as we accommodate, for example, smokers who are responsible for the diseases they develop as a consequence of their smoking).

[40] The issue of several policy options will be addressed in Chapter 7, section IV.2.

wants to use it for religious reasons claims that the prohibition violates her right to freedom of religion. Let us stipulate that the reason for the prohibition of the drug lies in considerations relating to harm to others (preventing the social problems associated with drug use, in particular crime), as opposed to paternalistic ones (protecting the potential drug user against her will); paternalism raises special problems which I have discussed elsewhere.[41] Let us further stipulate that the prohibition of the respective drug is, aside from the religious drug use issue, indeed justifiable (because if it were not, then the entire ban ought to be abolished and no separate issue regarding an exemption for religious drug use would arise).

The first question to ask is whether this is a case of harming others; and whether it is will depend on the circumstances. If the situation is such that by acquiring the drug, the religious drug user supports an illegal drug market and thus contributes, to a small extent, to its continued existence, then the case would indeed fall under the harm principle and the only hope of the religious person would lie in accommodation. More plausibly, however, the harm in such cases flows not from the individual contributions of the religious person but from the abuse of the permissive legal regime which allows the purchase of drugs under certain circumstances in order to protect religious drug users. This seems to have been the main concern in the South African case of *Prince*, which deals with the claim of Rastafari to be exempted from the general ban on Cannabis: '[I]t is difficult to imagine how the island of legitimate acquisition and use by Rastafari for the purpose of practising their religion could be distinguished from the surrounding ocean of illicit trafficking and use.'[42]

If the harm flows from the abuse of the permissive legal regime as opposed to from the actions of the religious drug user, then, just as in *Pretty*, there is no special relationship between the religious drug user and the victims of the permissive policy because the harm to the victims occurs independently of any activity of a religious drug user. It follows that interest balancing is appropriate, the question being whether the reduced social problems (i.e. crime) that come with a complete ban compared to a ban with an exemption for religious drug use outweigh the interests of the religious drug users in being allowed to acquire and use the drug. It seems plausible to assume that such a balance will

---

[41] Möller, *Paternalismus und Persönlichkeitsrecht* (Duncker & Humblot, 2005); see also my brief discussion of the issue in Chapter 5, section IV.4.b.

[42] *Prince v. President of the Law Society of the Cape of Good Hope* (2000) ZACC 28; 2001 (2) SA 388, para. 130.

normally go in favour of the avoidance of drugs-related crime. However, similarly to the case of assisted suicide discussed above, there exists an additional complexity in these cases, which provides the practically most promising avenue for a religious drug user: the question is whether the state might be under an obligation to accommodate her by spending scarce resources in order to set up a regulatory regime which allows the use of the drug for at least some religious purposes while at the same time preventing or minimizing abuse.[43]

There is an interesting disagreement between different justices of the US Supreme Court on the question of the correct balance in a similar case, *Oregon v. Smith*, where the Court held that the First Amendment does not require an exemption for religious purposes from a generally applicable law prohibiting the use of peyote.[44] Justice Scalia, speaking for the Court, expressed the view that the First Amendment does not require exemptions from generally applicable laws prohibiting certain drugs. The more interesting opinions for present purposes are those by Justice O'Connor on the one hand and Justices Brennan, Marshall and Blackmun on the other. All four agree that a balancing test (the 'compelling interest test') should be applied. While Justice O'Connor concludes that the state's interest in preventing drug abuse prevails, stressing that 'drug abuse is "one of the greatest problems affecting the health and welfare of our population" and thus "one of the most serious problems confronting our society today"',[45] the three other justices disagree. In their view, the prohibition of peyote was mere 'symbolism'[46] given that the State had 'not evinced any concrete interest in enforcing its drug laws against religious users of peyote',[47] that it offered 'no evidence that the religious use of peyote has ever harmed anyone',[48] and that there existed practically no illegal traffic in peyote.[49] It was 'simply . . . not a popular drug; its distribution for use in religious rituals has nothing to do with

---

[43] The extent to which accommodation is required was the crucial question in *Prince*, where Justice Sachs remarked that 'the real difference between the majority judgment and that of Ngcobo J relates to how much trouble each feels it is appropriate to expect the state to go to in order to accommodate the religious convictions and practices of what in this case is a rather small and not very popular religious community' (ibid., para 149). For a further discussion of this issue, see Chapter 7.

[44] *Employment division, department of human resources of Oregon v. Smith* (1990) 494 U.S. 872.

[45] Ibid., 904.

[46] Ibid., 911.

[47] Ibid.

[48] Ibid., 911–12.

[49] Ibid., 916.

the vast and violent traffic in illegal narcotics that plagues this country'.[50] The three justices also made it clear that religious claims involving drugs such as heroin or marijuana, 'in which there is significant illegal traffic, with its attendant greed and violence',[51] would not be successful. This indicates that where there are genuine risks to the public in terms of crime and violence flowing from a permissive policy, religious drug users cannot place much hope in the argument that their interests outweigh the interests of those affected by crime and violence; this seems to be the correct outcome. Thus, if at all, their claims can succeed only on grounds of accommodation under a system of state supervision which minimizes the risks but requires the spending of public resources.

d) *Regulating the behaviour of a person who is suspected of being a threat to others*

Sometimes there exists the *suspicion* that a person intends to engage in illegal, harmful activities, and certain limitations are imposed on the person's freedom, either to stop him or in order to establish whether he is indeed a threat. Nobody could complain about being stopped from actually engaging in illegal and harmful activities (such activities are impermissible under the harm principle as developed above). However, what principles apply when it has not been established whether the respective person really is a threat? Examples in this area range from relatively innocent cases involving body searches at airports or prisons[52] to some of the most controversial issues of our time, namely the treatment of terrorist suspects. The latter are particularly interesting in this context, not only because of their controversial nature and obvious importance, but also because the image regularly invoked in the respective discussions is that of the *'balance* between liberty and security': the idea is that in light of an increased terrorist threat to our security, some or all of us have to accept greater intrusions into our liberty.[53] The image of balance is normally invoked, of course, in order to justify those intrusive measures: the kind of balance that the proponents of the idea of 'striking a new balance' have in mind is a maximization or interest balancing approach, the idea being that the increase in security (i.e. the

---

[50] Ibid., 916.

[51] Ibid., 918.

[52] See for example *Wainwright v. United Kingdom* (2007) 44 EHRR 40.

[53] For an exploration of the meaning of this phrase, see Waldron, *Torture, Terror, and Trade-Offs: Philosophy for the White House* (Oxford University Press, 2010), 22–5.

protection of lives and physical integrity) of the many clearly outweighs the decrease in liberty of the few terrorist suspects. But this argument works only if interest balancing is indeed the appropriate kind of balancing in those cases.

Different states adopted different anti-terrorism measures post 9/11. In the UK, the first response was the policy of indefinite detention without trial for foreign terrorist suspects. Having been declared a violation of human rights by the House of Lords because of its discriminatory character (British terrorist suspects were not targeted by the policy),[54] the scheme was replaced by the control order system, which allows various restrictions on the liberty of the suspect, for example house arrest during certain hours of the day, electronic tagging, or limiting where a person can go or who he can see.[55] For present purposes the precise nature of the anti-terrorism measures, which can range from the imposition of control orders or indefinite detention without trial to torture in order to extract information about terrorist plots, is not crucial.[56] While of course these different measures vary greatly in the graveness of their interference with the rights of the suspects, they share the following structure: a suspect's freedom is limited in certain ways in order to prevent him from carrying out what might or might not be his plan, namely harming others.

As a theoretical experiment, let us stipulate that the policy targets not suspects but persons known to be completely innocent. So for some reason it is the case that it is possible to reduce the risk of a terrorist attack by imprisoning or otherwise restricting the liberty of innocent, non-threatening persons. This would amount to using them as a means for the purpose of protecting others, and this is normally prohibited under the approach proposed here. This example shows already that the simple image of the 'balance' between liberty and security is misleading if interpreted (as it usually is) as implying a kind of interest balancing or maximization approach. It cannot be assumed without further argument

---

[54] *A v. Secretary of State for the Home Department* (2004) UKHL 56.

[55] See s. 1 of the Prevention of Terrorism Act 2005. There has been extensive litigation about control orders and, connected to it, the special advocate system. See in particular *Secretary of State for the Home Department v. JJ* (2007) UKHL 45; *Secretary of State for the Home Department v. MB and AF* (2007) UKHL 46; *Secretary of State for the Home Department v. E* (2007) UKHL 47; *Secretary of State for the Home Department v. AF (No 3)* (2009) UKHL 28; the latter judgment was a response to *A v. United Kingdom* (2009) 49 EHRR 29 (Grand Chamber).

[56] Note that especially in the case of torture, special considerations might apply relating to the use of the *means* (torture) in the pursuit of an otherwise legitimate goal. I do not resolve this issue in this book.

that such balancing is appropriate—in the case of restricting the liberty of innocents, it is not.

The crucial question for the assessment of anti-terrorism measures involving not innocent people but suspects (who might well be innocent, or who might indeed be engaging in terrorist activities) is whether or to what extent their status as suspects changes the moral situation. I cannot resolve the issue here, but will offer some thoughts. The following analysis must proceed on the—controversial—basis that if it could be demonstrated that the suspects were indeed planning a terrorist plot, the measures would be justified. The assumption is controversial because it is questionable whether measures such as control orders are really preventative and not punitive in nature; if they were punitive, the guarantees attached to the criminal process (in particular the presumption of innocence and the guarantee of a fair trial before conviction by a court) would apply; thus, it would be impermissible to impose the orders as executive measures. Furthermore, there are, of course, problems relating to the proportionality of the measures, in particular their suitability and necessity as a means of preventing terrorist attacks. Finally, as indicated above, some measures (in particular, torture) might be impermissible even against people known to be planning a terrorist attack.

One could develop an argument against the permissibility of anti-terrorism measures targeted at suspects along the following lines: if there is no need to prove that there is a real threat emerging from the suspects, then it is clear that statistically speaking, the measure will be imposed on innocent people as well. We may never know which of the suspects were really innocent, but we do know with near certainty that some of them are, and that therefore some of them are being used as a means for the protection of the population. Thus, to avoid a situation where some are used as a means, it must be impermissible to impose anti-terrorism measures unless it has been established by a proper process that the recipient of the measure indeed poses a threat. This argument is not meant to resolve the issue, but rather to propose an idea worth exploring further. It is already sufficient to throw doubts upon the correctness of the approach of those who want to 'strike a new balance between liberty and security'. As argued above, while interest balancing is sometimes appropriate in the resolution of conflicts of autonomy interests, when it is, that is itself not the 'moral default' but rather the conclusion of a moral argument. It follows that the proponents of 'striking a new balance' would have to undertake a considerable amount of moral work to establish their point that interest balancing is indeed appropriate.

e) Regulating the behaviour of persons who claim the right to an exemption from an otherwise mandatory action

The scenarios discussed in the previous sections are all about agents actively pursuing their projects. Sometimes, however—in particular in cases involving conscience or religion—the concern of the agent is not about acting but about *avoiding* having to perform a certain action. In countries with military service, conscientious objectors want to *not* do their military service. An employee might *not* want to work on Saturdays or Sundays for religious reasons.

It would be wrong to resolve those cases by resorting to interest balancing, for example by asking how detrimental to national security a law allowing conscientious objection to military service would be on the one hand, and how important the autonomy interests of the conscientious objectors are on the other hand. The problem with interest balancing in such cases is that the agent, by not performing an action which all others perform, or all others in relevantly similar situations (e.g. all other employees), usually shifts the burden that he would normally have to carry on to others (those who do serve in the military; the colleagues who do not mind working on that particular day). When that is the case, the justification of exemptions becomes especially difficult because it seems clear that normally, claiming a right to get others to do one's own fair share of work must be unsuccessful. This situation is structurally comparable to that of harming others (possibly even harming others in a way which uses them as a means): the agent uses the resources of the others (their labour) to do the work of which he ought to shoulder an equal burden.

Just as in the case of the harm principle, in the situation discussed here it may, however, be appropriate to accommodate the agent. Sometimes such accommodation is possible without imposing the agent's fair share on others; for example there might be a civil service option for conscientious objectors to military service,[57] or it might be possible for an employee to take his favourite day off and work extra hours on other days. But even these cases are problematic because accommodating the agent will still involve some cost, for example a loss in flexibility or an administrative burden on the employer. This cost is the reason that a similar act of accommodation will normally not be awarded to others who do not have as subjectively important reasons. I could surely not

---

[57] Art. 12a (2) of the German Basic Law.

claim a right to be accommodated by not having to work on Wednesdays even if I offered to work extra hours on other days and even if there were colleagues willing to help out, if my only reason for this was that Wednesday is the day where I like to stay at home and watch my favourite TV series. Thus, the question is whether the special treatment that the agent demands can be justified by relying on accommodation, especially in cases where the agent is willing to contribute his equal share in a modified way. As I pointed out above, I do not develop a theory of accommodation here, but merely point to the proper structure which an argument about a claimed right to not having to perform an otherwise mandatory act would have to take: interest balancing is inappropriate; rather the 'default' is that no such right exists unless it can exceptionally be justified under the idea of accommodation.

f) Conclusion

This section has analysed the moral structure of conflicts of autonomy interests in the context of the regulation of harmful behaviour. The principles proposed show the complex ways in which it sometimes is and sometimes is not appropriate to put one person's autonomy interests on the scales together with everyone else's and perform a balancing operation (in the sense of interest balancing or autonomy maximization). On the one hand, it turns out that it is correct to say that every person is in some important ways protected from others in that he cannot normally be harmed by them in the pursuit of their projects. On the other hand, there are situations where the legitimacy of a policy indeed depends on the very interest balancing that is inappropriate in other cases. Thus, broad arguments in favour of or against interest balancing would not do justice to the complexity of the moral questions. A more subtle approach, focussing on the specific relationship which the agent's activity creates between him and other persons, helps to refine the analysis.

2. *Redistributive policies*

A considerable part of policy-making in welfare states deals with issues relating to redistribution. Should there be health care for those who cannot afford to pay for it? Should there be unemployment or other welfare benefits, and how high and extensive should they be? Should there be special protection of families and/or single parents? Such policies rely on the idea that distributive justice requires some redistribution of resources from, normally, the wealthier to the less wealthy.

Constitutional rights law deals with the same issues mostly under the heading of social rights, such as the rights to housing, food, drink, welfare and health care. Sometimes social rights theorists give the impression that the main question with regard to social rights is whether they exist as prima facie rights, and that once it has been concluded that they do, the main intellectual work has been done. However, under the theory of rights proposed here this is not true. Just as in the case of negative rights, the important question is not whether rights to housing, food, drink, welfare and health care are protected as prima facie rights: as a matter of political morality they clearly are, given their great importance for personal autonomy. Rather it is what their limits are, in particular in light of the fact of limited resources. For example, one of the morally difficult problems in this area is not *whether* there is a right to housing, but *how much* the state has to spend in the pursuit of providing housing for the homeless. Resolving this issue requires the striking of a difficult balance between the interests of those in need of housing and, in particular, the interests of those who are ultimately going to pay for it. This, however, is precisely one of the questions which redistributive theories address. Thus, it is not possible to develop a comprehensive theory of socio-economic rights without addressing the issue of distributive justice.[58]

Redistributive policies resolve conflicts of autonomy interests. For example, in the case of a policy taxing the rich to provide housing for the poor, the conflict of autonomy interests is between the wealthy people's autonomy interests in controlling their property[59] and the poor people's autonomy interests in having a home. How ought such conflicts to be resolved? The right answer cannot be interest balancing or autonomy maximization: the argument made in support of redistribution is not that the poor can gain more in terms of autonomy than the rich lose, and that this alone justifies redistribution. If that were true, then much more radical redistribution would not only be permissible, but obligatory. The state would have to tax the rich to such an extent that any further taxation would harm their autonomy more than the added resources would help the autonomy of the poor. Now, note that I am not saying

---

[58] For a similar conclusion see Waldron, 'Socioeconomic Rights and Theories of Justice', *NYU School of Law, Public Law & Legal Theory Research Paper Series*, Working Paper No. 10–79, November 2010, 30: 'I think it is better to let socio-economic rights emerge from a theory of justice than to try to defend them, line by line, on their own merits.'

[59] This is slightly simplistic; see above n 2.

that that would necessarily be the wrong policy. Remember that it follows from the approach developed in the last chapter that, in order to be constitutionally legitimate, redistributive policies must be based on a *reasonable* conception of equality (i.e. not necessarily the one correct conception). It must certainly be wrong to hold that anyone who does not agree with interest balancing in the case of redistributive policies is not only wrong (not correct) but actually even unreasonable in the sense that the only reasonable way to think about redistribution is to conduct an autonomy-maximizing calculation. But then interest balancing must be rejected as the standard for the assessment of the legitimacy of a redistributive policy. Rather, formal balancing is adequate: a moral argument which does not necessarily rely exclusively on the importance or weight of the respective autonomy interests must be constructed.

Let me make a few rough observations about the direction which this moral argument would have to take in social rights cases. The philosophical literature offers us some guidance on the issue of redistribution with a number of theoretical models, of which John Rawls's difference principle[60] and Ronald Dworkin's insurance model (equality of resources)[61] are among the best known ones. Under the reasonableness approach proposed in Chapter 5, it is clear that the state could pick and implement any of these models, or indeed any other model—as long as it is reasonable. The problem with the philosophical models is that they operate at a high level of abstraction and cannot without much further intellectual work be concretized and turned into policy proposals capable of being implemented in practical politics. So there is a great complexity at the theoretical level. The situation gets worse because the theoretical complexity is matched by a practical complexity: it is simply a fact of life that the laws of modern welfare states have become so complex that it is impossible for any legislature or government, however competent and good-willed, to coherently follow a given set of principles in all its policies. Major reforms in this area are usually fraught with unforeseeable effects; as a result only piecemeal reform, conducted in a trial and error fashion, is usually possible.[62] These theoretical and

---

[60] Rawls, *A Theory of Justice*, revised edition (Oxford University Press, 1999), 65–70.

[61] Dworkin, *Sovereign Virtue: The Theory and Practice of Equality* (Harvard University Press, 2000), ch. 2.

[62] It could be argued that this poses a problem of constitutional legitimacy because the reasonableness approach requires that any policy, including welfare policies, be reasonable. But that would be misguided: all that is required from the elected branches is what a well-working legislature and executive can reasonably be expected to deliver. It is important to recall the point of the reasonableness standard: I argued that the point of requiring the elected branches to come forward not with the one

practical problems make it extremely difficult for courts or indeed anyone to convince themselves of the reasonableness or unreasonableness of a specific social policy in light of possible alternatives, and this could potentially lead to a choice between courts either running the risk of making mistakes and declaring reasonable policies unconstitutional, or deferring to an extent that makes social rights toothless. Courts have developed strategies in response to this problem, for example proceduralizing the issue, or limiting themselves to more narrowly defined questions such as the internal coherence of a given scheme.[63] The important conclusion for present purposes is that turning to the idea of 'balancing' in order to determine the requirements of social rights, while correct in a technical sense (formal balancing is required), greatly under-emphasizes the moral and institutional difficulties with which social rights adjudication is fraught.

3. Policies supporting public goods and services

The state often requires its citizens to make sacrifices in order for it to be able to provide certain public goods and services. A core example is public infrastructure: everyone has to contribute to it (through taxation[64]), and everyone can use it in return. Other examples are public opera houses, sports centres, and libraries. While these cases raise relatively few problems for constitutional legitimacy, it is worth addressing them because there is an important insight about balancing to be gained from their discussion.

Policies supporting public goods and services involve conflicts of autonomy interests, but importantly, these conflicts differ in their moral structure from the other cases discussed in this chapter. In those

---

right answer but only with a reasonable one was to enable meaningful democratic debate about important policy questions. We cannot insist on a level of quality of the decisions of our elected representatives which is beyond what such representatives, working hard and making efforts in good faith, can reasonably be expected to deliver. If the economic and social welfare laws have reached a level of complexity which makes it impossible to control them in their entirety at any given moment, so that realistically only piecemeal reform is possible, then only this is required from a constitutional perspective.

[63] *Government of the Republic of South Africa v. Grootboom* (2000) ZACC 19; *Soobramoney v. Minister of Health (KwaZulu-Natal)* (1997) ZACC 17. In both cases the Court accepted without further inquiry the budget for, respectively, housing programmes and health services, but examined whether the ways in which these budgets were spent complied with constitutional standards. While in *Soobramoney* it concluded that it did, in *Grootboom* it found a breach of the constitution because there was no component providing relief for those most desperately in need of housing.

[64] This taxation might combine redistributive with non-redistributive elements. This slight complication does not present special problems, however.

cases one person wanted some autonomy-related benefit (for example, the right to engage in a particular activity) which she could only have at the cost of someone else's autonomy interests. So the 'balance' to be struck was between the autonomy interests of different persons. By way of contrast, in the case of public goods and services, on the correct analysis, the balance to be struck is (in Jeremy Waldron's terminology) *intra-personal*. One of Waldron's examples is airport security: everyone has to accept certain restrictions of his or her freedom in order to receive the benefit of increased security.[65] Or take the case of public infrastructure: everyone has to contribute his fair share to the construction and maintenance of infrastructure (such as streets), and everyone is free to use infrastructure in return. Looking at the issue in this way, it becomes clear that the real conflict of autonomy interests in the case of public goods and services is a conflict taking place *within* each person: is it more important for the respective person to have infrastructure, or is it more important for him to have that extra bit of money?[66] Is it more important not to have to go through the hassle of being searched by security personnel at airports, or is it more important to have the added safety that results from those practices? The point is that policies involving public goods and services are justified if *they make the people more autonomous than they would be without them.* The role of the state here is to facilitate the autonomous pursuit of its citizens' lives by demanding a sacrifice from them and using the sacrifice to deliver a public good or service, and to do this in a way that delivers more autonomy to the people than the sacrifice takes away from them. And precisely because the point of public goods and services is to increase each person's autonomy, it follows that balancing as autonomy maximization is appropriate.

V. INCOMMENSURABILITY?

An important objection to the idea of balancing could be that autonomy maximization, interest balancing and in some cases also formal balancing require comparing goods which are incommensurable. This is also a common objection to balancing in constitutional rights law generally.[67]

---

[65] Waldron, *Torture, Terror, and Trade-Offs: Philosophy for the White House* (Oxford University Press, 2010), 12.

[66] This discussion leaves aside the rather academic complication that some will use infrastructure less than others, and could therefore claim that they wanted to contribute less.

[67] Webber, *The Negotiable Constitution: On the Limitation of Rights* (Cambridge University Press, 2009), 90–100. Tsakyrakis, 'Proportionality: An Assault on Human Rights?', (2009) 7 *International Journal of*

The idea of incommensurability is that there are two values at stake and that it is not the case that value A is better than value B; it is not the case that B is better than A; and it is not the case that they are of equal value.[68] As a consequence, such incommensurability 'leave[s] us paralyzed, not knowing what to choose'.[69] 'Strong incommensurability implies that there is no basis in our knowledge of value to say that one decision rather than the other was the correct one',[70] and therefore all that is possible is to simply make a choice.

Applied to interest balancing in constitutional rights law, the question could be raised whether, taking as an example the *Pretty* case discussed above, the interest in dying with dignity and the interest in not being killed by a relative are really, as the balancing metaphor wants to make us think, commensurable. It would seem that to the extent that they are not, *any* choice made by an elected body, in particular the legislature, would be reasonable and should therefore be allowed to stand: by choosing one of the incommensurable options, the legislature did exactly the right thing.

This is not the place to discuss the issue of incommensurability comprehensively; rather I want to clarify one important aspect in which the theory of rights proposed here differs in structure from theories which rely on the idea that there exist goods which are *objectively* valuable and whose values are incommensurable.[71] For example, there may be objective value in engaging in profession A, and there may be objective value in engaging in profession B, and the two may be incommensurable, i.e. when a person has to make a choice between professions A and B, no alternative is superior, nor are both alternatives equally valuable. Under the theory advocated here, however, the moral setting is slightly but importantly different in that my model is not concerned with what is *objectively* valuable, but rather with the importance of certain activities and personal resources *from the perspective of the self-conception of the agent.* So while the values of

---

Constitutional Law 468, too, discusses and subscribes to incommensurability but has in mind a different ('weak') form which simply indicates that in the absence of a common metric a moral argument is needed to resolve a conflict. For a critical discussion of these views, see Afonso da Silva, 'Comparing the Incommensurable: Constitutional Principles, Balancing and Rational Decision', (2011) 31 *Oxford Journal of Legal Studies* 273.

[68] See Raz's definition of incommensurability: 'A and B are incommensurate if it is neither true that one is better than the other nor true that they are of equal value.' (*The Morality of Freedom* [Clarendon Press, 1986], 322).

[69] Waldron, 'Fake Incommensurability: A Response to Professor Schauer', (1993–94) 45 *Hastings Law Journal* 813, 816.

[70] Ibid.

[71] This is how Raz approaches the issue in *The Morality of Freedom*.

engaging in professions A and B may be incommensurable from an objective perspective, from the relevant perspective of the agent it may be absolutely clear which of the two corresponds more to the way he wants to lead his life. If I were faced with the alternatives of being a scholar or a tax advisor, there would be no trace of agony on my mind, and my preference would be crystal-clear, in spite of the fact that objectively, both professions may be valuable and their value may be incommensurable. But my personal decision about whether to become a scholar or a tax advisor is not concerned with objective value; it is about which of the two options sits better with *who I am* and *who I would like to be*, as well as *where I see myself as coming from* and *where I want to go* with my life: in other words, my personal decision will be guided by and flow from my self-conception. It may therefore be perfectly possible to compare the value of objectively incommensurable options *from the perspective of the self-conception of the agent*. While this difference in perspective does not necessarily make the problem of incommensurability go away in all cases, it may sometimes have this effect. To be sure, it may also be impossible to compare the values of professions A and B from the perspective of the self-conception of the agent, in which case the problem of incommensurability persists. However, often the self-conceptions of the people will be such that one of two or more options will correspond significantly better to their self-conceptions while possibly being incommensurable from an objective perspective. This is morally relevant because under the approach advocated here it is not the role of the state to decide for its citizens what is or is not objectively valuable, but to set up a scheme of policies which enables them to live their lives according to their own self-conceptions.

Let me apply this point to the example of the *Pretty* case. That case required a balance to be struck between the autonomy interests of people in situations like Ms Pretty's who want to die with dignity and the autonomy interests of mostly old and vulnerable people who might, if assisted suicide were made permissible, be killed or bullied into death by their relatives or carers. Someone might argue that it is impossible to compare the two interests: that both life courses (having a dignified death; not being bullied into suicide by a family member) are valuable, and that we cannot say that one of them is better or that they are equally valuable. But this would at the very least be rash. We could conduct an experiment and inquire into the self-conception of a single person, figuring out which of the two life courses would be better from the perspective of his self-conception. It might turn out that he has a religious belief which requires him not to commit suicide under any circumstances, in which case his autonomy interest in assisted suicide is zero and is outweighed by his other interest in not being killed by a family member or carer. Alternatively he might believe that the life course of an undignified death is so terrible that he would personally be willing to take the risk of being killed at a late stage of his life rather than having to take the risk of a distressing and possibly slow and painful death, with all the additional consequences that such a death has for his friends and family members and the ways in which they will remember him.

Now imagine that every member of a community has the same self-conception. In a community of religious believers it would make perfect sense to sum up the self-conceptions of the people and conclude that on balance, their autonomy interests are better served by a prohibitive policy, whereas in a community of persons with the alternative self-conception the opposite conclusion would apply. Thus, no issue of incommensurability arises. Of course, in reality there will be additional complexities; in particular, not all members of a community will have the same self-conception. This may lead to further problems but those problems have nothing to do with incommensurability.

In conclusion, I do not propose to completely explain away the problem of incommensurability. There may be cases where two policy options are genuinely incommensurable in that neither of them corresponds better, nor do they correspond equally well, to how people want to live their lives. Where this is so, the legislature can legitimately pick any of the incommensurable options. However, the relevance of incommensurability is at least reduced in the context of the theory of rights proposed here because the weight of the respective interests must be determined not objectively but according to the importance of those interests under each person's self-conception; and often one of two options will correspond better than the other to the way in which a person wants to live his life.

VI. CONCLUSION

Balancing is a powerful and useful metaphor for the resolution of conflicts of interests in both policy-making and constitutional rights law. It is also, however, potentially misleading because it may be seen as promising more than it can deliver: most importantly, balancing cannot offer a shortcut to morally attractive ways of resolving conflicts; moral reasoning cannot, under the label of balancing, be reduced to simple calculations or mechanical ways of quantifying and comparing values or interests. Rather, properly understood, balancing refers to the necessity of resolving a conflict of interests in line with sound moral principles. It turns out that these principles are of a variety of different kinds, depending on the nature of the policy as regulating harmful behaviour, redistributive, or providing public goods and services; and that in the first case, there are further distinctions to be made, depending on the specific relationship which the act in question creates between the respective persons. But this complexity is nothing that distracts from the value of the doctrine of balancing; it simply reflects the complexity of the underlying moral issues. We should embrace both the doctrine of balancing and the complexity of the moral questions.

༒ 7 ༒

Proportionality

I. INTRODUCTION

The principle of proportionality has become *the* major doctrinal tool in constitutional rights law around the world,[1] and in light of the previous chapters it is not hard to see why. The prima facie stage of rights, where every autonomy interest is protected,[2] does not operate as a filter. Thus, most of the hard analytical work, separating successful from unsuccessful rights claims, must be done at the justification stage, and the main doctrinal tool there is the principle of proportionality. It is therefore partly correct to say that human and constitutional rights law is all about proportionality: laws that are 'proportionate' respect constitutional rights and those which are 'disproportionate' violate them.[3]

Chapter 5 argued that a policy, to be constitutionally legitimate, must represent a reasonable, as opposed to the one correct, specification of the spheres of autonomy of equal citizens.[4] Chapter 6 identified as the key problem for this specification the issue of conflicts of autonomy interests.[5] It follows that proportionality analysis must assess precisely these issues. A policy which interferes with a person's general right to autonomy is proportionate and therefore justified if it resolves a conflict of autonomy interests in a reasonable way; and it is disproportionate and therefore violates her constitutional rights if it resolves such a conflict in an unreasonable way. But, someone might ask, why do we need the

---

[1] Stone Sweet and Mathews, 'Proportionality Balancing and Global Constitutionalism', (2008–9) 47 *Columbia Journal of Transnational Law* 72. See also Chapter 1.

[2] See Chapter 4, section I.

[3] As Webber puts it: '[T]he entire constitutional rights-project could be simplified by replacing the catalogue of rights with a single proposition: The legislature shall comply with the principle of proportionality.' (*The Negotiable Constitution: On the Limitation of Rights* [Cambridge University Press, 2009], 4).

[4] See Chapter 5, section IV.4.

[5] See Chapter 6, section II.

principle of proportionality to conduct this test? Why not start directly with the question of whether the policy resolves a conflict of autonomy interests in a reasonable way? What is the added value of the principle of proportionality?

The added value is that the proportionality test provides a *structure* which guides judges through the reasoning process as to whether a policy is constitutionally legitimate. It breaks down the complex question of whether a policy resolves a conflict of autonomy interests in a reasonable way into four smaller questions which can be analysed one by one, and in this way ensures (if properly applied) that the judicial analysis addresses comprehensively all the relevant issues. It is this link between the standard of constitutional legitimacy and the principle of proportionality which this chapter lays bare and explores. To this end, it provides an account of the principle of proportionality which shows the relevance of each of the four stages of the test for the overall assessment of the constitutional legitimacy of a policy. It starts with a brief account of the principle as it has developed in constitutional rights law (section II). The following sections (III–V) provide accounts of the different stages of the test.

II. THE PRINCIPLE OF PROPORTIONALITY

The statement that constitutional rights law is all about proportionality must be qualified slightly because proportionality is generally applied only with regard to negative civil and political rights in their vertical dimension. It does not make much sense with regard to, in particular, socio-economic rights and positive obligations because in almost all circumstances the realization of those rights requires scarce resources; therefore any limitation will always further the legitimate goal of saving resources and will always be suitable and necessary to the achievement of that goal. The only meaningful test would be the balancing stage. In light of this it makes sense that the ECtHR uses indeed a 'fair balance' test with regard to positive obligations[6] and that the South African Constitutional Court uses a reasonableness test with regard to socio-economic rights.[7] Those tests are not different in substance, but they

---

[6] For a comprehensive study of the fair balance principle, see Mowbray, 'A Study of the Principle of Fair Balance in the Jurisprudence of the European Court of Human Rights', (2010) 10 *Human Rights Law Review* 289.

[7] For a critical analysis of this approach see Bilchitz, *Poverty and Fundamental Rights: The Justification and Enforcement of Socio-Economic Rights* (Oxford University Press, 2007), ch. 5.

acknowledge the fact that the first three stages of the proportionality test are unhelpful in determining the content of resource-sensitive rights under conditions of scarcity. In cases involving positive obligations, the ECtHR routinely stresses that the applicable principles with regard to positive and negative obligations are 'similar'[8] in that the fair balance test requires the same balance that for negative rights is conducted at the final stage of the proportionality test. This lends further support to my view that any difference between proportionality and fair balance or other balancing tests is largely terminological.

The focus of this chapter will be on those rights where proportionality has its proper place, namely civil and political rights. Even here, it is an overstatement to say that proportionality is applied to all rights; for example, under the ECHR, the rights to freedom from torture and inhuman or degrading treatment or punishment (Article 3 ECHR) and the rights not to be held in slavery or servitude and not to be required to perform forced or compulsory labour (Article 4 ECHR) are absolute and thus not limitable. Some procedural rights are also absolute, such as the right to a fair trial (Article 6 ECHR) and the principle of legality (Article 7 ECHR). But the principle of proportionality does apply to the bulk of civil and political rights of the ECHR, in particular the rights to life (Article 2 ECHR), physical integrity (which is read into Article 8 ECHR), private and family life, home and correspondence (Article 8 ECHR), thought, conscience and religion (Article 9 ECHR), expression (Article 10 ECHR), assembly and association (Article 11 ECHR), and property (Article 1 of the First Protocol).

Proportionality is used to determine whether an interference with a prima facie right is justified. It thus only comes into play when it has been established that there is an interference with a right, i.e. if a person's autonomy has been limited. Such an interference requires a justification because the possibility exists that the policy in question is based on a scheme which fails to specify the right-holder's sphere of autonomy in a reasonable way and which is therefore constitutionally illegitimate. Thus, the point and purpose of the principle of proportionality is to determine whether a policy is constitutionally legitimate in the sense proposed in Chapter 5.

There are several slightly different formulations of the principle. I will, in line with the German Federal Constitutional Court and the leading

---

[8]   See for example *von Hannover v. Germany* (2005) 40 EHRR 1, para. 57.

theorists of proportionality, take proportionality to imply the following test.[9] First, the policy interfering with the right must pursue a legitimate goal (legitimate goal stage). Second, there must be a rational connection between the policy and the achievement of the goal; in other words, the law must be a suitable means of achieving the goal at least to a small extent (rational connection or suitability stage). Third, the law must be necessary in that there must not exist a less intrusive but equally effective alternative (necessity stage). Fourth and finally, the law must not impose a disproportionate burden on the right-holder (balancing stage; proportionality in the strict sense). The proportionality test is at its core about the resolution of a conflict of autonomy interests, and this conflict is ultimately resolved at the balancing stage.[10] But before engaging in the balancing exercise it is important to establish that there exists a genuine conflict (suitability) between relevant interests (legitimate goal) which cannot be resolved in a less restrictive way (necessity). In the following sections, I will go through the stages of the test one by one, and I will in each case first explain the relevance of the respective stage for the overall assessment of the reasonableness of the policy at stake, and then address special problems arising at the respective stages.

III. THE LEGITIMATE GOAL STAGE

The legitimate goal stage raises two questions: first, what does it mean to speak of a 'goal' of a policy; and second, which goals are and which are not legitimate. I will deal with each issue in turn.

---

[9] Cf. Alexy, *A Theory of Constitutional Rights* (Oxford University Press, 2002), 66–9; Kumm, 'Political Liberalism and the Structure of Rights: On the Place and Limits of the Proportionality Requirement', in Pavlakos (ed.), *Law, Rights and Discourse: The Legal Philosophy of Robert Alexy* (Hart Publishing, 2007), 131, 138–9.

[10] This is controversial. In particular, the Canadian version of the proportionality test tends to read the balancing exercise, which, in my view, should be carried out at the final stage, into the earlier stages. This is criticized by Denise Réaume who argues that 'this question [the question of which of the values is more important], which has so often been disguised and hidden elsewhere in the steps of the *Oakes* test, or simply not been addressed, properly belongs at the end of the process, with the other steps serving simply to disqualify bad justificatory arguments and refine the ultimate contest.' See Réaume, 'Limitations on Constitutional Rights: The Logic of Proportionality', (2009) *University of Oxford Legal Research Paper Series*, Paper No. 26/2009, 26. Dieter Grimm makes essentially the same point in his 'Proportionality in Canadian and German Constitutional Jurisprudence', (2007) 57 *University of Toronto Law Journal* 383. The issue will be discussed in more detail below.

1. The goals of policies

Speaking of goals or aims of policies is slightly misleading. Having a goal or an aim is a state of mind; therefore policies cannot have goals or aims. One might think that what counts are the goals or aims of the respective decision-makers, for example parliamentarians or civil servants. But that, too, would be misleading: courts do not normally inquire into the states of mind of the respective decision-makers, and rightly so. What matters is whether the policy is *objectively* justifiable, not whether the persons who made it had the right considerations on their minds. Thus, it may have been the case—indeed it is quite plausible to assume—that in the scenario leading up to *Smith and Grady v. United Kingdom*[11] one of the subjective goals of the policy-makers deciding that homosexuals should be banned from serving in the army was simply to give expression to their homophobia. But that psychological fact was irrelevant for the question of whether the policy violated the right to private life under Article 8 ECHR. Rather than relying on psychological facts, the idea of a goal of a policy should be understood in the following way. The first question to answer when assessing the legitimacy of a policy which interferes with a right is whether there are any interests which are *candidates* for justifying the interference in the sense that it is *not entirely implausible* that they will at least be rationally connected to the policy. Take the case of a prohibition of a demonstration on the ground that it might attract counter-demonstrations which could lead to violence. An interest which would be a candidate for justifying the prohibition is the need to protect the rights to physical integrity of those who might be harmed by the violence; therefore, the protection of their rights qualifies as a goal (which would obviously also be legitimate). As a matter of principle nothing speaks against counting the protection of some completely unrelated interest—say, an interest in good schools—as a (legitimate) goal; it clearly is a goal which the state may and should pursue. But the reason that we do not seriously consider it as a goal in this particular case is that it is blatantly obvious that this interest cannot justify the ban of the demonstration—it simply has nothing to do with it, and it would therefore not pass the suitability test at the next stage. Thus, it is just a matter of intellectual efficiency not even to consider it as a goal pursued by the ban.

---

[11] *Smith and Grady v. United Kingdom* (2000) 29 EHRR 493.

2. The legitimacy of a goal

a) General observations

Most goals pursued by policies are obviously legitimate, in particular the goals of protecting a person's physical or psychological integrity, his property, liberty or other autonomy interests. In general, for a goal to be legitimate it must be autonomy-related. This follows from the point and purpose of state policies, which is the specification of the spheres of autonomy of equal citizens.[12] In particular, any goals relating to so-called 'public' goods must be shown to actually be about personal autonomy. In some cases there is a straightforward way to reformulate a public good as autonomy-serving, for example in the case of the protection of national security, which is just a short form of referring to the protection of the autonomy of the people from the many evils that come with war (in particular, but not limited to, threats to life and physical integrity). In other cases it will be controversial whether a goal can be reformulated as serving personal autonomy, for example in the case of the goals of promoting 'secularism' or 'respect for human life'; then, further argument is needed to establish the legitimacy of the goal.

b) Goals connected to ethical disapproval of certain lifestyles

One particularly important problem in constitutional rights law is the state's or majority's treatment of certain lifestyles of which it disapproves. The core example, now largely a matter of legal history at least in the Western world, is the prohibition of sodomy on the perceived ground of its immorality, or as I would prefer to say, following Ronald Dworkin, ethical worthlessness.[13] This section will explore the role and relevance of ethical disapproval in the context of the theory of rights proposed here. Within the proportionality structure, this issue properly belongs to the legitimate goal stage: the question is whether the goal of prohibiting, discouraging or attaching any negative consequences to the pursuit of certain lifestyles held to be ethically worthless is legitimate.

Mattias Kumm is the first author who has linked the philosophical idea of anti-perfectionism to proportionality-based rights analysis.[14]

---

[12] See Chapter 5, section IV.4.

[13] Cf. Dworkin's distinction between ethics and morality: morality concerns duties we have to others, whereas ethics concerns duties we have to ourselves (*Is Democracy Possible Here? Principles for a New Political Debate* [Princeton University Press, 2006], 21).

[14] Kumm, 'Political Liberalism and the Structure of Rights: On the Place and Limits of the Proportionality Requirement', in Pavlakos (ed.), *Law, Rights and Discourse: The Legal Philosophy of Robert Alexy* (Hart Publishing, 2007), 131.

His goal is not primarily to make a case for anti-perfectionism, but rather to show how anti-perfectionism can be integrated into the proportionality test. He uses a straightforward example: suppose a state makes school prayers compulsory, arguing that this is a valuable goal because it furthers a Christian way of life. It seems clear that this goal must be constitutionally impermissible even if it were correct that school prayers helped crafting souls worthy of salvation. Thus, 'the class of reasons that can legitimately be used to limit individual liberty are few', in particular '[i]t is more limited than the class of reasons that are of interest to someone trying to seek orientation and meaning in her life'.[15] More precisely, reasons relating to the realization of *perfectionist ideals* are *excluded*. Kumm integrates this general point into the proportionality test by arguing that perfectionist goals ought to be excluded from counting as legitimate at the first stage of the test.

I agree with Kumm on this structural point. Adding to his analysis, I want to present a more fully developed moral argument in defence of anti-perfectionism which will then help identify more precisely the kinds of goals that are illegitimate (not all cases are as obvious as the school prayer example). It may be appropriate to approach the issue with a discussion of Ronald Dworkin's views, because Dworkin is famous for both his theory of rights and his commitment to anti-perfectionism.

> I presume that we all accept the following postulates of political morality. Government must treat those whom it governs with concern, that is, as human beings who are capable of suffering and frustration, and with respect, that is, as human beings who are capable of forming and acting on intelligent conceptions of how their lives should be lived. Government must not only treat people with concern and respect, but with equal concern and respect. It must not distribute goods or opportunities unequally on the ground that some citizens are entitled to more because they are worthy of more concern. It must not constrain liberty on the ground that one citizen's conception of the good life of one group is nobler or superior to another's.[16]

Dworkin's famous right to equal concern and respect thus consists of two separable ideas: the idea that all citizens have equal worth and that therefore no policy must be based on the grounds that someone is worth less, and the idea that the state must respect each person's conception of

---

[15] Ibid., 143.

[16] Dworkin, *Taking Rights Seriously* (Duckworth, 1977), 272–3.

the good and therefore not limit his liberty on the ground that his conception of the good is deficient. The first idea is uncontroversial and sits well with the theory of rights proposed here. I argued in Chapter 5 that policy-making is directed at the specification of the spheres of autonomy of equals. A policy which awards to someone, say, a black member in a predominantly white community, less than to others, on the grounds that he is considered to be worth less ('Blacks don't deserve more because they are inherently worth less than whites') involves a blatant denial of the status of the person as an equal. It cannot, therefore, rest on a reasonable specification of the autonomy spheres of equals; thus, it is constitutionally illegitimate.

I believe that the second idea is correct, too. Read narrowly, it argues that the fact that the government, rightly or wrongly, considers someone's activity to be ethically worthless provides no reason for the prohibition of that activity. In this narrow formulation most people would agree with it. This becomes clear when placing oneself in the position of the person to be coerced. It is one thing to accept someone—say, the Pope—as an authority and obey his directives prohibiting certain activities even when on occasion one disagrees with them. It is quite a different thing to have certain activities prohibited by someone whom one does *not* accept as an authority and with whom one disagrees about the ethical value of these activities. I cannot see how I, personally, could in the event of such a clash of conceptions of ethical value regard as legitimate someone else's orders to obey him; and I also believe that almost everyone holds the same view with regard to himself. But if we, individually, think that such coercion would always be wrong when administered on ourselves, then we cannot without contradiction hold that it would sometimes be right to administer it on someone else. As Joel Feinberg puts it with regard to a parallel point: 'Demonstration of the doctrine is not possible, but the reader may find that it resonates with something in his most fundamental moral attitudes—particularly some of the attitudes he holds towards himself.'[17]

There is, however, a wider reading of Dworkin's thesis, which goes beyond prohibiting activities regarded as ethically worthless, namely the idea that the state should be neutral with regard to the good life; or as I would prefer to say, the state should be neutral with regard to questions of ethics, i.e. duties a person owes to herself. The state has

---

[17] Feinberg, *The Moral Limits of the Criminal Law, v. 3: Harm to Self* (Oxford University Press, 1986), 52.

many ways of taking sides in questions of ethics without prohibiting activities. Joseph Raz agrees with the narrow reading presented above in that he objects to the state resorting to coercion to further the well-being of its citizens, but he is very much in favour of the state resorting to non-coercive means: the state should, for Raz, create valuable options and remove (non-coercively) worthless ones; it should tax worthless activities and subsidize valuable ones, and it should encourage people to engage in valuable activities and discourage them from engaging in worthless ones.[18] This distinction between coercive and non-coercive means to get people to do the ethically right thing is, however, deeply problematic. Raz rejects coercion because of the *disrespect* it shows for the agent's autonomy.[19] But taxation, or imposing oneself as an unwanted ethical adviser, in order to discourage a person from engaging in certain activities, or refraining from creating a specific option on the ground of ethical disapproval, equally shows disrespect for the person's ethical views:[20] the state makes it impossible for a person to pursue her project (removal of option), or it attaches negative consequences to a person pursuing her project (taxation, discouragement), on the ground of ethical disapproval. Thus, it is impossible to pursue perfectionist policies in the way Raz envisages without showing exactly the kind of disrespect to people which he rightly wants to avoid; and this strikes me as offensive to the idea of personal freedom. Therefore the wider reading of Dworkin's comment on equal respect, namely a commitment to state neutrality in questions of ethics, should be adopted.

The problem with Dworkin's right to equal concern and respect, as quoted above, is that it does not reflect the ways in which governments or legislatures actually reason about policies. The arguments used are (fortunately) only very rarely of this vulgar kind. No legislature endowed with any traces of democratic culture makes a law against a certain group 'on the ground that some citizens are entitled to more because they are worthy of more concern'; and only rarely do legislatures make laws limiting an unpopular group's freedom 'on the ground that one citizen's conception of the good life of one group is nobler or superior to another's'. Rather, policy-makers rely on much subtler, *autonomy-related* arguments. In the times when homosexual sex was still a constitutional

---

[18] Raz, *The Morality of Freedom* (Clarendon Press, 1986), 417.

[19] Ibid., 410.

[20] Waldron, 'Autonomy and Perfectionism in Raz's *Morality of Freedom*', (1988–89) 62 *Southern California Law Review* 1097, 1141–52.

issue in the Western world, one of the strategies to rephrase the debates about the prohibition of homosexual sex in terms of autonomy was to argue that permitting such sex would lead to an estrangement of the majority from the community because they could not regard themselves in a genuine community with people engaging in what they regarded as degraded lifestyles.[21] Since from the perspective of most people, being in a community with people who hold ethical views similar to one's own is of value, this is an autonomy-based argument: the autonomy of some (homosexuals) has to be limited in order to protect the autonomy interests of the majority in identifying more closely with their community.[22] The example Kumm discusses in various places is the prohibition of gays from serving in the army. Again, the reason given for this policy was not that 'gays are worth less than others', or that 'gay lifestyles are inferior, and therefore options should be removed from them' but rather that allowing gays to serve in the army would lead to a decline in its military strength because of anticipated tensions between the gay and the straight soldiers.[23]

Here are more examples. The prohibition or regulation of headscarves or other forms of religious dress in schools and universities might be justified not on the ground that 'Muslims are worth less than Christians', or that 'Islam is a degraded religion', but rather on the ground that headscarves might impermissibly influence or impose pressure on others to also dress in certain ways, or that the permissibility of a specific form of religious dress might encourage the parents of the student to exert pressure on her to make use of this option.[24] A demonstration of fascists might be prohibited not because the fascists are regarded as worth less than other people, but because the expression of their views offends or scares the people living in the area;[25] pornographic or blasphemous speech, too, might be prohibited because of its offensiveness, which affects the offended people's ability to lead their lives without being

---

[21] See Dworkin's subtle discussion of the various arguments against liberal tolerance in *Sovereign Virtue: The Theory and Practice of Equality* (Harvard University Press, 2000), ch. 5.

[22] I argued in Chapter 5 (section IV.4.a) that we should not conceive of autonomy as being only about activities; rather it is more generally about control over one's life; and since the ability to identify with one's fellow citizens may be a part of one's goals in life, a policy which promotes this kind of identification enables people to realize their projects; thus it is autonomy-based.

[23] *Smith and Grady v. United Kingdom* (2000) 29 EHRR 493, paras. 77–80.

[24] Cf. *R (SB) v. Governors of Denbigh High School* (2006) UKHL 15, paras. 97, 98 (Baroness Hale).

[25] Cf. *National Socialist Party of America v. Village of Skokie* (1977) 432 U.S. 43. (where the US Supreme Court however held in favour of the fascists).

exposed to such influences and attitudes,[26] or in order to prevent harm to minors.[27] What these arguments have in common is that they do not openly rely on a denial of the status as an equal or a denial of the equal respect to be shown for an ethical view, but that at the same time some of them may seem uncomfortably close to such impermissible arguments. They are the kinds of argument which would be readily embraced by someone who disliked a particular group or lifestyle but was aware that citing his and his fellow citizens' dislike would not count as an acceptable reason for limiting their autonomy.

As a preliminary point, when trying to resolve these cases, it is important to understand that the threats to autonomy invoked by the majority are not necessarily unreal. Sometimes, of course, they are bogus arguments put forward by those who want to discriminate against some group and are trying to save their policies by appealing to some autonomy-related argument. But sometimes they are not. I find it very plausible to assume that someone who intensely dislikes gays may find it easier to live his life in a way which corresponds to his self-conception in an environment where they and their views are not prevalent. This is in principle just the same as someone who intensely dislikes fascists, and who will have a life which corresponds better to his idea of giving his life meaning and value in a community where he does not constantly face fascist neighbours and work colleagues. The point is that our social environment *does* make a difference to our ability to lead our lives according to our own set of values: while being confronted with life-styles that are very different from one's own may be enriching, it can also be perceived as unsettling and it may make it more difficult to form close ties with one's fellow citizens. Or imagine there was evidence that children were likely to learn less in the presence of a teacher wearing a headscarf because, say, they were not able to connect to the teacher on a personal level in a way which is beneficial for studying. Of course, this might be based on dislike or simple prejudices, but the loss in education and therefore autonomy would be real.

In resolving the issue of when autonomy-related harm which arises 'in the neighbourhood' of moralism counts, I shall distinguish between two scenarios. The first situation concerns cases where *the harm rests on the ethical dislike of one person or group for another*: when, for whatever reason,

---

[26] Cf. *Wingrove v. United Kingdom* (1997) 24 EHRR 1, para. 47: the goal of the anti-blasphemy legislation was to prevent the causation of 'justified indignation'.

[27] *Handyside v. United Kingdom* (1979–80) 1 EHRR 737, para. 52.

the dislike fades away, the harm disappears as well. For example, let us say that one possible reason for prohibiting headscarves in the classroom could be that the children and their parents simply disapprove of Islam. Forcing the children to attend school with Muslim teachers will quite plausibly lead to some real harm for the education of the children because it will be harder for them to build up a good relationship with the teacher. Another example is that homophobic people may experience a real loss when having to live in an environment where homosexuals are present. The third example is the offence caused by the existence of pornographic or blasphemous expression in the respective community. In all cases, when the dislike fades away, so does the harm to autonomy: when the children and their parents stop disliking Muslims, they will no longer have a problem connecting to the teacher and will therefore suffer no harm in their education; when the homophobic people stop disliking homosexuals they will no longer see any disadvantage in sharing their social environment with them; and when the pornography and blasphemy haters stop being ethically opposed to pornography and blasphemy, they will no longer be offended by its mere existence and thus no longer suffer a harm to their autonomy.

The proper way of dealing with the problem of whether to acknowledge harm flowing from ethical dislike is straightforward: it must not be accorded any weight in a political community committed to personal freedom. While, to repeat, the loss in autonomy may be real, the price to pay for a commitment to freedom must be that others use their freedom in ways which one finds ethically wrong. Therefore, permitting the harm flowing from ethical disapproval as a reason for the restriction of the other person's autonomy would undermine the commitment to personal freedom.

The situation where the harm rests on ethical disapproval must be distinguished from the second scenario where, while ethical disapproval may be present, *it does not cause the harm*. Take the case of a Nazi demonstration in a Jewish neighbourhood.[28] Presumably the Jews in the area will intensely dislike (ethically disapprove of) Nazi lifestyles. But that in itself could not justify the prohibition of the demonstration. Rather, the question must be whether the demonstration involves an independent harm to their autonomy, for example an attack on their sense of self-worth.[29] As a second example, take the case of gays in the army, and

---

[28] *National Socialist Party of America v. Village of Skokie* (1977) 432 U.S. 43.

[29] As I have stated in Chapter 6 (section IV.1.b), I believe that people have an important autonomy interest in their recognition as equals, or at least the absence of denial of their equal importance.

assume (counterfactually[30]) that the argument against allowing gay soldiers to serve is that doing so would lead to the possibility of sexual tensions
between gay and straight soldiers and that such tensions would detract
from the army's fighting power. This argument is not based on dislike of
gay people (for example, it applies in the same way to heterosexual men
and women serving together). It is therefore a permissible autonomy-based
argument. This does not imply, of course, without further argument that it
will justify the proposed policy. Rather, whether or not it does will depend
in particular upon whether it survives the balancing stage of the proportionality test and whether it is coherent[31] (it seems unlikely that it would be
coherent to let heterosexual men and women serve together but not
homosexual and heterosexual men because the kinds of sexual tensions
which might arise would presumably be similar).

So when assessing the legitimacy of a goal as part of the first stage of the
proportionality test, one may start by excluding openly moralistic goals such
as 'this particular form of sex ought to be prohibited because it is morally
wrong'. However, one must not stop there. When goals are offered which
are about protecting others from a certain harm to their autonomy—such as
the harm flowing from offence—we must ask whether this harm rests on
ethical disapproval. When it does, the goal is impermissible.

The conception of the legitimate goal stage of the proportionality test
advocated here has at least three important advantages. First, its mere
existence as a doctrine of constitutional law has a disciplining effect on
public authorities in that they will from the very beginning of the
legislative or executive decision-making process—long before the matter
comes before a court—be aware of the impermissibility of reasons based
on ethical dislike, and will therefore from the outset design policies
around permissible reasons. Second, when the matter does eventually
reach a court, public authorities will usually not even try to rely on
impermissible reasons.[32] With regard to *Smith and Grady*, Kumm rightly
points out that it is highly plausible to assume that homophobia fea-
tured, as a matter of psychological historical fact, in the motivation of
the ban on gays to serve in the army: arguments such as 'gays are

---

[30] The real argument relied on was not about sexual tensions, but rather about the dislike that the
heterosexual soldiers would feel towards their homosexual colleagues, which would then lead to a
decline in cohesion and thus affect the army's fighting power.

[31] On the relevance of coherence as an aspect of equality, see Chapter 5, section V.

[32] Kumm, 'Political Liberalism and the Structure of Rights: On the Place and Limits of the
Proportionality Requirement', in Pavlakos (ed.), *Law, Rights and Discourse: The Legal Philosophy of Robert
Alexy* (Hart Publishing, 2007), 131, 146.

disgusting'; 'we don't want gays here'; 'the military is an institution for real men'.[33] Interestingly, none of these 'arguments' made it to the UK's submissions before the ECtHR; rather the Court was presented with what Kumm calls *'sanitized'* arguments[34] about operational effectiveness, unit cohesion and the like. So what had happened in the meantime is that the clearly impermissible homophobic arguments had been replaced with arguments that are permissible but—and this, too, is typical—eventually did not justify the policy in its entirety. Third, for the constitutional judge, the legitimate goal stage performs an important function within the proportionality assessment because it excludes, right from the start, impermissible goals and thus pushes him on the right track by forcing him to identify permissible arguments whose actual strength can then be examined at the later stages of the test.

The gist of my argument in the preceding paragraphs is neither new nor original; in fact anti-perfectionism has for a long time been a dominant strand in political theory, and for the reasons I have given, I regard Raz's more recent attempts to challenge it as unconvincing. However, when it comes to the record of the courts, the picture is more mixed. My point here, in line with my reconstructive account, is not to argue that the courts have indeed accepted the argument developed above; rather it is that even if they have not, they *should*, on the basis of their own record, subscribe to it. Or, to put it differently: I believe that there is no other principled approach to the issue of moralism which fits the case law better than the approach developed above. Let me illustrate this with a couple of cases from the ECtHR relating to sexual orientation. In *Dudgeon v. United Kingdom*,[35] the ECtHR declared a law prohibiting homosexual sex a violation of Article 8 ECHR. That may seem like a confirmation of the argument made here, but the Court was very vague in its reasoning. It first accepted that the policy pursued a legitimate goal, namely the protection of morals.[36] The fact that the Court even regarded the protection of morals as a legitimate goal seems to run against the approach defended here; but the Court was forced to this conclusion because the protection of morals is explicitly listed as a legitimate goal in Article 8(2) ECHR. However in the next step it denied that there was a pressing social

---

[33] Ibid.

[34] Kumm, 'Institutionalising Socratic Contestation: The Rationalist Human Rights Paradigm, Legitimate Authority and the Point of Judicial Review', (2007) 1 *European Journal of Legal Studies*, 19.

[35] *Dudgeon v. United Kingdom* (1982) 4 EHRR 149.

[36] Ibid., para. 46.

need for the prohibition of sodomy in Northern Ireland,[37] and thus let the policy fail at this early stage of the proportionality assessment. It could have stopped there: when there is no pressing social need, nothing can save an interference with a right from amounting to a violation. However, the Court carried on in its assessment of the proportionality of the measure and also declared the law disproportionate to the legitimate aim (of protecting morals).[38] This seems to indicate that it did indeed see some merit in the law because otherwise there would have been nothing against which the privacy interest of the applicants could have been balanced. So while the judgment has been hailed as a triumph for gay rights, its language is highly guarded and its reasoning is (possibly deliberately) vague and confusing. In *Laskey, Jaggard and Brown v. United Kingdom*,[39] decided a few years later, the issue was whether the UK had been justified in prosecuting men who had participated in homosexual sadomasochistic group sex orgies involving considerable violence. Here the Court tried to avoid the issue of moralism altogether by not at all referring to the protection of morals. It decided against the applicants on the grounds that the activities involved significant physical injury,[40] completely ignoring the obviously important point that all participants had consented to the injury. I do not express a view on whether this case was decided rightly or wrongly, but it is plainly impossible to assume that the Court itself was convinced by its obviously *incomplete* argument. But the tendency to dodge the hard issues about the general permissibility of moralism is probably typical. This lends support to my view that there is not even a consistent doctrinal approach, let alone a coherent one, in the case law of the courts on this issue; in other words, there is no viable alternative to the view which I expressed above and the core elements of which are supported by the dominant strand of liberal thinking.

One might say, presumably with some support from the case law, that the extent to which specific moralistic preferences are accepted as valid reasons by the courts will partly depend on the prevalence of those views in society at large. Judges will by and large have the same moralistic views (or prejudices) as society at large, and it is therefore unrealistic to assume that they will exclude moralism in general from their deliberations.[41]

---

[37] Ibid., para. 60.   [38] Ibid., paras. 60–1.

[39] *Laskey, Jaggard and Brown v. United Kingdom* (1997) 24 EHRR 39.   [40] Ibid., paras. 43–6.

[41] This point can be seen as a facet of the debate about the desirability of judicial review because it raises doubts about whether courts will significantly improve the overall protection of rights. See Waldron, 'The Core of the Case Against Judicial Review', (2005–6) 115 *Yale Law Journal*, 1346, 1404–5.

That may or may not be true as an empirical observation, but it is not my concern here because this view could not possibly form the basis of a plausible reconstructive theory of rights. To repeat, I am not interested in what judges, as a matter of fact, are likely to do, or which views of moralism they are likely to hold, but in the different question of which coherent set of principles makes most sense of the practice of constitutional rights law, implying that judges *ought* to adopt it, independently of whether they as a matter of fact *have* adopted or *will* adopt it. But it would be incoherent to hold that judges should follow the views of their society in accepting or excluding moralistic preferences. It would, for example, imply that in a generally homophobic society, it is morally permissible to punish active homosexuals, or that in a generally Islamophobic society, it would be permissible to deny Muslims advantages that other groups enjoy simply on the basis of them being disliked. However accurate as a *de*scription of what is actually happening, this theory must be unattractive as a *pre*scription and cannot therefore claim to reconstruct the practice in a coherent way.

IV. THE SUITABILITY AND NECESSITY STAGES

1. General

The point of the *principle of suitability* is to establish the extent to which the two (or more) relevant autonomy interests at stake clash. Put negatively: the point of the suitability stage is to sort out those cases where upon a closer look there does not actually exist a conflict of autonomy interests. The principle of suitability holds that there must be a *rational connection* between the act that interferes with the right and the legitimate goal; the interference must be a *suitable means* of contributing to the realization of the legitimate goal at least to a small extent. If it does not contribute to its realization at all, then there is no conflict between the two autonomy interests at stake: a conflict of interests means that one can realize one interest only at the cost of the other; however, here the right is limited with no corresponding gain for the legitimate goal. Conversely, if the interference contributes to the achievement of the goal to some extent, however small, then the suitability test is satisfied because it has been established that there is indeed a clash of the two interests.

The *principle of necessity* holds that there must be no other, less restrictive policy that achieves the legitimate goal equally well. There are two basic situations where a policy is unnecessary. In the first, the state does all that is necessary, *and more*. To the extent that the state goes beyond what is necessary, there is, again, no clash of values. It would therefore also be possible to resolve such a case under the suitability principle by arguing that to the extent that the measure goes beyond what is necessary, it is not a suitable means of achieving the goal (because the goal has already been achieved). For example, if, similar to the case of *Handyside v. United Kingdom*,[42] a book is banned in order to remove it from circulation (and let us assume that this happens for a legitimate reason, such as the protection of minors), then, depending on the circumstances, it may not be necessary to seize, forfeit and destroy all existing copies of the book or to punish the publisher, because the goal may already have been achieved by the ban itself, unaided by seizure, forfeiture and destruction.

The second situation is where the state has a choice between two or more different ways of achieving the goal, and one of them is less restrictive of the right. Contrary to the first situation, even if the state chooses the more intrusive policy, there does exist a genuine conflict of interests. For example, assume that the code of conduct policy in *Smith and Grady v. United Kingdom* would have avoided any tensions between homosexual and heterosexual soldiers just as well as the dismissal of the homosexual soldiers. It is still the case that there is a conflict of interests between the homosexual soldiers' interest in remaining in the army and the national security interest in that national security can be protected at the cost of the soldiers' interest in remaining in the army. But the point is that the alternative measure would have achieved the goal at a lesser cost for the homosexual soldiers.

2. A range of possible policies

The traditional formulation of the necessity test, which asks whether there is a less restrictive but equally effective means, is in some ways simplistic. The problem is that often there exists an alternative policy which is indeed less restrictive but has some disadvantage. One can distinguish three scenarios. First, the alternative policy is less restrictive but not equally effective. For example, the code-of-conduct policy in *Smith and Grady* probably would not have been equally effective: surely

---

[42] *Handyside v. United Kingdom* (1979–80) 1 EHRR 737. Note that the facts in this case were slightly different; the example serves only to illustrate the argument.

dismissing all gay soldiers resolves the problem of possible tensions between gay and straight soldiers very effectively because there will simply not be any openly gay soldiers left. It is therefore doubtful that the code-of-conduct policy would have achieved the goal just as well.

Second, an alternative policy which is less restrictive may require additional resources to be provided by the state. For example, in *Pretty v. United Kingdom*[43] the Court could, and indeed should, have considered not only the alternatives of permitting or prohibiting assisted suicide, but also the possibility of making assisted suicide permissible within a regulatory framework designed to minimize the danger of abuse, for example by requiring certain procedures to be followed, such as the involvement of a physician. But such a scheme would involve a certain bureaucratic effort and thus require a certain amount of resources to be spent; so while the alternative is less restrictive of the right, it involves an extra cost to be borne by the public. Another example is that of religious drug use, where one way of controlling the harm associated with making certain drugs available for religious purposes would be a regulatory regime designed to limit abuse; but again this involves the spending of resources.

Third, there may be a policy option that is less restrictive but imposes a burden on a third party. The difference to the second scenario is that here a private person as opposed to the political community has to carry the extra burden. Rather than prohibiting the activity of person A, the state imposes a lesser burden on person B in order to enable A to follow her project. Cases involving accommodation often fall into this category: rather than requiring a religious believer to act against her religious duty, a relatively light burden is imposed on others to accommodate her.

Structurally, there are two ways to deal with such cases: they can either be resolved at the necessity stage or the balancing stage. The necessity stage may be considered the proper place because the question is whether, in light of a less restrictive alternative, the more restrictive policy is really 'necessary'. This seems to be the way favoured in Canada.[44] Alternatively, one could conclude at the necessity stage that the more restrictive policy is indeed necessary because the alternative involves an extra cost and cannot therefore be considered equally effective; the problem then has to be resolved at the balancing stage.

---

[43] *Pretty v. United Kingdom* (2002) 35 EHHR 1.

[44] Grimm, 'Proportionality in Canadian and German Constitutional Jurisprudence', (2007) 57 *University of Toronto Law Journal* 383.

This is the solution favoured in Germany.[45] But while I believe that the German approach is preferable for reasons of structural clarity, the important point is not whether to deal with the issue of a range of policy options at this or that stage of the test, but, rather, to adequately address the substantive problem at issue. This problem is that the original proportionality test is simplistic in suggesting that all we need to look for is a less restrictive alternative which achieves the legitimate goal just as well. There will often be a range of possible responses to a social problem; some will be more restrictive, others more effective; some will burden one group, others another group. The proper way to handle such a situation must be to assess all possible policies relative to each other.[46] This follows from the purpose of constitutional judicial review, namely ensuring that the state picks one of the reasonable policies, as opposed to an unreasonable one. Whether a policy is reasonable can only be assessed by comparing it to *all other* possible policies. In particular, it *cannot* be assessed by comparing it only to the alternative policy of non-interference.

Let us apply this approach to the first and second scenario presented above.[47] In the first, the alternative policy is less restrictive but not quite as effective. The question is whether the more restrictive policy can be regarded as superior to both the less restrictive and the permissive policy. On the assumption that the more restrictive policy can be defended in relation to the permissive policy, the crucial question is whether the policy-maker could also reasonably conclude that the more restrictive policy was superior to the less restrictive one. Thus, the question is whether the additional gain of the more restrictive policy (the difference between what the more restrictive policy achieves relative to the less restrictive policy) justifies the additional burden on the right-holder. In *Smith and Grady*, the question would be whether the dismissal policy can be regarded as superior to the code-of-conduct policy *and* the tolerance policy. Let us stipulate for the sake of the argument that relative to the tolerance policy, the dismissal policy avoids a harm of 100 units to national security. If most but not all of this harm can be avoided by introducing the code-of-conduct policy—let us say, only a harm of 10 units would remain—then the question is whether the

---

[45] Ibid.

[46] A similar approach has been proposed by Hickman, 'The Substance and Structure of Proportionality', (2008) *Public Law* 694, 711.

[47] The third one does not raise special structural problems: to the extent that accommodation of, for example, the religious believer is required, a limitation of his freedom would be either unnecessary or disproportionate, depending on whether one follows the Canadian or the German approach.

policy of dismissing the gay soldiers could also be justified if the gain was only 10 instead of 100 units.[48]

In the second scenario, the question is whether the state can reasonably conclude that prohibiting a certain activity is superior both to the absence of any regulation and to a regulatory policy scheme which avoids or minimizes risks but requires some additional resources. The problem with the regulatory regime is that the right-holder demands that the state spend a certain amount of resources to enable him to follow his project, and that he thereby shifts the cost of his project on to others (the public). This raises the question whether the state may be under a duty to *accommodate* him.[49] While I do not offer a comprehensive theory of accommodation in this book, I will make a proposal for this particular scenario. A proponent of what I called 'the dominant narrative'[50] could try to justify the need for accommodation by arguing that accommodation was necessary where a human or constitutional right, as opposed to a simple interest, is at stake: under the dominant narrative, rights carry a special importance which is intimately connected with their special normative force. Because of this, the argument would be, the community will not normally be entitled to limit an activity protected by a right if it is possible to accommodate the agent.

But this approach must fail because, as has been demonstrated, the twin ideas of special importance and special normative force, while intuitively appealing to many, are incoherent: there is no principled way of distinguishing between rights and mere interests; and because of this impossibility this book concluded, supported by the practice of the global model, that there is a constitutional right to everything which is in the interest of a person's autonomy.[51] But then we cannot rely on the ideas of special importance and special normative force to justify the need for accommodation unless we hold that there is the need for accommodation in every case where someone's interests are affected; and that would surely go too far.

I want to make a different proposal which offers a more convincing way of making sense of the widely held intuition that some accommodation of

---

[48] This is on the assumption that the burden of the code of conduct on the soldiers would be considered negligible. It also leaves aside the issue of the possible bureaucratic cost of setting up and enforcing the code of conduct.

[49] On accommodation, see Chapter 6, section IV.1.b.

[50] See Chapter 1, section II.

[51] See Chapter 4, section I.

the kind discussed here may be required, and I will use the example of assisted suicide to explain it. As a theoretical experiment, imagine that every person in the community had an interest in being able to receive assistance with her suicide should she need it to realize her project of dying with dignity at some point. Under these circumstances it would make sense for the state to provide the option of a regulatory regime designed to minimize the dangers associated with an unrestricted permissibility of assisted suicide (i.e., abuse). While this would create an additional cost to be borne by everyone, it would also enable everyone to pursue the project of dying with dignity should this become necessary.[52] The provision of the regulatory regime would be what I called the 'provision of a public service' in Chapter 6. It is not different in principle from the provision by the state of infrastructure or swimming pools: it enables people to give their lives meaning and direction by providing them with an option they would otherwise not have (swimming pool) or that could otherwise be limited (as arguably in the case of assisted suicide). The creation of such options is justified, as argued in the previous chapter, if it creates more freedom than it takes away. So if in a society of adherents to the idea of a self-determined death the state could enable people to live (and end) their lives according to their common self-conception by providing a system that minimized the risk of abuse but required a moderate amount of public resources, then the state could be justified or possibly required to introduce such a system.

The problem is that, of course, not all people will value this particular option: for those who reject the idea of assisted suicide, the state creating and supporting a regulatory regime to enable people to engage in assisted suicide is analogous to the situation where the state funds opera houses which are not appreciated by rock fans. Thus, someone could argue that the state cannot be under an obligation to create a particular option if this required the spending of public money: it would oblige some to pay for the projects of others. But this argument would be rash. If it were correct, then the state could never provide any public good or service if there were just one person who did not want to use it; and that would make the provision of such goods and services almost impossible in practice. Thus, it would be a mistake to declare the provision of a specific public good or service impermissible or not

---

[52] There might be the additional problem that even a regulatory regime could not prevent all instances of abuse. This problem should be dealt with according to the principles developed above for the first scenario (the alternative policy is less restrictive but not equally effective).

required just because it would not be used and welcomed by all. Instead, the preferable way of thinking about the issue is not to focus on one *specific* option—such as assisted suicide—but rather on the *general* availability of some measure of accommodation where it is needed in order to enable persons to pursue their important projects. Thus, every person who has or develops at some point in her life an important autonomy interest in an activity which is not in itself harmful to others but whose permissibility has negative side effects which can only be controlled by a regulatory regime, knows that the state will provide the necessary regulatory regime rather than prohibit the respective activity, in order to enable her to pursue her project. Every person has to contribute the—marginal—cost towards the funds required for the respective regulatory regimes, and every person gets in return the security that the pursuit of important projects will not normally be made impossible because of side effects which could be prevented by a regulatory regime. A state that follows this general policy increases the overall level of autonomy of its citizens at a marginal cost for each citizen.

This way of explaining why there may be the need for accommodation in the scenario discussed in this section avoids the mistake of defending such necessity simply on the ground that a 'right' is at stake, and additionally it offers an explanation as to why others should be under a duty to pay for an agent's pursuit of his project. Furthermore, just like the approach of the proponent of the dominant narrative, the approach proposed here will limit the need for accommodation to particularly important autonomy interests—such as arguably autonomy interests in engaging in certain religious duties or in a dignified death—because it would seem absurd to require the state to set up regulatory regimes for every trivial interest that a person might have or develop (such as feeding the birds). Thus, it achieves the same result of endorsing the need for accommodation under certain circumstances; but it does so in a morally coherent way.

V. THE BALANCING STAGE

1. *General*

When reaching the balancing stage, it has already been established that there is a genuine conflict of autonomy interests which cannot be resolved in a less restrictive but equally effective way. The point of the balancing stage is to determine which of the two (or more) autonomy interests takes priority in the specific circumstances of the case. To this end, the two interests have to be 'balanced' against each other.

In the previous chapter I presented a theory of balancing; I will only briefly summarize some of the main points here. Balancing is sometimes taken to refer to simple consequentialist trade-offs or mechanical ways of quantification. But that is not what it means in constitutional rights law, where at the most general level it simply points to the necessity of resolving a conflict of autonomy interests in line with sound moral principles (*balancing as reasoning*). Those principles will sometimes indeed require that the respective interests be placed on an imaginary set of scales (*autonomy maximization; interest balancing*); however in most cases the moral argument will be more complex and what I called *formal balancing* will be required.

The insight that balancing in constitutional rights law does not necessarily refer to consequentialist approaches or to mechanical ways of quantification can sometimes lead to results that may seem paradoxical at first glance. For example, it is uncontroversial that it would be impermissible for the state to set up a policy which makes it permissible to kill one person in order to use his organs to save the lives of five. Thus, killing the *one* would be *disproportionate* to the goal of saving the *five*. This may sound paradoxical because, *on balance*, five lives seem to outweigh one life. But the paradox disappears when we realize that contrary to some common usage, balancing in constitutional rights law is not always about autonomy maximization or interest balancing. Rather it is about *the sacrifice that can legitimately be demanded from one person for the benefit of another*, and it cannot be demanded of a person to sacrifice his life to enable others to be saved through the use of his body parts.

2. The margin of appreciation

One of the conclusions of Chapter 5 was that the acts of the elected branches are legitimate when they rely on a *reasonable* (as opposed to the one correct) specification of the spheres of autonomy of equal citizens. It is primarily at the balancing stage that the reasonableness requirement comes into the proportionality test: rather than asking whether the balance has been struck *in the one correct way*, the question is whether it has been struck in a *reasonable* way. Different doctrinal tools have been developed by courts to integrate the reasonableness requirement into the proportionality test; I will briefly discuss the approaches of the

ECtHR, the Canadian Supreme Court and the German Federal Constitutional Court.

The ECtHR relies on the doctrine of the *margin of appreciation*. As George Letsas has pointed out,[53] this concept is used in two different ways by the Court. First, the Court refers to it in the context of whether the member state struck an acceptable balance between the right and the competing public good (this is what Letsas calls the *substantive concept*, and what British lawyers sometimes call, misleadingly, *democratic deference*). Second, the Court uses the margin of appreciation doctrine in a sense which Letsas calls *structural* and which British lawyers would refer to as *institutional deference*: it awards member states a margin of appreciation on the grounds that they are in principle in a better position than an international court to set up and assess policies. So this concept 'has to do with the relationship between the European Court of Human Rights and national authorities, rather than with the relationship between human rights and public interest.'[54]

The margin of appreciation which I have in mind here is the substantive concept. While considerations relating to institutional deference have a (limited) role to play in constitutional rights law,[55] the issue here is not (institutional) deference but the acceptable balance between conflicting interests; and according to the substantive concept of the margin of appreciation, the elected branches enjoy a certain leeway in this regard. This leeway or margin reflects and integrates into the proportionality test the fact that for democratic decision-making to be legitimate, all that is required is that the elected branches come forward with a reasonable (as opposed to the one correct) solution to a conflict of interests.[56]

The version of the proportionality test used in Canada varies slightly from the European one in that the balancing is often conducted at the minimal impairment stage (which in European terminology would be the necessity stage).[57] While the Canadian Supreme Court does not seem to have developed a uniform approach to the issue yet, it seems

---

[53] Letsas, 'Two Concepts of the Margin of Appreciation', (2006) 26 *Oxford Journal of Legal Studies* 705.

[54] Ibid., 721.

[55] See Chapter 5, section VI.2.

[56] For an argument which reaches a similar conclusion on the basis of an Alexian framework, see Afonso da Silva, 'Comparing the Incommensurable: Constitutional Principles, Balancing and Rational Decision', (2011) 31 *Oxford Journal of Legal Studies* 273.

[57] For an insightful comparison of the tests used in Canada and Germany, see Grimm, 'Proportionality in Canadian and German Constitutional Jurisprudence', (2007) 57 *University of Toronto Law Journal* 383.

clear that it has considerably softened its strict approach in *Oakes*,[58] which, taken literally, would have left the legislature only one constitutionally acceptable option when limiting a Charter right.[59] Occasionally the Court refers to the idea of the legislature enjoying a 'margin of appreciation'[60]: the term has been imported from Europe. In other places the Court states that 'the legislature must be given reasonable room to manoeuvre',[61] a phrase whose point is to indicate that the legislature need not find the one right answer to the rights question. This sits well with the approach proposed here.

The German Federal Constitutional Court employs a different terminology to achieve the same result: rather than insisting that the public interest outweigh the right—which would indicate the employment of a correctness test—it often uses a negative formulation, stating that the balancing test is satisfied if the interference is 'not disproportionate' or 'not out of proportion'.[62] So rather than requiring positively that the policy be proportionate, the Court demands negatively that it not be disproportionate. The effect of this is to give the necessary leeway to the elected branches. Occasionally the Court uses formulations that indicate even more clearly that the approach it uses is really a reasonableness approach, for example when it states that there must be 'a relationship [between the seriousness of the interference and the weight of the reasons supporting the interference] that can still be considered as reasonable'.[63]

Understanding the doctrine of the margin of appreciation as incorporating the reasonableness requirement into constitutional rights law helps clarify a mistake, or at least an overstatement, made by some critics of judicial review who argue that judicial review removes questions of rights from the democratic process. The opposite is true for the theory of rights underlying the global model: judicial review leaves the specification of the spheres of autonomy of equal citizens—the specification of their rights—to the democratic (majoritarian) process. It does not

---

[58] *R. v. Oakes* (1986) 1 SCR 103.

[59] For an account of this development in the Court's jurisprudence see Choudhry, 'So What Is the Real Legacy of *Oakes*? Two Decades of Proportionality Analysis under the Canadian *Charter's* Section 1', (2006) 34 *Supreme Court Law Review* 501.

[60] *Irwin Toy Ltd. v. Quebeck (Attorney General)* (1989) 1 SCR 927, 999.

[61] *R. v. Edwards Books and Art* (1986) SCR 713, 795.

[62] See for example BVerfGE 65, 1, 54.

[63] BVerfGE 76, 1, 51.

require the elected branches to conform to the preferences of the constitutional court; the constitutional court will not even make public its favourite way of specifying rights in any given case. Rather, it will only step in when the specification of the spheres of autonomy of the citizens has been carried out in an unreasonable way, meaning that it is outside the state's margin of appreciation and therefore beyond the range of reasonable responses to a conflict of autonomy interests. Some examples from the ECtHR's jurisprudence will clarify this point. In *Pretty*,[64] the Court did *not* decide the issue of how to resolve the conflict between the right to die with dignity and the interests of old or weak persons in being protected from abuse, thus taking away this important issue from the elected branches. Rather, it decided that both policy options—making assisted suicide legal, thus protecting the autonomy interests of terminally ill persons to die with dignity, and prohibiting assisted suicide, thus preventing an abuse of a permissive policy which could lead to vulnerable persons being killed or bullied into suicide by relatives—were acceptable specifications of the rights of the people in the given circumstances. In *Şahin*,[65] the Court did *not* decide how to best resolve the conflict between a Muslim woman's autonomy interest in wearing a headscarf in a public university in Turkey and an assumed public interest in secularism, thus removing this important issue of rights from the elected branches; rather it held that both allowing and prohibiting the headscarf was a permissible specification of the spheres of autonomy of Muslim women wishing to wear headscarves. In *Odievre*,[66] the Court did *not* decide the rights issue of whether adopted children ought to have the entitlement to be informed of the identity of their biological parents; rather it held that both policy options were within France's margin of appreciation and therefore acceptable specifications of the rights of the affected persons.

Now, one might object to the use of the above examples because in each case the Court decided that there was no violation of rights. Would it be true to say that the Court claims to have found the correct interpretation of the rights issue, thus removing it from the legislature, in a case where it holds that there is indeed a violation of rights? It would not be true, as the following example will show. In *Jersild*,[67] the Court decided that the punishment for promoting racist speech of a journalist who had produced a documentary about the problem of racism among

---

[64] *Pretty v. United Kingdom* (2002) 35 EHHR 1.   [65] *Şahin v. Turkey* (2007) 44 EHRR 5.

[66] *Odievre v. France* (2004) 38 EHRR 43.   [67] *Jersild v. Denmark* (1995) 19 EHRR 1.

some Danish youths violated his right to freedom of expression. The Court did *not* decide for Denmark how to deal with racist speech, thus removing this important issue from the democratic agenda. Rather, it accepted that Denmark enjoys a margin of appreciation with regard to the issue of how to deal with racist speech, but that by punishing a journalist who had tried, without any racist intentions, to raise awareness for a serious social problem, the Danish authorities had gone too far and stepped outside their margin of appreciation.

Of course it is possible to have a debate in all constitutional rights cases about whether the respective constitutional court correctly determined the limits of the reasonable; and of course there will be cases where the respective court did *not* get them right. But whether or not a court made a mistake in a given case, or whether or not a court is on the whole more likely to get right or wrong the question of the margin of appreciation and thus the limits of the reasonable, is a debate which must be conducted independently from the point which is at issue here, namely the overstated objection to judicial review which claims that constitutional courts, even when they identify the margin of appreciation correctly, unjustifiably remove issues of rights from the democratic process.

VI. CONCLUSION

This chapter presented an account of the principle of proportionality, and given that that principle is at the heart of the global model of constitutional rights, we now also have a theory of the global model. In a nutshell it is this. At the centre of most policy-making and constitutional rights law lies the issue of conflicts of autonomy interests. A proper understanding of the value of democracy requires that these conflicts be resolved in a way which is reasonable (as opposed to correct). Thus, the role of the courts is to police whether a conflict of autonomy interests has been resolved in a reasonable way by the elected branches. The proportionality test is the doctrinal tool which enables them to carry out this task. At its first stage—legitimate goal—it identifies a relevant autonomy interest which is a candidate for conflicting with the right; moralistic goals are impermissible in spite of sometimes being autonomy-related. At the next two stages—suitability and necessity—it ensures that there is in fact a conflict between the interest protected as a right and the conflicting interest, which cannot be resolved in a way which is equally effective but less restrictive of the right. At the final stage—balancing—it determines whether the conflict has been resolved in a reasonable way, relying on the margin of appreciation (or parallel) doctrine in order to award the elected branches the necessary leeway. Thus, the principle of proportionality provides a structure which guides judges in their task of assessing whether an act of a public authority is constitutionally legitimate in that it respects the conditions of democracy.

∽ 8 ∾

Conclusion

The theory of the global model of constitutional rights which this book proposes and defends employs a number of abstract concepts and values which it interprets in sometimes conventional, sometimes original ways. The value of *personal autonomy* was introduced in Chapter 2 in a relatively innocent way as having some explanatory force with regard to some of the features of the global model. But in subsequent chapters it became clear that it is indeed, next to equality, the controlling value not only in constitutional rights law but in politics as well. (Almost) all policies are autonomy-related in that they must be directed at creating the conditions for people to live their lives freely (autonomously). In particular, the value of autonomy pushes a rival value, well-being, out of the picture; as has been shown, even when we might intuitively think of the state as protecting our well-being (such as arguably in the case of social rights, or in the case of so-called community values), this is actually better explained as serving autonomy.

Equality is, next to autonomy, the second abstract value which is important for both reasoning with rights and reasoning about policies. It is the controlling value in the common case of a conflict of autonomy interests: such conflicts must be resolved in a way which respects the equal importance of the agents whose autonomy interests clash.

The third important value, *democracy*, requires the introduction of a further dimension of autonomy, in addition to the personal autonomy protected by constitutional rights: *political autonomy*, which is about the citizens of a state collectively governing themselves. While collective self-government is based on the ideal of the consent of the governed, it must rely on the procedure of majority voting in practice. The resulting gap between ideal and reality necessitates the acknowledgment of a substantive requirement, namely that a policy, to be truly democratic and thus constitutionally legitimate, must represent a reasonable, as opposed to the one correct, way of specifying the spheres of autonomy of equals.

The concept of *constitutional rights* is given an interpretation here which flows from this understanding of democracy. Every citizen has an entitlement to have his or her autonomy interests treated adequately at all times, where 'adequate' means: in line with a reasonable specification of the spheres of autonomy of equal citizens. This philosophical point is translated into a doctrine of rights by protecting every autonomy interest of a person as a prima facie constitutional right, and assessing the reasonableness of an interference with the autonomy interest at the justification stage.

Balancing and *proportionality* are the concepts used by constitutional lawyers to conduct this inquiry. They are doctrinal tools the merit of which is to guide lawyers through or at least direct them towards the important moral issues in the resolution of constitutional rights cases, namely conflicts of interests. Their danger is that, if misunderstood, they may suggest a mistaken simplicity about reasoning with rights: the idea that the difficult questions about rights can be resolved by recourse to a largely mechanical exercise of quantification. However, reasoning with rights will often be extremely complex, and this complexity is reflected in the complexity of the doctrines of balancing and proportionality properly understood.

For a theory of constitutional, as opposed to moral or fundamental, rights, the moral concepts, in the particular interpretations given to them, must become part of an *institutional arrangement* involving *legislatures, executives* and *courts*. While some believe that questions of institutional competence are really at the core of any attractive theory of constitutional rights, the view proposed here is that the moral questions occupy this privileged place. The institutional design follows by and large the moral parameters, entrusting to well-designed courts working under well-designed procedural rules the task of enforcing constitutional rights by conducting an inquiry into whether the policy in question represents a reasonable specification of the spheres of autonomy of equal citizens.

Under the theory proposed here, the main entitlement which rights confer upon a person is that to be treated with a certain *attitude*: an attitude that takes seriously his project of living his life. Every feature of the theory flows from this basic proposition. The *two-stage test*, dividing rights analysis into the prima facie stage and the justification stage, reflects a useful way of splitting the question of whether the person's autonomy interests have been taken seriously into two: the first question, to be considered at the prima facie stage, is whether the policy at stake affects a person's control over his life; the second question, to be considered at the justification stage, is whether it does so in a way which takes his autonomy interests adequately into account and thus is justifiable to him. The *wide scope of rights* with its arguably counter-intuitive inclusion of trivial and even immoral activities reflects the fact that respect for a person's autonomy requires taking all his projects seriously, including those of lesser importance and those which are ethically worthless; this implies that they cannot without further consideration be excluded from the scope of rights. The *proportionality test* stands for the idea that respect for a person's autonomy demands that any measures restricting it must pursue a legitimate aim and be suitable, necessary and not disproportionate to the achievement of that aim. Underlying the idea of *balancing* is the insight that taking everyone's autonomy interests seriously will involve the necessity of resolving conflicts of autonomy interests in line with the respective agents' status as equals. The doctrine of the *margin of appreciation* reflects the fact that 'adequate' protection of a person's autonomy must, particularly in the interest of democracy, leave a certain leeway to the elected branches.

This, then, is the core of the theory of rights proposed here: the entitlement of every person to be treated with an attitude of respect for her autonomy. There is something both simple and radical about this proposition. It is simple in that it is a straightforward reinterpretation of mainstream liberal views about the conditions under which an exercise of state authority is legitimate. What is radical about it is the institutional implementation and constitutionalization of this simple idea: the constitutional acknowledgment of every person's right to challenge acts of public authorities before courts who have the final say with regard to whether the respective act shows adequate respect for his or her autonomy.

This radicalism was made possible by two groups of actors. The first is that of the framers of the respective constitutions. They seized the opportunity that arose, in particular, after the collapse of fascism, communism and apartheid, and set up constitutional arrangements which awarded judges the enormous powers that they have especially under strong systems of judicial review. But the more important contribution came from another group: the global model of constitutional rights is mostly the creation of judges all over the world, and it has flourished and matured in their hands. It is striking that none of its features is explicitly mentioned in the respective constitutions and that some of them even contradict both what the respective texts clearly state and what their framers intended. Rights inflation, horizontal effect, positive obligations and, to a lesser extent, socio-economic rights, as well as balancing and proportionality are all phenomena and doctrines which were first developed by judges. They gradually created a bold jurisprudence which, guided as much by intuition as by theoretical reflection, engages in the difficult but crucially important work of making the abstract formulations used by constitutions meaningful and effective in legal practice.

The result of their combined efforts is the global model of constitutional rights: a practice which is not just a collection of cases but one which also developed a set of general and abstract doctrines, including most prominently the doctrines that form part of the global model: the broad scope of rights; negative and positive obligations; vertical and horizontal effect; balancing and proportionality. The goal of this book is to add a further layer of abstraction and integrate those doctrines into a comprehensive theory of constitutional rights which is coherent, fits the practice, and reflects attractive conceptions of other constitutional values, in particular the values of democracy and the separation of powers. If this project has been successful, then it is true to say that the global model is, in its simplicity and its radicalism, a success: not only does it work in practice in a way which has earned it the respect of many people and makes it a role model for young (and old) democracies; it also reflects a valuable and coherent political philosophy and, indeed, it has been an important inspiration for the very development of that philosophy.

But of course, while it has merits, it also has its instances of failure in the past and risks for the future; and while it is widely endorsed, it also has its critics. Furthermore, the global model is still a young practice and many of its features are in flux. Thus, it is not only predictable but crucially important that there should be ongoing conversation about it: at the practical level of judges and other practitioners deciding or participating in actual cases and bringing in their unrivalled experience in dealing with questions of rights; at the more theoretical level of scholars; and at the political level of the citizens and their representatives of whose system of government constitutional judicial review is (or is not) a part. As a contribution to this conversation, this book has, first, tried to improve our understanding of the global model and, inseparably from this, assessed its moral justifiability. Second, it has raised the bar for critics of the practice: they must, in order to avoid fighting against a straw man, make the strongest case in favour of the practice before attempting to demolish it; thus, they are invited to engage with the account proposed here and show that their model is really superior to this one. These and other conversations are something to look forward to, and therefore this book can conclude on a happy note: the inspiring and important philosophical, legal and political discussions about constitutional rights and judicial review, dealing with moral concepts such as autonomy, equality, rights, and democracy and institutions including constitutional courts, parliaments, governments, and public agencies, are far from over. On the contrary, and particularly in light of the relative youth of the success of the global model of constitutional rights, it is closer to the truth to say that they have only just begun.

Bibliography

Afonso da Silva, Virgílio, 'Comparing the Incommensurable: Constitutional Principles, Balancing and Rational Decision', (2011) 31 *Oxford Journal of Legal Studies* 273

Aleinikoff, T. Alexander, 'Constitutional Law in the Age of Balancing', (1987) 96 *Yale Law Journal* 943

Alexander, Larry (ed.), *Constitutionalism: Philosophical Foundations* (Cambridge: Cambridge University Press, 1998)

Alexy, Robert, *A Theory of Constitutional Rights* (Oxford: Oxford University Press, 2002)

—— 'Constitutional Rights, Balancing, and Rationality', (2003) 16 *Ratio Juris* 131

—— 'On Balancing and Subsumption. A Structural Comparison', (2003) 16 *Ratio Juris* 433

—— 'Balancing, Constitutional Review, and Representation', (2005) 3 *International Journal of Constitutional Law* 572

Alldridge, Peter and Brants, Chrisje (eds.), *Personal Autonomy, the Private Sphere and the Criminal Law* (Oxford: Hart Publishing, 2001)

Barak-Erez, Daphne and Gross, Aeyal M. (eds.), *Exploring Social Rights: Between Theory and Practice* (Oxford: Hart Publishing, 2007)

Barber, N. W., 'Prelude to the Separation of Powers', (2001) 60 *Cambridge Law Journal* 59

Barendt, Eric, 'The United States and Canada: State Action, Constitutional Rights and Private Actors', in Oliver and Fedtke (eds.), *Human Rights and the Private Sphere* (Abingdon: Routledge-Cavendish, 2007), ch. 13

Beatty, David M., *The Ultimate Rule of Law* (Oxford: Oxford University Press, 2004)

Bellamy, Richard, *Political Constitutionalism: A Republican Defence of the Constitutionality of Democracy* (Cambridge: Cambridge University Press, 2007)

Berlin, Isaiah, *Liberty* (Oxford: Oxford University Press, 2002)

—— 'Two Concepts of Liberty', in Berlin, *Liberty* (Oxford: Oxford University Press, 2002), 166

Besson, Samantha and Tasioulas, John (eds.), *The Philosophy of International Law* (Oxford: Oxford University Press, 2010)

Bilchitz, David, *Poverty and Fundamental Rights: The Justification and Enforcement of Socio-Economic Rights* (Oxford: Oxford University Press, 2007)

Brems, Eva, 'Indirect Protection of Social Rights by the European Court of Human Rights', in Barak-Erez and Gross (eds.), *Exploring Social Rights: Between Theory and Practice* (Oxford: Hart Publishing, 2007), 135

Butler, Andrew, 'Constitutional Rights in Private Litigation: A Critique and Comparative Analysis', (1993) 22 *Anglo-American Law Review* 1

Chemerinsky, Erwin, 'Rethinking State Action', (1985) 80 *Northwestern University Law Review* 503

Choudhry, Sujit, 'So What Is the Real Legacy of *Oakes*? Two Decades of Proportionality Analysis under the Canadian *Charter*'s Section 1', (2006) 34 *Supreme Court Law Review* 501

Cohen-Eliya, Moshe and Porat, Iddo, 'The Hidden Foreign Law Debate in *Heller*: The Proportionality Approach in American Constitutional Law', (2009) 46 *San Diego Law Review* 367

—— 'American Balancing and German Proportionality: The Historical Origins', (2010) 8 *International Journal of Constitutional Law* 263

Craig, Paul and de Búrca, Gráinne, *EU Law* (5th edition, Oxford: Oxford University Press, 2011)

Davis, Dennis M., 'Socio-Economic Rights: The Promise and Limitation—The South African Experience', in Barak-Erez and Gross (eds.), *Exploring Social Rights: Between Theory and Practice* (Oxford: Hart Publishing, 2007), 193

Denninger, Erhard, 'Freiheitsordnung—Wertordnung—Pflichtordnung', (1975) *Juristenzeitung* 545

Dworkin, Ronald, *Taking Rights Seriously* (London: Duckworth, 1977)

—— 'Rights as Trumps' in Waldron (ed.), *Theories of Rights* (Oxford: Oxford University Press, 1984)

—— *A Matter of Principle* (Cambridge, MA: Harvard University Press, 1985)

—— *Law's Empire* (Oxford: Hart Publishing, 1986)

—— *Freedom's Law: The Moral Reading of the American Constitution* (Cambridge, MA: Harvard University Press, 1996)

—— *Sovereign Virtue: The Theory and Practice of Equality* (Cambridge, MA: Harvard University Press, 2000)

—— *Is Democracy Possible Here? Principles for a New Political Debate* (Princeton: Princeton University Press, 2006)

—— *Justice in Robes* (Cambridge, MA: Harvard University Press, 2006)

—— *Justice for Hedgehogs* (Cambridge, MA: Harvard University Press, 2011)

Ely, John Hart, *Democracy and Distrust: A Theory of Judicial Review* (Cambridge, MA: Harvard University Press, 1980)

Fabre, Cécile, *Social Rights under the Constitution: Government and the Decent Life* (Oxford: Oxford University Press, 2000)

Feinberg, Joel, *The Moral Limits of the Criminal Law, v. 2: Offense to Others* (Oxford: Oxford University Press, 1985)

—— *The Moral Limits of the Criminal Law, v. 3: Harm to Self* (Oxford: Oxford University Press, 1986)

Fleming, James E., *Securing Constitutional Democracy: The Case of Autonomy* (Chicago: Chicago University Press, 2006)

Foot, Philippa, *Moral Dilemmas* (Oxford: Oxford University Press, 2002)

Forst, Rainer, 'The Justification of Human Rights and the Basic Right to Justification: A Reflexive Approach', (2010) 120 *Ethics* 711

Fredman, Sandra, *Human Rights Transformed: Positive Rights and Positive Duties* (Oxford: Oxford University Press, 2008)

Gardbaum, Stephen, 'The "Horizontal Effect" of Constitutional Rights', (2003–4) 102 *Michigan Law Review* 387

—— 'Where the (State) Action is', (2006) 4 *International Journal of Constitutional Law* 760

Gearty, Conor, 'The Paradox of United States Democracy', (1991–2) 26 *University of Richmond Law Review* 259

Gewirth, Alan, 'Are There Any Absolute Rights?', in Waldron (ed.), *Theories of Rights* (Oxford: Oxford University Press, 1984)

Griffin, James, *On Human Rights* (Oxford: Oxford University Press, 2008)

Grimm, Dieter, 'Proportionality in Canadian and German Constitutional Jurisprudence', (2007) 57 *University of Toronto Law Journal* 383

Gunther, Gerald, 'The Supreme Court, 1971 Term—Foreword: In Search of Evolving Doctrine on a Changing Court: A Model for a Newer Equal Protection', (1972) 86 *Harvard Law Review* 1

Habermas, Jürgen, *Justification and Application* (Cambridge, MA: MIT Press, 1994)

Harel, Alon and Kahana, Tsvi, 'The Easy Core Case for Judicial Review', (2010) 2 *Journal of Legal Analysis* 227

Hart, H. L. A., 'Between Utility and Rights', in Hart, *Essays in Jurisprudence and Philosophy* (Oxford: Clarendon Press, 1983), 198

—— *Essays in Jurisprudence and Philosophy* (Oxford: Clarendon Press, 1983)

Hickman, Tom, 'The Substance and Structure of Proportionality', (2008) *Public Law* 694

Hunt, Murray, 'The "Horizontal Effect" of the Human Rights Act', (1998) *Public Law* 423

Huscroft, Grant (ed.), *Expounding the Constitution: Essays in Constitutional Theory* (Cambridge: Cambridge University Press, 2008)

Kamm, Frances Myrna, *Morality, Mortality. Volume II: Rights, Duties, and Status* (Oxford: Oxford University Press, 1996)

—— *Intricate Ethics: Rights, Responsibilities, and Permissible Harm* (Oxford: Oxford University Press, 2007)

Kavanagh, Aileen, 'Participation and Judicial Review: A Reply to Jeremy Waldron', (2003) 22 *Law and Philosophy* 451

—— 'Deference or Defiance? The Limits of the Judicial Role in Constitutional Adjudication', in Huscroft (ed.), *Expounding the Constitution: Essays in Constitutional Theory* (Cambridge: Cambridge University Press, 2008), 184

—— *Constitutional Review under the UK Human Rights Act* (Cambridge: Cambridge University Press, 2009)

Khosla, Madhav, 'Proportionality: An Assault on Human Rights?: A reply', (2010) 8 *International Journal of Constitutional Law* 298

Kleinig, John, *Paternalism* (Manchester: Manchester University Press, 1983)

Kumm, Mattias, 'Constitutional Rights as Principles: On the Structure and Domain of Constitutional Justice', (2004) 2 *International Journal of Constitutional Law* 574

—— 'Who is Afraid of the Total Constitution? Constitutional Rights as Principles and the Constitutionalization of Private Law', (2006) 7 *German Law Journal* 341

—— 'Institutionalising Socratic Contestation: The Rationalist Human Rights Paradigm, Legitimate Authority and the Point of Judicial Review', (2007) 1 *European Journal of Legal Studies*

—— 'Political Liberalism and the Structure of Rights: On the Place and Limits of the Proportionality Requirement', in Pavlakos (ed.), *Law, Rights and Discourse: The Legal Philosophy of Robert Alexy* (Oxford: Hart Publishing, 2007), 131

—— 'The Idea of Socratic Contestation and the Right to Justification: The Point of Rights-Based Proportionality Review', (2010) 4 *Law & Ethics of Human Rights* 141

Kumm, Mattias and Ferreres Comella, Victor, 'What is so Special about Constitutional Rights in Private Litigation? A Comparative Analysis of the Function of State Action Requirements and Indirect Effect', in Sajó and Uitz (eds.), *The Constitution in Private Relations: Expanding Constitutionalism* (The Hague: Eleven, 2005)

Letsas, George, 'Two Concepts of the Margin of Appreciation', (2006) 26 *Oxford Journal of Legal Studies* 705

—— *A Theory of Interpretation of the European Convention on Human Rights* (Oxford: Oxford University Press, 2007)

Matscher, F. and Petzold, H. (eds.), *Protecting Human Rights: The European Dimension* (Cologne: Carl Heymanns Verlag, 1990)

McCrudden, Christopher, 'A Common Law of Human Rights?: Transnational Judicial Conversations on Human Rights', (2000) 20 *Oxford Journal of Legal Studies* 499

—— 'Human Dignity and Judicial Interpretation of Human Rights', (2008) 19 *European Journal of International Law* 655

Michelman, Frank, 'Law's Republic', (1988) 97 *Yale Law Journal* 1493

Mill, John Stuart, *On Liberty and Other Essays* (Oxford: Oxford University Press, 1991)

Möller, Kai, *Paternalismus und Persönlichkeitsrecht* (Berlin: Duncker & Humblot, 2005)

—— 'On Treating Persons as Ends: The German Aviation Security Act, Human Dignity, and the Federal Constitutional Court', (2006) *Public Law* 457

—— 'Balancing and the Structure of Constitutional Rights', (2007) 5 *International Journal of Constitutional Law* 453

—— 'Two Conceptions of Positive Liberty: Towards an Autonomy-based Theory of Constitutional Rights', (2009) 29 *Oxford Journal of Legal Studies* 757

—— 'The Right to Life Between Absolute and Proportional Protection', in Bronitt, Gani, and Hufnagel (eds.), *Shooting to Kill: Socio-Legal Perspectives on the Use of Lethal Force* (Oxford: Hart Publishing, 2012)

Mowbray, Alastair, 'A Study of the Principle of Fair Balance in the Jurisprudence of the European Court of Human Rights', (2010) 10 *Human Rights Law Review* 289

Mulhall, Stephen and Swift, Adam, *Liberals and Communitarians* (2nd edition, Oxford: Blackwell Publishers, 1996)

Murphy, Liam and Nagel, Thomas, *The Myth of Ownership: Taxes and Justice* (Oxford: Oxford University Press, 2002)

Nagel, Thomas, *Concealment and Exposure* (Oxford: Oxford University Press, 2002)

—— 'The Problem of Global Justice', (2005) 33 *Philosophy & Public Affairs* 113

Nozick, Robert, *Anarchy, State, and Utopia* (Oxford: Basil Blackwell, 1974)

Oliver, Dawn and Fedtke, Jörg (eds.), *Human Rights and the Private Sphere: A Comparative Study* (Abingdon: Routledge-Cavendish, 2007)

Otsuka, Michael, 'Kamm on the Morality of Killing', (1997) 108 *Ethics* 197

—— 'Double Effect, Triple Effect and the Trolley Problem: Squaring the Circle in Looping Cases', (2008) 20 *Utilitas* 92

Pavlakos, George (ed.), *Law, Rights and Discourse: The Legal Philosophy of Robert Alexy* (Oxford: Hart Publishing, 2007)

Pildes, Richard, 'Why Rights Are Not Trumps: Social Meanings, Expressive Harms, and Constitutionalism', (1998) 17 *Journal of Legal Studies* 725

—— 'Dworkin's Two Conceptions of Rights', (2000) 29 *Journal of Legal Studies* 309

Rawls, John, *A Theory of Justice* (revised edition, Oxford: Oxford University Press, 1999)

—— *Collected Papers* (Cambridge, MA: Harvard University Press, 1999)

—— *Justice as Fairness: A Restatement* (Cambridge, MA: Harvard University Press, 2001)

Raz, Joseph, *The Morality of Freedom* (Oxford: Clarendon Press, 1986)

—— (ed.), *Authority* (New York: New York University Press, 1990)

—— 'Introduction', in Raz (ed.), *Authority* (New York: New York University Press, 1990), 1

—— *Ethics in the Public Domain: Essays in the Morality of Law and Politics* (new edition, Oxford: Clarendon Press, 1995)

—— 'Disagreement in Politics', (1998) 43 *American Journal of Jurisprudence* 25

—— 'On the Authority and Interpretation of Constitutions: Some Preliminaries', in Alexander (ed.), *Constitutionalism: Philosophical Foundations* (Cambridge: Cambridge University Press, 1998), 152

—— 'The Problem of Authority: Revisiting the Service Conception', in Raz, *Between Authority and Interpretation* (Oxford: Oxford University Press, 2009), 126

—— 'Human Rights without Foundations', in Besson and Tasioulas (eds.), *The Philosophy of International Law* (Oxford: Oxford University Press, 2010), 321

Réaume, Denise, 'Limitations on Constitutional Rights: The Logic of Proportionality', (2009) *University of Oxford Legal Research Paper Series*, Paper No. 26/2009

Regan, Donald H., 'Paternalism, Freedom, Identity, and Commitment', in Sartorius (ed.), *Paternalism* (Minneapolis, MN: University of Minnesota Press, 1983), 113

Roberts, Paul, 'Privacy, Autonomy and Criminal Justice Rights: Philosophical Preliminaries', in Alldridge and Brants (eds.), *Personal Autonomy, the Private Sphere and the Criminal Law* (Oxford: Hart Publishing, 2001), 59

Rubenfeld, Jed, 'Legitimacy and Interpretation', in Alexander (ed.), *Constitutionalism: Philosophical Foundations* (Cambridge: Cambridge University Press, 1998), 194

Sager, Lawrence, 'The Domain of Constitutional Justice', in Alexander (ed.), *Constitutionalism: Philosophical Foundations* (Cambridge: Cambridge University Press, 1998), 235

Sajó, András and Uitz, Renáta (eds.), *The Constitution in Private Relations: Expanding Constitutionalism* (The Hague: Eleven, 2005)

Sartorius, Rolf (ed.), *Paternalism* (Minneapolis, MN: University of Minnesota Press, 1983)

Schermes, Henry G., 'The international protection of the right to property', in Matscher and Petzold (eds.), *Protecting Human Rights: The European Dimension* (Cologne: Carl Heymanns Verlag, 1990), 569

Shiffrin, Sheana Valentine, 'Egalitarianism, Choice-Sensitivity, and Accommodation', in Wallace, Pettit, Scheffler, and Smith (eds.), *Reason and Value* (Oxford: Clarendon Press, 2004), 270

Stone Sweet, Alec and Mathews, Jud, 'Proportionality Balancing and Global Constitutionalism', (2008–9) 47 *Columbia Journal of Transnational Law* 72

Strauss, David A., 'Due Process, Government Inaction, and Private Wrongs', (1989) *Supreme Court Review* 53

Thomson, Judith Jarvis, 'A Defense of Abortion', (1971) 1 *Philosophy & Public Affairs* 47

—— 'The Trolley Problem' (1985) 94 *Yale Law Journal* 1395

Tsakyrakis, Stavros, 'Proportionality: An Assault on Human Rights?', (2009) 7 *International Journal of Constitutional Law* 468

—— 'Proportionality: An Assault on Human Rights?: A Rejoinder to Madhav Khosla', (2010) 8 *International Journal of Constitutional Law* 307

Waldron, Jeremy (ed.), *Theories of Rights* (Oxford: Oxford University Press, 1984)

—— 'Autonomy and Perfectionism in Raz's *Morality of Freedom*', (1988–9) 62 *Southern California Law Review* 1097

—— 'Homelessness and the Issue of Freedom', (1991–2) 39 *UCLA Law Review* 295

—— 'Fake Incommensurability: A Response to Professor Schauer', (1993–4) 45 *Hastings Law Journal* 813

—— *Law and Disagreement* (Oxford: Oxford University Press, 1999)

—— 'Pildes on Dworkin's Theory of Rights', (2000) 29 *Journal of Legal Studies* 301

—— 'The Core of the Case Against Judicial Review', (2005–6) 115 *Yale Law Journal* 1346

—— 'Do Judges Reason Morally?', in Huscroft (ed.), *Expounding the Constitution: Essays in Constitutional Theory* (Cambridge: Cambridge University Press, 2008), 38

—— 'Socioeconomic Rights and Theories of Justice', *NYU School of Law, Public Law & Legal Theory Research Paper Series*, Working Paper No. 10–79, November 2010

—— *Torture, Terror, and Trade-Offs: Philosophy for the White House* (Oxford: Oxford University Press, 2010)

Walen, Alec, 'Doing, Allowing, and Disabling: Some Principles Governing Deontological Restrictions', (1995) 80 *Philosophical Studies* 183

Wallace, R. Jay, Pettit, Philip, Scheffler, Samuel and Smith, Michael (eds.), *Reason and Value* (Oxford: Clarendon Press, 2004)

Webber, Grégoire C. N., *The Negotiable Constitution: On the Limitation of Rights* (Cambridge: Cambridge University Press, 2009)

Wilkinson, T. M., 'Dworkin on Paternalism and Well-Being', (1996) 16 *Oxford Journal of Legal Studies* 433

Yowell, Paul, 'A Critical Examination of Dworkin's Theory of Rights', (2007) 52 *American Journal of Jurisprudence* 93

Index